英美报刊选读
（第2版）

吴潜龙　盛　婧　编著

华中科技大学出版社
中国·武汉

内 容 提 要

《英美报刊选读》(第 2 版)继承了第一版两个方面的特点:一是选材丰富多彩,具有时代性,信息量丰富;二是从英语新闻学的角度介绍了阅读英语报刊的一些基本知识,而不是简单谈论阅读理解的方法。《英美报刊选读》(第 2 版)重新遴选了 54 篇新闻,按内容分成 18 个单元,每篇新闻的长度在 700～900 个词之间。每篇新闻后面都附有两大类内容。第一类帮助学生理解文章,如生词、重要的专有名词、内容要点和句子翻译,用中文写出。第二类属于"考"学生的,也就是"练习",练习紧扣选文,从词语和全文理解两个方面设计练习,同时布置一些自主学习的思考题,供学生自己上网搜索和阅读。此外,还有报刊英语常识介绍。

图书在版编目(CIP)数据

英美报刊选读/吴潜龙,盛婧编著. —2 版. —武汉:华中科技大学出版社,2017.1(2023.7 重印)
ISBN 978-7-5680-0928-7

Ⅰ.①英… Ⅱ.①吴… ②盛… Ⅲ.①英语-阅读教学-高等学校-教材 Ⅳ.①H319.4

中国版本图书馆 CIP 数据核字(2015)第 120078 号

英美报刊选读(第 2 版) 吴潜龙 盛 婧 编著
Yingmei Baokan Xuandu

策划编辑:刘 平
责任编辑:刘 平
责任校对:曾 婷
封面设计:原色设计
责任监印:周治超

出版发行:华中科技大学出版社(中国·武汉)   电话:(027)81321913
武汉市东湖新技术开发区华工科技园   邮编:430223
录   排:华中科技大学惠友文印中心
印   刷:武汉开心印印刷有限公司
开   本:787mm×1092mm 1/16
印   张:18
字   数:457 千字
版   次:2009 年 5 月第 1 版 2023 年 7 月第 2 版第 6 次印刷
定   价:48.00 元

本书若有印装质量问题,请向出版社营销中心调换
全国免费服务热线:400-6679-118   竭诚为您服务
版权所有 侵权必究

第 2 版前言

本书于 2009 年初完稿付印,2010 年 3 月,我便作为"孔子学院"的中方院长,外派到南非的开普敦大学。去年底接到通知,开始准备修订,于是在工作之余,多少抽出时间收集材料和考虑如何修订。

几年之后回头看看原来的书,才感觉到修订是十分必要的。首先,"世事多变",这个世界上每天发生的事情确实太多了。几年工夫,地球上发生了很大的变化,作为让人们及时了解变化、应对变化的媒体手段之一的新闻,也紧跟事件的发生发展,不停地更新报道。原来的选文,已经有很多过时了,不更换不行。其次,原来选文的标准和注释说明的力度,存在很多不足之处,也不乏错漏的地方。而且,配合选文所编写的一些知识和练习,也存在不少的错漏。因此,不修订不行,不改不行。

本次修订,在选文上的考虑是:与其修修补补,不如更换新的。如去掉一些文章,补充一些新的文章,这样虽然比较简单,但有些章节已经没有必要保留了,如 The Iraq War;再看有些单元,原来的选文也不是很有价值。所以,各单元的主题做了改动,大多数选文也是新的。从新闻内容的角度来看,这样的修订,使新版和原版能相互补充和照应。当然,对于已经使用过这本教材的教师来说,就必须重新备课。

本书继续保留原版的编写体例,但也做了一些微调,如"句子翻译"这一部分增加了对新闻句子特点的简单分析,并不再重复原句,而是在选文中以数字序号标示;在"新闻介绍"中增加了对新闻背景的介绍,以帮助读者理解选文的内容。练习则尽量紧扣选文,从词语和全文理解两个方面设计练习,同时布置一些自主学习的思考题,供学生自己上网搜索和阅读,并将结果写成书面报告,有条件的可以让学生在课堂上交流和讨论。

最后,随着电脑和通讯技术的发展,新闻报道也发生了急剧的变化。报刊这一曾经是人们获取新闻的唯一媒体,已经全面立体化了。报刊网站上的声音、丰富的照片和视频,使阅读新闻更加生动和现实。但是,是否也使阅读语言变得不重要了呢?因为图片和视频基本就可以让读者明白所发生的一切。其次,新闻报道的时效性更强了,由于互联网的广泛使用,使在世界上某一地点发生的事情,几乎是同时地被用各种不同的语言传遍到世界各地。任何英文报刊上的重大消息,几乎马上就可以在互联网上找到中文的报道。阅读英文报刊作为学习英语的一种手段,是否也变得可有可无了呢?还有,许多大学已经在进行"零课时"的课程教学改革,基本上已经把阅读、听力、写作等变成以学生为主的课程了,这使"英美报刊选读"课是否有必要继续存在成为一个很大的疑问和悬念。

这也是对编写报刊阅读教材提出的挑战。不管怎样,学习、掌握和应用一门外语还是需要付出劳动的,至于怎么学、怎么用,就要根据实际情况了。教师只是引路人,教材只是他手中的拐杖。由于在南非教学等工作的影响,使得修订工作赶赶停停,进度较慢,不能如期完成,请多原谅。

吴潜龙
2014 年 12 月 26 日

第1版前言

应华中科技大学出版社之约，为"高等学校英语专业规划教材"编写其中的《英美报刊选读》一书，自2007年底开始构思至2009年2月脱稿，历时一年半始得完成。

"英美报刊选读"是一门比较传统的课程。所谓"传统"，是指该课程在我国高校英语专业的教学大纲上早已列出，许多院校均开设此课程，对提高学生的英语水平和增加阅读量、扩大知识面等都有帮助。

读报和读书一样是语言教学的一种重要手段。坚持阅读英语报刊对于我国学习英语的学生来说，不仅是入门的时候提高兴趣、增加词汇的好办法，也是在学习中不断训练阅读技巧、扩大词汇量的必经过程，更是学成以后温习英语、获取信息和了解世界的好助手。因此，本书并不一定只适用于理工科院校、综合院校和师范类院校的英语专业学生，它应该对所有希望学好英语的学生都有用。

本书的主要特点应该说有两个方面：第一，选材注重丰富多彩及拥有足够的信息量，同时具有时代性；第二，从英语新闻学的角度介绍了阅读英语报刊的一些基本知识，而不是简单谈论阅读理解的方法。本书共选了54篇新闻，按内容分成18个单元。每篇新闻的长度在700~900个词之间，对比较长的新闻均做了节选，但保留原文的主要内容，使选文和标题保持一致。每篇新闻的生词在20~30个之间，个别可能会多一些。全书共有2 000左右词汇。

从编排体例来讲，每篇新闻后面都附有两大类的内容。第一类属于帮助学生理解文章的，如生词、重要的专有名词、内容要点和句子翻译，已用中文写出，因为我国学生的母语绝大部分是汉语。第二类的内容属于"考"学生的，也就是"练习"，题目不多，一道题是阅读理解题，以选择题形式回顾新闻的主要内容；另一道题是词汇题，从新闻中选出约10个词，重复出现，帮助学生温习、记忆，最后学会应用这些词；最后一道题是讨论和写作题，可以在课堂上进行，也可以布置给学生在课后完成，不论采用哪种形式，题目都是与文章的内容密切相关的。因此，练习是紧扣文章的。

另外，每个单元后面附上一幅生动的漫画或一张新闻照片，可让学生在轻松的气氛中获得信息，理解文章并得到提高。同时还有报刊英语常识介绍。

最后是关于使用本书教学的小建议。每位老师都有自己的习惯和风格，课堂教学形式也是多样的。本书可用一个学期，每周2~4节均可。如要使用一学年，最好就是结合形势，补充一些当前的新闻，或让学生上网阅读有关新闻。无论采用什么方式进行教学，重要的是不仅要讲课文，还要使学生掌握课文的语言材料，同时学会查找相关信息，获取即时新闻。至于具体的教学方法，可由任课老师充分发挥。

吴潜龙
中山大学外语学院
2009年2月

Contents

Unit 1 Regional Focuses: Domestic Turmoil and War ·········· 1
  1. After Benghazi attacks, Islamist extremists akin to al-Qaeda stir fear in eastern Libya ·········· 1
  2. Syrian unrest spills into Lebanon ·········· 5
  3. North Korea moves missile to coast, but limited threat seen ·········· 9

Unit 2 Conflicts in the Middle East ·········· 15
  1. "Terrorist" explosion on Tel Aviv bus jeopardises Hamas truce deal ·········· 15
  2. Hizbollah debates dropping support for the regime of President Bashar al-Assad ·········· 19
  3. The Israel-Palestine conflict won't go away ·········· 24

Unit 3 The African Scene ·········· 30
  1. Boko Haram: Borno residents want permanent military presence ·········· 30
  2. What are Western and African powers up against in Mali, Algeria? ·········· 34
  3. CAR: how Bozizé lost his piece of Africa ·········· 39

Unit 4 Violence and Terrorist Attacks in the U.S. ·········· 46
  1. Terrorists hijack 4 airliners, destroy World Trade Center, hit Pentagon; hundreds dead ·········· 46
  2. "I Saw Bodies Falling Out— Oh, God, Jumping, Falling" ·········· 52
  3. 2nd bombing suspect caught after frenzied hunt paralyzes Boston ·········· 56

Unit 5 American Election 2012 ·········· 62
  1. With debates over, candidates race to clinch vital states ·········· 62
  2. Heated fight for presidency goes to voters ·········· 67
  3. Will we be better off in 2016? ·········· 72

Unit 6 Social News—the U.S. ·········· 78
  1. Storm barrels through region, leaving destructive path ·········· 78
  2. Nation reels after gunman massacres 20 children at school in Connecticut ·········· 83

3. Some give up their guns as others rally against tighter laws ········· 87

Unit 7   National News—the UK ········· 93

   1. David Cameron's critics are wrong. He's on the verge of something great
      ·· 93
   2. MPs to escape expenses investigations after paperwork destroyed by Parliament
      ·· 98
   3. Thatcher's death has Britain peering back through time ········· 102

Unit 8   Social News—South Africa ········· 109

   1. Bloody gunfight ········· 109
   2. Marikana: 900 bullets ········· 112
   3. Nelson Mandela's condition "unchanged", officials say ········· 117

Unit 9   Social News—Life and Lawsuits ········· 123

   1. Victim's friend tells of brutal gang attack ········· 123
   2. Family sues over Hout Bay tragedy ········· 127
   3. Oscar Pistorius charged with Reeva Steenkamp murder ········· 131

Unit 10   Environmental Protection—Saving Wild Lives ········· 138

   1. Rangers in isolated Central Africa uncover grim cost of protecting wildlife
      ·· 138
   2. Saving two-ton giraffe a tall order ········· 143
   3. Cape's abalone is well on the way to extinction ········· 148

Unit 11   Computer Technology and the Internet ········· 155

   1. The web is the most conservative force on Earth ········· 155
   2. Google pledge to downgrade piracy sites under review ········· 160
   3. Simultaneous translation by computer is getting closer ········· 164

Unit 12   Science and Technology ········· 172

   1. Grandma's curse ········· 172
   2. It's snowing, and it really feels like the start of a mini ice age ········· 176
   3. Climate change alters ecosystems from Walden Pond to "The Shack" ········· 181

Unit 13   World Economy ········· 186

   1. The economy is holding up surprisingly well in a year of austerity ········· 186
   2. IMF calls on UK to do more to boost economy ········· 191
   3. EU, South Korea to ally on faster mobile access ········· 195

Unit 14   Business News ········· 201

   1. Chinese trade with Africa keeps growing; fears of neocolonialism are overdone
      ·· 201
   2. "We're happy" — Frenzy drives traffic to retailers ········· 205

    3. EU duties on Chinese solar panels losing member state support ·············· 210

Unit 15　The London 2012 Olympics ·············· 216

    1. London Olympics opening ceremony quirky, fun, loud, British ·············· 216

    2. Licence to thrill! London welcomes the world with spectacular three-hour Olympic Opening Ceremony celebrating Great Britain ·············· 220

    3. Don't Deny the Joy of Usain Bolt ·············· 225

Unit 16　Culture News ·············· 231

    1. Eid Al-Adha, the story and traditions ·············· 231

    2. Coming to bad ends: stories that refuse closure ·············· 235

    3. The Box and the Keyhole ·············· 240

Unit 17　The British Pub and Drinking Culture ·············· 247

    1. A Pub Crawl through the Centuries ·············· 247

    2. Still the Moon under Water ·············· 252

    3. Booze buses and drunk tanks to tackle Britain's drinking culture ·············· 256

Unit 18　Entertainment News ·············· 261

    1. Scarlett Johansson in Broadway's *Cat on a Hot Tin Roof*: What did critics think? ·············· 261

    2. Story of Young Woman's Awakening Is Top Winner ·············· 265

    3. Jennifer Lawrence, interview: 'I do worry that I'm too in your face' ······ 268

Keys to Understanding Ideas in the News ·············· 274

Unit 1　Regional Focuses: Domestic Turmoil and War

We begin the first chapter of this book with news on some countries that attract the attention of the media because there have been civil wars and turmoil in the countries, or because they create tensions in the region. The first report is about the recent happenings in Libya, where the Gaddafi regime was overthrown and Gaddafi himself died a tragic death in 2012. The second is about the civil war in Syria, which is still going on; and the third is about North Korean's threat of using nuclear weapons against the South and the U.S..

当今世界上,有些国家和地区还处在内战和动乱之中,或处在战争的威胁之下。有关这些国家的报道,便常常成为世界各地报刊的头条新闻,成为人们关注的重点。每天的新闻电讯和报纸,都充满了对这些国家或地区所发生事情的消息。记者用他们富有煽动性的语言,配以现场的照片甚至视频,常常把刚发生的事件以最快的速度绘声绘色地呈现在读者面前。这些地方主要有:非洲的利比亚(以及北非的一些阿语国家)、中东的叙利亚,以及朝鲜半岛上的朝鲜和韩国。本章第一篇新闻是关于利比亚卡达菲政权倒台以后的国内形势,第二篇是关于正在叙利亚发生的战争对邻国黎巴嫩的影响,第三篇是关于朝鲜在核试验之后对韩国和美国发出的威胁和挑战。

1. After Benghazi attacks, Islamist extremists akin to al-Qaeda stir fear in eastern Libya

An explosion destroyed a building of the Abu Slim Martyrs Brigade, an extremist militia in Darna, Libya.

By Abigail Hauslohner
The Washington Post
Saturday, October 26, 2012

DARNA, Libya — Operating from the shadows, armed Islamist extremists are terrorizing the eastern Libyan city of Darna, six weeks after the deadly attack on the U.S. mission in Benghazi threw a spotlight on Libya's growing religious extremism. ①

A campaign of bombings and death threats aimed at Libyan government targets is being blamed on armed Islamist extremists, including the city's most powerful militia, the Abu Slim Martyrs Brigade, whose ideology residents say is akin to al-Qaeda's.

What is unfolding here may be the most extreme example of the confrontation underway across Libya, underscoring just how deeply the fundamentalists have sown their seeds in the security vacuum that has defined Libya since the fall of Moammar Gaddafi last September. ②

The extremists have continued to operate here despite the popular backlash that followed last month's attack in Benghazi, 156 miles to the west, and despite fears of possible retaliation by the United States, whose unmanned drone aircraft can now be heard humming overhead almost every day. ③

For now, the militants appear to have taken cover in urban homes and farms in the remote Green Mountains that surround the city. But officials say the local government remains powerless to stop them, even as the extremists push their ideology just as fervently as before.

"No one will stop anyone from doing anything," said Fathalla al-Awam, the head of the largely toothless local council, and militants are free to come and go from the city and surrounding areas as they please. "There's no police, no army and no militias. Nothing. It's an open city from east and west."

Some Libyans say the extremist views are held much more broadly than just among the Islamist militias themselves, a fact they said the United States has failed to understand in the wake of the Benghazi attack. ④ Not all of the extremists in Darna or elsewhere in Libya belong to a group, they said. But those who share al-Qaeda's ideology are many, they said, and that creates ample opportunity for recruitment.

"It's a way of thinking," said Saad Belgassim, who used to work as a bureaucrat in Darna's now defunct court system. "They kidnap people like they do in Afghanistan. They delude young people and send them off to bomb themselves."

In some ways, the sway that Islamists hold here is not a surprise. Neglected, conservative and desperately poor under Gaddafi, Darna stood out for its fierce Islamist resistance to the old regime — and for sending more jihadists to Iraq during the U.S. occupation than any other place in Libya.

The latest bombing here came early Thursday morning, when an explosion ripped through a building on the city's eastern outskirts that local authorities had hoped to use to support a new security force. ⑤ Often, the locals say, the target is a car belonging to an official or journalist who has dared to defy the militias. A newly appointed police chief was slain in broad daylight last March with a quick round of bullets to the back as he filled up his tank at the gas station.

Until a month ago, the Abu Slim Martyrs Brigade occupied buildings and ran checkpoints around the city, operating alongside like-minded groups, including the local branch of Ansar al-Sharia, the prime suspects in the Benghazi attack.

"They were the police and they were the criminals at the same time," said Hussein al-Misary, a local journalist. They pushed aggressively for Islamic law and threatened those who favored Tripoli's vision of a central government and constitution. They even posted kill lists on anonymous jihadist Facebook pages, he said. (592 words)

Words and Expressions

extremist	n.	极端主义分子	fervently	ad.	强烈地
stir	v.	激起	in the wake of		作为……的余波
terrorize	v.	恐吓	defunct	a.	已不存在的
militia	n.	民兵	bureaucrat	n.	官僚
militant	n.	好战分子	delude	v.	迷惑, 蛊惑
underscore	v.	强调	hold sway over		控制
backlash	n.	强烈反对	jihadist	n.	圣战者, 伊斯兰主义者
drone aircraft		无人驾驶飞机	rip	v.	撕, 剥
akin to		类似的	defy	v.	违抗, 使……难于
fundamentalist	n.	原教旨主义者	slay	v.	杀死
retaliation	n.	报复			

Proper Nouns

Darna(又作 Derna) 迪纳尔

Benghazi 班加西(利比亚城市)

Abu Slim Martyrs Brigade 伊斯兰基地组织。利比亚内战期间, al-Hasidi 率领该组织活跃在利比亚东部城市迪纳尔。

al-Qaeda 基地组织。基地这个词来源于阿拉伯语, 可以直译为"基地"、"营地"之意, 但还有"组织"、"原则"和"普遍真理"的意思。它是伊斯兰教逊尼派的组织, 成立于1988年。

Moammar Gaddafi 卡扎菲, 原利比亚总统

Ansar al-Sharia 伊斯兰民兵组织, 在利比亚内战期间形成, 鼓吹在利比亚执行严格的伊斯兰法律, 在卡扎菲死后, 该组织迅速发展。

Tripoli 的黎波里(利比亚首都)

News Summary

2011年2月15日,在北非"阿拉伯之春"的影响下,利比亚民众开始和平示威,但遭到政府军的镇压,导致了"2月17日革命"、卡扎菲政权垮台和卡扎菲本人死亡。10月23日,"全国过渡委员会"宣告全国解放、战争结束。但直到现在,地区和部落冲突时有发生,尤其是伊斯兰极端主义者和"基地"组织的渗入,造成了人民的恐惧和社会的不安定。本文介绍的就是利比亚东部城市迪纳尔受到伊斯兰极端主义组织操控的情况。

Understanding Sentences

① 在班加西美领馆遭受致命袭击引起人们开始注意利比亚越来越厉害的宗教极端主义六周之后,躲在阴暗角落里的武装伊斯兰极端主义分子正在利比亚东部城市迪纳尔制造恐怖,威胁人民生命财产安全。

② 正在这里发生的一切可能是目前在利比亚全国所发生的冲突中最极端的例子,进一步说明了原教旨主义者如何在去年九月份卡扎菲死后安保的真空里深深地散下他们的种子。

③ 尽管上个月对西面156公里以外的班加西的袭击遭到人们的强烈反对,尽管担心美国可能采取报复行动——现在几乎每天都可以听到美国无人驾驶飞机的轰鸣声,极端主义者仍继续在这里活动。

④ 一些利比亚人说,持极端主义观点的人远不止伊斯兰民兵自己,这是美国在班加西袭击事件发生以后仍不明白的。

⑤ 最近的一次爆炸发生在星期四早晨,在城市东部郊区的一栋房子里发生了一声巨响,这座当局准备作为一个新的保安队伍基地的楼房轰然倒塌。

Exercises

Ⅰ. Understanding Ideas in the News

1. Who are held responsible for the terrorist attacks in Libya?
   A. Islamist extremists.   B. Al-Qaeda.   C. Libya government.
2. How are the Islamist extremists terrorizing the eastern Libyan city of Darna?
   A. By fervently advocating their ideology.
   B. By hiding themselves in and around the city.
   C. By attacking the government.
3. "The fundamentalists", "the militants" and "the extremists" refer to _____.
   A. the security vacuum   B. Moammar Gaddafi's soldiers
   C. the same people
4. What has the United States failed to understand in the wake of the Benghazi attack?
   A. The Islamists in Darna or elsewhere in Libya belong to a group.
   B. The Islamists still resist the old regime.
   C. There are many Libyans who share the Islamist extremists views.

5. What are likely targets for bombing attacks in the city?
A. Official or journalist cars.　　　　　　B. Buildings.
C. Police checkpoints.

Ⅱ. Language Points

stir fear, akin to, in the wake of, hold sway over 这几个短语都是由简单的单音节词构成,常见于新闻英语,特别是标题中。

stir:(激起、激发某种情感)to excite or arouse (passion); prompt or evoke (anger, affection, suspicion, a memory, etc.)

akin:(类似于)similar; having some of the same qualities　e.g. *They speak a language akin to French.*

wake:(紧接……之后发生)If something happens <u>in the wake of</u> something else, it happens after and often because of it　e.g. *Airport security was extra tight in the wake of yesterday's bomb attack.*

hold sway:(影响,控制) to have power or a very strong influence　e.g. *Fundamentalist beliefs hold sway over whole districts, ensuring the popularity of religious leader.*

Ⅲ. Questions for Further Study

This short news report tells the readers that Islamist extremists are carrying out a series of terrorist attacks in eastern Libya. It is reporting facts and using quotes from people the report has interviewed. But the tone is negative to the extremists, for terrorism itself implies violence and killing. Find more expressions in the article that indicate the reporter's attitude.

2. Syrian unrest spills into Lebanon

— Kidnapping vendetta between Syrian rebels and Lebanese Shi'a clan

Lebanese gunmen from the Al-Meqdad clan in Beirut's southern suburbs (AFP Photo)

By Rana Muhammad Taha
The Daily News
August 16, 2012

  The Shi'a Lebanese Meqdad clan abducted tens of Syrians and one Turk in Lebanon on Wednesday, in retaliation for the abduction of a member of the Meqdad family by Syrian rebels.①

  The Meqdad clan is threatening to kidnap more Saudi, Turkish, and Qatari nationals until Al-Meqdad is released, according to Reuters. The three countries are accused of supporting the Syrian rebels. *The New York Times* quoted Hatem Al-Meqdad, Hassan's brother, vowing to kill all the hostages if his brother isn't released.②

  The Turkish Foreign Minister confirmed Wednesday the kidnapping of Turkish citizen, Aydin Tufan Tekin, according to *The Wall Street Journal*. Gulf countries including Saudi Arabia and Kuwait are urging their citizens to leave Lebanon immediately, citing security concerns.

  Twelve flights instead of the usual five daily are being sent by Lebanon's national carrier, Middle East Airlines, to Saudi Arabia, according to Lebanon's *The Daily Star*.

  Hassan Al-Meqdad, who arrived in Syria along with 1,500 members of Hezbollah, was kidnapped by the Free Syrian Army (FSA) on Monday, according to Al-Arabeya. Al-Meqdad was accused by the FSA of being part of a Hezbollah group sent to Syria to aid Bashar Al-Assad and fight the Syrian opposition; they released a video of Al-Meqdad on Tuesday where he admitted as much, according to BBC news.③ Both his family and Hezbollah deny the accusations, however.

  Kidnapping has been increasingly used as a tool by the Syrian rebels. Two weeks ago, they kidnapped 48 Iranians whom they accused of being members of the Iranian Revolutionary Guard, sent to Syria to quell the uprising. However, Monday's abduction is the first to generate retaliation.

  Tensions were further heightened in Lebanon on Wednesday by news that a building in Azaz, north of Aleppo, sheltering 11 Lebanese pilgrims abducted by Syrian rebels in May had been shelled by Al-Assad's forces.④ A spokesperson for the FSA's higher military council, Louay Mokdad, told *The Wall Street Journal* that two of the Lebanese hostages were injured in the bombing incident, while the fate of another four remains unknown.

  Following news of the shelling, families of the hostages took to the streets in Lebanon, where they blocked the Beirut airport highway.

  The conflict in neighbouring Syria has been spilling over into Lebanon for some time. The north Lebanese city of Tripoli, seen as an Al-Assad stronghold, witnessed several clashes between members of its Alawite Shi'a community and security forces in June.

Unit 1　Regional Focuses: Domestic Turmoil and War

Syrian refugees in Lebanon have been targeted by cross-border Syrian shelling which has killed Lebanese citizens also. Lebanon is currently sheltering 37,000 Syrian refugees, according to the United Nations High Commissioner for Refugees. (433 words)

Words and Expressions

clan	n.	部落	quell	v.	镇压
abduct	v.	劫持	tension	n.	紧张局势
kidnap	v.	绑架	shelter	n.	庇护所
vendetta	n.	宿怨,世仇	pilgrim	n.	朝圣者
rebel	n.	叛军	shell	v.	轰炸
carrier	n.	载运器,航空公司	spill	v.	溢出,波及
release	v.	释放	clash	n.	冲突

Proper Nouns

Al-Meqdad　黎巴嫩什叶派的一个部落
Shi'a Muslim　什叶派[教徒]
Damascus　大马士革(叙利亚首都)
Hatem & Hassan Al-Meqdad　该部落的两个兄弟
Hezbollah　(黎巴嫩)真主党
Al-Arabeya(应为 Al-Arabiya)　沙特阿拉伯拥有的一个泛阿拉伯地区电视台
Bashar Al-Assad　巴沙尔·阿萨德,叙利亚总统
Beirut　贝鲁特,黎巴嫩首都
Azaz, Aleppo　阿扎斯,阿利颇,黎巴嫩地名
Alawite　阿拉维,黎巴嫩地名

News Summary

　　2011年初,叙利亚发生反政府示威活动,并演变成为武装冲突,以阿萨德为首的政府军与反对派一直在打打停停,持续至今。在这个过程中,反对派的"自由军"的背后推手一直非常神秘,但逐渐显露出伊斯兰极端组织的控制,其中有些组织与"基地"存在直接的联系,这些曾经在伊拉克、利比亚、阿尔及利亚、阿富汗、索马里和车臣战斗过的伊斯兰极端主义者已经渗入到"反对派"领导层,并已操纵了国家局势。由于地理及宗教等原因,在叙利亚所发生的动乱已经波及了邻国黎巴嫩,本文就是报道这方面的一些消息。

Understanding Sentences

　　① 黎巴嫩什叶派的阿梅达部落星期三绑架了数十名在黎巴嫩的叙利亚人和一名土耳其人,作为对叙利亚反对派绑架阿梅达部落一名成员的报复。
　　②《纽约时报》引述哈桑的兄弟哈蒂姆阿梅达的话说,如果不释放他的兄弟,他将杀死所有人质。

③ 叙利亚自由军指控阿梅达属于被派到叙利亚支援巴沙尔·阿萨德并与叙利亚反对派作战的一个真主党组织;据英国广播公司消息,他们公开了星期二拍摄的一段视频,阿梅达在上面承认了这点。

④ 星期三,黎巴嫩的局势进一步紧张,有消息说,阿利颇以北的城市阿扎斯一栋关押11名五月份被叙利亚反对派绑架的黎巴嫩朝圣者的楼房遭到阿萨德力量的轰炸。

Exercises

Ⅰ. **Understanding Ideas in the News**

1. Who were kidnapped by the Shi'a Lebanese Meqdad in Lebanon?
   A. A member of the Meqdad family.　　B. Some Syrians and one Turk.
   C. Some Syrian rebels.
2. What did the Shi'a Meqdad demand for the kidnapping?
   A. The release of Hassan Al-Meqdad.　　B. The death of Hatem Al-Meqdadrian.
   C. To kill all the hostages.
3. What did the FSA accuse the Al-Meqdad of?
   A. Being part of a Hezbollah group.　　B. Supporting the Syrian rebels.
   C. Supporting the Syrian government.
4. How is Lebanon affected by the fighting between the Syrian unrest?
   A. Kidnapping has been commonly used by Syrian rebels.
   B. Cross-border Syrian bombing of refugee camps also killed Lebanese citizens.
   C. Lebanon is currently sheltering 37,000 Syrian refugees.
5. Which countries in the region are accused of supporting the Syrian rebels?
   A. Saudi, Turkey and Qatar.　　B. Saudi Arabia, Kuwait and Lebanon.
   C. Lebanon, Iran and Iraq.

Ⅱ. **Language Points**

abduct, kidnap, quell, shell, spill 这几个单音节词常用在新闻报道和标题中,它们表达强烈的感情,也容易记住。

abduct:(劫持) to lead or take away (a person, esp. a woman or child) by illegal force or fraud　e.g. *His car was held up and he was abducted by four gunmen.*

kidnap:(绑架) to carry off by illegal force or fraud, abduct, (a person, esp. a child) formerly, to provide servants or labourers for the American plantations, now esp. to obtain ransom　e.g. *Police in Brazil uncovered a plot to kidnap him.*

quell:(镇压) to stop something, esp. by force　e.g. *This latest setback will have done nothing to quell the growing doubts about the future of the club.*

shell:(这里用来表示"轰炸,炮击") to bombard (an enemy position etc.) with shells.

spill:(溢出,涌流) to (cause to) flow, move, fall or spread over the edge or beyond the limits of something　e.g. *Crowds of football fans spilled onto the field at the end of the game.*

III. Questions for Further Study

Since the beginning of 2011, the turmoil in northern African Arabic countries spread to Western Asian countries, and the rebels in Syria, led by the Free Syrian Army, started to fight the government Army, the country fell into a serious civil war. Try to find out more information and introduce to the class the causes of the Syrian civil unrest.

3. North Korea moves missile to coast, but limited threat seen

By CHOE SANG-HUN
From *the New York Times*
April 4, 2013

SEOUL, South Korea — South Korea's defense chief said on Thursday that North Korea had moved to its east coast a missile with a "considerable" range, but that it was not capable of reaching the United States. The disclosure came as the Communist North's military warned that it was ready to strike American military forces with "cutting-edge smaller, lighter and diversified nuclear strike means."①

North Korea has been issuing a blistering series of similar threats in recent weeks, citing as targets the American military installations in the Pacific islands of Hawaii and Guam, as well as the United States mainland. In its latest threat on Thursday, it did not name targets but said it was authorized to "take powerful practical military counteractions" against the threats from B-2 bombers from the United States, B-52 bombers from Guam and F-22 Stealth jet fighters from Japan that have recently run missions over the Korean Peninsula during joint military exercises with South Korea.②

"The moment of explosion is approaching fast," the general staff of the North Korean People's Army said in a statement carried by the North's official Korean Central News Agency. "The U.S. had better ponder over the prevailing grave situation."

Most analysts do not believe that North Korea has a missile powerful enough to deliver a nuclear warhead to the United States mainland or that it is reckless enough to strike the American military in the Pacific. Still, with the North's bellicose postures showing no signs of letting up, the United States announced Wednesday that it was speeding the deployment of an advanced missile defense system to Guam in the next few weeks, two years ahead of schedule in what the Pentagon said was "a precautionary move" to protect American naval and air forces from the threat of a North Korean missile attack. ③

Testifying before a parliamentary hearing, defense minister Kim Kwan-jin of South Korea said the missile North Korea has moved to the east coast, possibly "for demonstration or for training," appeared not to be a KN-08, which analysts say is the closest thing North Korea has to an intercontinental ballistic missile, though its exact range is not known. The new missile was unveiled during a military parade in the North Korean capital, Pyongyang, last April.

South Korean media quoted unnamed military sources as saying that the missile was a Musudan. Deployed around 2007, Musudan is a ballistic missile with a range of more than 1,900 miles, according to the South Korean Defense Ministry. Guam is nearly 2,200 miles from North Korea.

Col. Wee Yong-sub of the army, deputy spokesman of the Defense Ministry, would only say that the South Korean and American military have been closely monitoring the movements of all North Korean missiles, including Musudan.

"Chances are not high that they will lead to a full-scale war," said Mr. Kim, the defense minister, referring to the North Korean threats. "But given the nature of the North Korean regime, it's possible that they will launch a localized provocation."

For a second straight day, North Korea blocked South Koreans from crossing the border to enter a jointly operated industrial park, threatening the future of the last remaining symbol of inter-Korean cooperation. It also warned that it would pull out more than 53,000 North Korean workers from the joint factory park, located in the North Korean city of Kaesong, if taunts from the South Korean news media continued.

After the North's threat to close the industrial complex last week, some South Korean media reports have said that the North Korean leader, Kim Jong-un, would be all talk but no action when it came to the park because he did not want to risk one of his most precious sources of hard currency. ④

After the United Nations Security Council imposed further sanctions against the North for its launching of a three-stage rocket in December and its third nuclear test in February, North Korea has appeared to harden its stance considerably. It said it would never negotiate away its nuclear weapons arsenal but would expand it. On Tuesday, it declared it would restart a nuclear reactor that gave it a small stockpile of plutonium and would readjust its uranium-enrichment plant for weapons efforts. (704 words)

Unit 1 Regional Focuses: Domestic Turmoil and War

Words and Expressions

missile	n.	导弹		posture	n.	摆姿势，做出姿态
range	n.	射程，范围		deployment	n.	部署
strike	v.	打击		ballistic	a.	弹道的
cutting-edge	a.	尖端的，前沿的		provocation	n.	挑衅
diversified	a.	多样的		taunt	v.	辱骂，嘲讽
blistering	a.	严厉的		sanction	n.	制裁
ponder over		沉思，深思		stance	n.	姿态，态度
prevailing	a.	主要的		arsenal	n.	兵工厂
grave	a.	严重的		stockpile	n.	积蓄，库存
reckless	a.	不计后果的		plutonium	n.	[化] 钚
bellicose	a.	好战的				

Proper Nouns

Guam   关岛

B-52 bombers   B-52 轰炸机

F-22 Stealth jet   F-22 隐形喷气战斗机

Pentagon   (美)五角大楼

Pyongyang   平壤

Musudan   木水端导弹(也叫 BM25 导弹)，朝鲜研制的一种中程导弹

Kaesong   开城

News Summary

近年来，朝鲜不停地利用核试验和发射导弹做文章，在国际社会引起一波接一波的风浪，也在朝鲜半岛制造了紧张局势。2013 年 3 月份以来，除了宣布已成功进行核试验，朝鲜还威胁要把远程导弹部署在其东海岸并处于发射状态，直接威胁韩国、日本和美国在夏威夷和关岛的军事目标。此外，他们还单方面关闭了开城工业区，撤回朝方工人等。这篇报道就是针对朝鲜部署导弹的消息，但美国的记者也一针见血地指出"威胁有限"，因为人们已经熟悉了他们的做法只不过是虚张声势而已。

Understanding Sentences

① 这一消息是随着共产主义北方的军事警告一起被泄露出来的，说它现在能够用"新式的、更小、更轻和多样化的核弹头"打击美国军事力量。

② 在其星期四发表的最新威胁中，没有说明具体的目标，但是，说它有权对从美国本土起飞的 B-2 轰炸机、从关岛起飞的 B-52 轰炸机和从日本起飞的 F-22 隐形喷气战斗机"采取强有力的、实际的军事反击行动"，这些飞机在最近的美韩联合军事演习中在朝鲜半岛上空执行任务。

③ 但是，由于朝鲜的好战姿态并没有表现出有所收敛的迹象，美国星期三宣布在接下

来的几周时间里将加快在关岛部署一种先进的导弹防御系统,比原定计划提前了两年,据五角大楼宣布,这是为了应对朝鲜的导弹攻击,是保护美国海军和空军的"一种预防性的行动"。

④ 在朝鲜上星期威胁要关闭这个工业园区之后,一些韩国媒体的报告说,在工业园问题上,朝鲜的领导人金正恩只是在口头上威胁,不会采取行动,因为他不愿意冒着失去他最宝贵的硬通货币来源之一的危险。

Exercises

Ⅰ. Understanding Ideas in the News

1. What did North Korea threaten to do in the recent weeks?

A. To counter-attack American bombers.

B. To move a missile to its east coast.

C. To strike American military forces with nuclear bomb.

2. What weapon did they claim to use to strike American military forces?

A. Advanced nuclear warheads.　　　　B. F-22 Stealth jet.

C. Nuclear bombs.

3. What did the U. S. decide to speed up in response to North Korea's bellicose postures?

A. The deployment of a missile defence system to Guam.

B. The deployment of a KN-08 missile.

C. Intercontinental ballistic missiles.

4. After North Korea's threat to close the Kaesong Industrial Complex, how did South Korean media respond?

A. They criticized the North.　　　　B. They taunted the North.

C. They disagreed with the North.

5. What's North Korea's attitude to its developing nuclear weapons?

A. It would negotiate away its nuclear weapon arsenal.

B. It would continue to expand its nuclear weapon arsenal.

C. It would restart a nuclear reactor.

Ⅱ. Language Points

blistering, bellicose 这两个词用来描述朝鲜方面那种严厉的口气和姿态。

blistering:(严厉的) A blistering remark expresses great anger or dislike　e.g. *The president responded to this with a blistering attack on his critics.*

bellicose:(好战的) wishing to fight or start a war　e.g. *The general made some bellicose statements about his country's military strength.*

stance, taunt, provocation 这几个名词也是新闻英语中常用的。

stance:(姿态,态度) a way of thinking about something, especially expressed in a publicly stated opinion   e. g. *The doctor's stance on the issue of abortion is well known.*

taunt:（辱骂，嘲讽）to intentionally annoy and upset someone by making unkind remarks to them, laughing at them, etc.   e. g. *The other children used to taunt him in the playground because he was fat and wore glasses.*

provocation:（挑衅）an action or statement that is intended to make someone angry   e. g. *He'd fly into a rage at the slightest provocation.*

III. Further Study

This news story is about North Korea's threat to the south with the missiles and nuclear bombs it claimed to have launched. The reporter uses proof from officials in South Korea to analyze the threats issued by North Korea. See who are quoted and what they want to prove. Find more information about the negotiation between North and South Korea on the re-opening of the Kaesong Industrial Complex and the current situation there.

英语报刊知识介绍

新闻学与新闻要素

新闻学（journalism）是关于收集、撰写和报道新闻的一门学科，即报道那些发生在现实社会中的、尚未被大众知道的事情。新闻学首先研究的是：什么是新闻。在人们的日常生活中，每时每刻都在发生着各种各样的事情。哪些事情才能成为新闻，得到传播呢？西方新闻界有一句名言："新闻就是人咬狗"。因为在生活中，狗咬人的事情时有发生，不足为奇，而人咬狗就成了怪事，于是也就成了新闻。

新闻是报道在某一特定地方和时间发生的事件，它必须交代清楚时间、地点、什么事情、涉及的人、产生的结果和影响，等等。在英语新闻上，人们常说的就是新闻的五个 W 和一个 H：Who? What? Where? When? Why? 和 How? 我们在阅读英语新闻的时候，必须围绕这六个方面来理解新闻的内容。

报刊新闻指刊登在各种报纸和杂志上的新闻。本书主要采用英美报刊刊登的新闻，学生通过阅读来获取信息，掌握更多词汇，通过练习提高英语水平。

1. A clip of front page of the *New York Times*

2. A stack of English newspapers

Unit 2 Conflicts in the Middle East

The Middle East is another "hot spot" in the world, as there have been conflicts and fightings over the past 60 years or so. Since the establishment of Israel in the Middle East, the Palestinians have been engaged in several major battles and suicidal bombing became one of the major means of terrorism targeting the Israelis. Although peace agreements have been signed between the two sides, conflicts still exist, and in the wider area of the Middle East, wars between countries, international intervention and domestic turmoil in many Arabic countries, etc. are still focus of news, hence it is worthwhile to put some news reports about this area in a separate chapter as a regional focus.

英语的"中东"地区是指跨越欧洲以东的亚洲区域,对我们来说应该是西亚地区。中东地区的冲突,首先是以色列和巴勒斯坦的冲突,从20世纪中期开始一直延续了半个多世纪。目前虽然相对稳定,但自杀式炸弹爆炸的事件还是时有发生,局部战争还是绵延不断地发生。就整个中东地区来说,从20世纪的阿富汗战争、科威特战争至21世纪初的伊拉克战争,战火从未停息,国际社会的介入又使问题更加复杂化,各国的统治阶层和人民、部落和宗教教派之间的矛盾也日益突出,因而在这个地区发生的事件几乎都是新闻,这里我们用一章来介绍几篇有关中东地区的新闻。

1. "Terrorist" explosion on Tel Aviv bus jeopardises Hamas truce deal

An explosion has hit a public bus in the heart of Tel Aviv, wounding at least 10 people, even as frantic diplomatic efforts continued to secure a truce between Israel and Hamas.

A witness said there were few passengers on the bus when it exploded. Photo: BBC

By Damien McElroy and agencies
The Daily Telegraph
10:16AM GMT, 21 Nov., 2012

"A bomb exploded on a bus in central Tel Aviv. This was a terrorist attack. Most of the injured suffered only mild injuries," said Ofir Gendelman, a spokesman for Prime Minister Benjamin Netanyahu.

The bus was charred and blackened, its side windows blown out and its glass scattered on the asphalt. ①

An Israeli driver who witnessed the explosion told Army Radio the bus was "completely charred inside." Another witness said there were few passengers on the bus when it exploded.

Police spokesman Micky Rosenfeld said authorities were investigating whether the bomb had been planted and left on the bus or whether it was the work of a suicide bomber.

Witnesses told the BBC that they saw a man leave something on the bus near the nation's military headquarters.

The attack happened on the eighth day of an Israeli offensive against the Gaza Strip which it launched with the stated aim of preventing rocket strikes from the Palestinian enclave. ②

Celebratory gunfire rang out in Gaza City when local radio stations reported news of the Tel Aviv explosion.

The last time Israel's commercial capital was hit by a serious bomb blast was in April 2006, when a Palestinian suicide bomber killed 11 people at a sandwich stand near the city's old central bus station. ③ "There are about 10 people wounded of whom three are in serious condition," emergency services spokesman Zaki Heller told public radio.

"There was an apparent explosion on a bus in Shaul HaMelech Street in Tel Aviv. The background and circumstances are not clear yet," police spokesman Luba Samri told AFP.

News of the explosion came as Hillary Clinton, the U.S. secretary of state, is engaged in strenuous shuttle diplomacy to wring an elusive truce deal from Israel and Gaza's militant Hamas rulers, after earlier attempts to end more than a week of fighting broke down amid heavy overnight bombing. ④

Mrs. Clinton joined other diplomats in shuttling between Jerusalem, the West Bank and Cairo, trying to piece together a deal after a week of fighting and mounting casualties.

After meeting Benjamin Netanyahu, the Israeli Prime Minister, in Jerusalem on Tuesday night, Mrs. Clinton conferred with Palestinian President Mahmoud Abbas in the West Bank on Wednesday morning.

She then returned to Jerusalem for further talks with Mr. Netanyahu, Ehud Barak, the defence minister and Avigdor Lieberman, the foreign minister.

She was due to travel to Cairo, carrying Israeli demands for further Egyptian assurances that the flow of arms to Hamas, the militant faction that controls Gaza, can be cut off.

Protesters angered by the eight-day Israel operation to bomb Gazan rocket arsenals gathered outside the Ramallah complex housing the Palestinian Authority as Mrs. Clinton met Mahmoud Abbas, its president.

The U. S. envoy arrived in Israel last night and met Benjamin Netanyahu, the Israeli prime minister who launched Operation Pillar of Defence last Wednesday. He said the U. S. and Israel would take the opportunity to align their positions so that diplomacy could draw the conflict to a close.

"If there is a possibility of achieving a long-term solution to this problem with diplomatic means, we prefer that," he said. "But if not, I'm sure you understand that Israel will have to take whatever action is necessary to defend its people."

Sources in Gaza reported the death toll in Gaza had reached 139 by Wednesday morning.

Instead of an expected cessation, Israel's military laid on a heavy bombardment of artillery and aerial bombing on Gaza after warning residents to move to designated "safe areas".

In the hours of darkness, Israeli forces targeted dozens of "terrorist infrastructure sites". More than 30 strikes overnight also included government ministries and a banker's empty villa.

At least four strikes within seconds of each other pulverised a complex of government ministries covering a city block, rattling nearby buildings and shattering surrounding windows.⑤ Hours later, clouds of acrid dust still hung over the area and smoke still rose from the rubble. (658 words)

Words and Expressions

jeopardize	v.	危害,危及	wring	v.	(通过努力)达成
truce	n.	停战协议	elusive	a.	难以捉摸的
char	v.	烧成炭	confer	v.	协商
asphalt	n.	沥青	align	v.	使结盟,使成一行
frantic	a.	疯狂的	cessation	n.	停止
suicide bomber		自杀式炸弹	artillery	n.	炮兵
enclave	n.	被包围的领土	pulverise	v.	粉碎
blast	n.	爆炸	rattle	v.	发出咔嗒声
strenuous	a.	紧张的	shatter	v.	粉碎

Proper Nouns

Benjamin Netanyahu 本杰明·内塔尼亚胡(以色列总理)
Gaza Strip 加沙地带
Tel Aviv 特拉维夫(以色列首都)
Hamas 哈马斯(巴勒斯坦解放阵线的一个激进派别)
Jerusalem 耶路撒冷
Mahmoud Abbas 阿巴斯(巴勒斯坦总统,哈马斯负责人)
Twitter 推特

News Summary

"在特拉维夫市中心的一辆公共汽车上一颗炸弹发生了爆炸。"这是这则新闻的中心内容。由于炸弹爆炸,特别是自杀式炸弹爆炸,在以色列已经是司空见惯的事情了,所以这条新闻也没有在爆炸发生的具体情况上多做文章,只是简单地引用见证人的话,说明当时汽车上的乘客不多,大部分伤者也只是受了轻伤。文章接着笔锋一转,点出了爆炸事件发生在以色列为了打击巴勒斯坦人向以色列发射火箭而开展的军事打击行动的第八天,正是美国国务卿希拉里忙着在巴以之间穿梭调停,希望能达成一个和平协议的时候,所以新闻的标题用了"特拉维夫公共汽车上的爆炸危及了哈马斯的停战协议"。

Understanding Sentences

① 整辆汽车被烧成焦黑了,两边的窗户被弹出,破碎的玻璃洒落在马路的沥青上面。

② 这次袭击发生在以色列针对加沙地带发动攻击的第八天,以色列公开声明,攻击的目的是阻止从巴勒斯坦被包围的地区发射火箭。

③ 上次以色列的商务首都遭受严重的炸弹袭击是在2006年4月份,一名巴勒斯坦自杀式炸弹携带者在旧的汽车总站附近一个快餐档口引爆炸弹,导致11人死亡。

④ 爆炸的消息传来的时候,正是美国国务卿希拉里·克林顿忙于进行穿梭外交,试图在以色列和加沙好战的哈马斯领导人之间达成勉强的停战协定之时,在此之前,试图结束一周来的战斗的努力被一个晚上的炮火打破了。

⑤ 至少四次间隔非常短的轰炸瞬间把占据一个街区的政府部门办公室大楼夷为平地,震动了附近的大楼,使四面窗户的玻璃成为碎片。

Exercises

Ⅰ. Understanding Ideas in the News

1. What is unsure about the bus explosion in central Tel Aviv?
   A. Whether it is a suicidal bombing.   B. The number of injured.
   C. The location of bombing.

2. What is the purpose of the eight-day offensive against the Gaza Strip?
   A. To bomb the Ramallah complex.
   B. To bomb the Gaza Strip.

C. To prevent rocket strikes from the area.

3\. Between what places are diplomats, including Mrs. Clinton, travelling?

A. Israel, the United States and Egypt.

B. Tel Aviv, Gaza City and Egypt.

C. Jerusalem, the West Bank and Cairo.

4\. Will a long-term solution to this problem be achieved with diplomatic means, as from this news report?

A. Not likely.　　　　B. Yes.　　　　C. No.

5\. Which of the following is not included in the targets by the Israeli military forces?

A. Government complex.　　　　B. The Ramallah complex.

C. Pillar of Defence.

II. Language Points

wring, confer, align, rattle, shatter 这些是文章中使用的简单、有力的动词。

wring：("绞,拧",这里表示"达成某种协议") ring sth. from/out of somebody: to force or persuade someone to give you something　e.g. *They managed to wring a few concessions from the government.*

confer：(协商,交换意见) to exchange ideas on a particular subject, often in order to reach a decision on what action to take　e.g. *I should like some time to confer with my lawyer.*

align：(对齐,对准) to put two or more things into a straight line　e.g. *When you've aligned the notch on the gun with the target, fire!*

rattle：(震动,震响) to (cause to) make a noise like a series of knocks　e.g. *The explosion rattled the cups on the table.*

shatter：(粉碎) to (cause something to) break suddenly into very small pieces　e.g. *The glass shattered into a thousand tiny pieces.*

III. Questions for Further Study

This news report presents mainly two parts of information. The first is about the bomb explosion in a Tel Aviv bus. The reporter quotes several witness to tell people the seriousness of the explosion. The second is about the U. S.'s diplomatic efforts to mediate the two sides, together with some background about Israeli's offensive. Notice the typical news reporting language and analyze how information is effectively conveyed in the news.

2. Hizbollah debates dropping support for the regime of President Bashar al-Assad

Hizbollah has been one of the staunchest supporters of the regime of President Bashar al-Assad, but now there are bitter arguments within its ranks about whether it is time to change course.

In Hizbollah's South Beirut stronghold Mr. Assad is still a hero. Photo: Ali Hashisho/REUTERS

By Nick Meo, Ruth Sherlock, and Carol Malouf in Beirut
The *Daily Telegraph*
5:00PM BST, 27 Oct., 2012

The giant banner with a portrait of Bashar al-Assad, strung across a busy street in South Beirut, proclaimed loyalty to the Syrian president — and cursed his enemies.

"Those who hate the Lion of Syria are sons of bitches," it read, in Arabic slang with a play on the meaning of the Assad name.

Elsewhere in the Arab world he may be hated as a bloody tyrant, but in Hizbollah's South Beirut stronghold Mr. Assad is still a hero.

A couple of streets away, the British hostage Terry Waite was held captive for four years until his release in 1991, and nearby is the site of the notorious massacre of Sabra and Shatila where perhaps as many as 3,500 people were murdered by pro-Israeli militias in 1982.

Hizbollah's reclusive leader Hassan Nasrallah, the undisputed head of Lebanon's Shia Muslims, lives nearby in a heavily guarded apartment complex. Hizbollah's own police force, in khaki fatigues, patrol the streets, which are noticeably more crowded and scruffier than in the centre of Beirut with its nightclubs and fashionable shops.

Hizbollah—"the party of God"—needed help from neighbouring Syria to become the most powerful force in Lebanese politics, and it could always depend on the ruling family in Damascus during its wars with Israel. ①

Now in Mr. Assad's time of need Lebanon's Shias have mostly been loyal in return — providing logistical and moral support and even sending fighters into Syria's civil war to kill his enemies.

But in Lebanon there are as many Christians and Sunni Muslims as there are Shia. Now, as doubts grow that Mr. Assad will survive and Syria's civil war begins to spread into Lebanon, The *Sunday Telegraph* has been told of secret arguments raging inside Hizbollah's ranks about whether the time has come to stop backing Mr. Assad. ②

To many in South Beirut, where Hizbollah runs hospitals, schools, and rubbish collections, and pays pensions to the families of slain fighters, that would be unthinkable.

Many Hizbollah supporters insist it is Assad who is the victim, not the opposition, and that he is worthy of their support.

"In Syria there are terrorist attacks, torture, killing and beheading, all done by the enemies of the regime," Mr. Suleiman said. "This is not a revolution like the one in Egypt. Ninety per cent of the Syrians support Bashar. He is a good man and he will survive.

"If it looks as if he is in real danger, we will send thousands of our men into Syria. And if America or Nato is stupid enough to intervene, we will be there defending Arab lands."

There were reports of fresh fighting in Syria on Saturday, with opposition activists claiming Syrian artillery bombarded cities, in breach of a truce meant to mark the Muslim Eid al-Adha holiday. ③ Both the government and rebels agreed a truce. Mohammed Doumany, an activist from the Damascus suburb of Douma, said he had counted 15 explosions in an hour and said at least two civilians had been killed. There were also reports of heavy fighting along the Syria-Turkey border.

Some Hizbollah members, including clerics, fear that their support for Mr. Assad is dragging them into a dangerous fight with Sunni Arabs — the other side of Islam's main sectarian divide — in Syria and Lebanon, he said. ④

They say it is now urgent to end their support for Mr. Assad, so that a new relationship can be formed with whoever comes to power in Syria next.

The most dramatic sign of dissent within Hizbollah is the cancellation of a forthcoming party convention that is usually held every three years — the first time anybody can remember it being dropped. The official explanation is that it would be a security risk.

But a Shia politician from an important political family said: "They are not able to hold their convention because they are afraid they cannot agree on Syria."

Disagreement is said to be strongest between civilian Hizbollah members, who are more likely to favour cutting links with Damascus, and its powerful military wing, trained and indoctrinated by Iran and still fiercely loyal to the Syrian regime. ⑤

Car bombings and clashes between militias, alarming signs that Syria's violent struggle is spreading to Lebanon, have forced many of his followers to wonder where their involvement with Mr. Assad is leading them. (726 words)

Words and Expressions

staunch	a.	忠诚的,坚定的	rage	n.	愤怒
proclaim	v.	声明,显示	rank	n.	职位,官级
notorious	a.	声名狼藉的	in breach of		违反
massacre	v. & n.	屠杀	cleric	n.	牧师
undisputed	a.	无可争议的	sectarian	a.	教派的
khaki fatigue		卡其布工作服	dissent	n.	反对者,持异议者
patrol	v.	巡逻	indoctrinate	v.	灌输
scruffy	a.	肮脏的	logistical	a.	后勤的

Proper Nouns

Bashar al-Assad 巴沙尔·阿萨德(叙利亚总统)

Sabra and Shatila 萨布拉和沙提拉

Shia 什叶派

Sunni 逊尼派

Eid al-Adha (穆斯林)开斋节

Damascus 大马士革(叙利亚首都)

News Summary

这一则有关中东地区的新闻从另一个侧面反映了当前阿拉伯世界的一些变化。叙利亚和黎巴嫩是相邻的两个阿拉伯国家,他们曾经长期联合在一起对抗以色列。自2011年初开始的"阿拉伯之春"已经导致了统治利比亚长达42年的卡扎菲政权垮台和同样统治埃及几十年的穆巴拉克政权更换,并且在叙利亚引发了内战。这又影响到它的邻国黎巴嫩。本文在描述了贝鲁特南部真主党控制地区仍然表现出对叙利亚阿萨德政权的支持情况之后,简单说明真主党依靠阿萨德政权的根本原因,然后转而介绍说,由于叙利亚的战争影响到黎巴嫩,迫使一些真主党成员开始考虑是否有必要继续支持阿萨德。由于国际社会各方面的干预,叙利亚的战争还在继续,它对黎巴嫩的进一步影响还有待"下回分解"。

Understanding Sentences

①真主党——"神的党"——需要来自邻近的叙利亚的帮助,以成为黎巴嫩政治上最强大的力量,而它在和以色列开战的时候,一直就是依靠大马士革的这个当权家族的。

②现在,由于对阿萨德能否坚持到底产生怀疑,随着叙利亚内战开始蔓延到黎巴嫩,《星期日电讯》报收到消息说,在真主党内的各个级别都在秘密地激烈争论是否该停止支持阿萨德。

③有报道说星期六叙利亚又发生新的战斗,反对派活跃分子声称叙利亚政府军炮兵违反了庆祝阿拉伯节日的停战协定,轰炸了城市。

④他说,一些真主党成员,包括牧师,担心他们对阿萨德的支持正在把他们拖进与逊尼派阿拉伯人——伊斯兰的另一个主要的教派——的危险战争中。

⑤ 据说,在真主党的平民成员中存在着最强烈的不同意见,他们更可能倾向于切断和大马士革以及它的由伊朗训练和灌输思想、仍然非常忠于叙利亚当前政权的强大军事力量的联系。

Exercises

Ⅰ. Understanding Ideas in the News

1. What indicates the support of Mr. Assad by the Hizbollah in Lebanon?
   A. Hizbollah's police in khaki fatigues.
   B. The Lion of Syria.
   C. A giant banner with a portrait of Mr. Assad in the street.
2. Why do the Hizbollah need help from neighbouring Syria?
   A. They want to become the most power force in Lebanese politics.
   B. They provide Syria with logistical and moral support.
   C. They are fighting Israel.
3. What cause the Hizbollah's rank to debate on whether they should still support Assad?
   A. The Shias won't be dragged into a fight with Sunni Arabs.
   B. Syria's civil war begins to spread into Lebanon.
   C. Doubts on Mr. Assad grow among people.
4. What did supporters of the Hizbollah believe about the situation in Syria?
   A. It is the opposition that is to be blamed.
   B. Assad is not a good man.
   C. They will send thousands of men into Syria.
5. What did the opposition activists accuse Syria government of?
   A. The cancellation of a forthcoming convention.
   B. Breach of a truce to mark the Eid-al-Adha holiday.
   C. Heavy fight along the Syrian-Turkey border.

Ⅱ. Language Points

staunch, reclusive, notorious, scruffy, sectarian 这些是文章中使用的一些描述性质、特点等的形容词。

staunch:(忠诚的,坚定的) always loyal in supporting a person, organization or set of beliefs or opinions e. g. *He gained a reputation as being a staunch defender/supporter of civil right.*

reclusive:(隐居的) A reclusive person or animal lives alone and deliberately avoids the company of others e. g. *She had been living a reclusive life in Los Angeles since her marriage broke up.*

notorious:(声名狼藉的) famous for something bad e. g. *The company is notorious for paying its bills late.*

scruffy: (肮脏的) untidy and dirty   e. g. *They live in a rather scruffy part of town.*

sectarian: (教派的) denoting or concerning a sect or sects   e. g. *Among the sectarian offshoots of Ismailism were the Druze of Lebanon.*

III. Questions for Further Study

This news story gives us information about the Hizbollah in southern Lebanon. They have been supporting the Syrian president Assad, but since the civil war in Syria, they are thinking about changing it. This is the main idea of the news. But there are also other information about the sectarian sections and their conflicts. Analyze the news report carefully to see how it is presented.

3. The Israel-Palestine conflict won't go away

The trail of an Israeli missile launched in response to an incoming rocket from Gaza.

By YOSSI ALPHER
The New York Times
November 16, 2012

THE Israel-Hamas clash in and around the Gaza Strip offers an important reminder to the second Obama administration: You can ignore the Israeli-Palestinian conflict for only so long.

You can, with wishful thinking, derogate that conflict to a low priority on your list of Middle East tasks — well below Iran, Syria, Afghanistan and the democratizing of political Islam.① But it will contrive to bounce right back up to the top of your list.

Currently, the administration confronts two urgent developments related to the conflict: the Gaza fighting and the determination of the Palestinian Authority leader,

Mahmoud Abbas, to seek U. N. General Assembly recognition of Palestine as a quasi-state.

Washington's natural inclination is to fall back on shopworn formulas for pushing these issues back off the immediate agenda: another Egyptian-mediated cease-fire, however temporary, in Gaza; and promises to Abbas that if he just backs away from the U. N. the administration will sponsor yet again discussion of the Oslo-begotten formula for a two-state solution. ②

These tactics might even work for a while, at least until the new administration gets organized and Israel gets through its Jan. 22 elections. But they are just that: tactics. They reflect the prolonged absence in Washington, Jerusalem and Arab capitals of a viable and realistic strategy for dealing with the Palestinian issue in all its complexity.

Looking at the Gaza Strip, five years of economic blockade failed to weaken or moderate Hamas, while giving Israel a bad name. Military reoccupation is justifiably shunned by Israel as counterproductive; every incursion into the Strip has a quick exit plan. Hamas refuses to talk with Israel and Israel, backed by Washington, refuses to talk with Hamas.

Now, with the support of Egypt's Muslim Brotherhood government and the deep pockets of the Qataris, Hamas feels more confident than ever, despite the bashing it has received from Israel. ③ It confronts us with the specter, in a best-case scenario, of a three-state solution. In a worst-case scenario, its provocations could bring Egypt and Israel to the brink of dangerous armed tensions.

Turning to the West Bank, where the Palestinian Authority is close to bankrupt and the P. L. O. still pretends it can represent Gaza in the U. N. and in talks with Israel, the absence of substantive negotiations for the past four years points to the effective demise of the Oslo process, the strategy of the past 20 years.

The failure of the Olmert-Abbas talks back in September 2008 was far more than a tactical setback. In retrospect, it must be understood as a reflection of the parties' true inability to bridge their "narrative" gaps regarding refugee right of return and the Temple Mount in Jerusalem. ④ Under these sad circumstances, "Just get to the damn table" (Leon Panetta, Dec. 2, 2011) is not a strategy for resolving this conflict. These issues will not go away.

The coming months of transition in Washington provide a unique opportunity to review failed strategies in the Israeli-Palestinian context and examine new ones, even if the objective is stabilization and limited progress rather than an elusive end-of-conflict.

For starters? West Bank unilateral-withdrawal proposals by the Israeli political center and strategic think tanks deserve serious consideration.

The new Egyptian leadership could be pressed by Washington to persuade Hamas to negotiate directly with Israel, where many would welcome this opportunity.

And conceivably, Abbas's U. N. initiative could be leveraged into a useful "win-

win" formula for partial progress toward a two-state framework. (603 words)

Words and Expressions

wishful	a.	一厢情愿的	incursion	n.	侵入
derogate	v.	贬低	specter	n.	幽灵
contrive	v.	安排,设计	beget	v.	招致,产生,引起
quasi-state		准国家的	scenario	n.	情景
shopworn	a.	陈旧的	bashing	n.	重打,猛击
formula	n.	方式	substantive	a.	有实质的
viable	a.	可行的	demise	v.	让渡,转让
tactic	n.	战术,策略	retrospect	n.	回顾
blockade	v. & n.	封锁	unilateral	a.	单方的
shun	v.	避开	leverage	n.	支撑,影响力

Proper Nouns

Oslo　（挪威）奥斯陆
The Muslim Brotherhood　（埃及）穆斯林兄弟会
P. L. O　巴勒斯坦解放组织
Temple Mount　圣殿山,耶路撒冷的一个宗教圣地

News Summary

　　这是《纽约时报》上的一篇时事评论。美国2012年大选刚结束,以色列和巴勒斯坦在加沙地带又发生了激烈的火箭袭击和反袭击战斗。评论用第二人称,给奥巴马的下一任政府出谋划策,并一针见血地指出,以巴冲突将不会消失。文章指出,美国政府目前面临的两个紧迫问题是加沙地区的战斗和阿巴斯寻求联合国大会支持巴勒斯坦立国,但是,美国采取的仍然是拖延的态度。文章指出,美国可以趁政府换届的机会,重新审视以前的政策和目前中东的局势,采取一些行动来支持该地区实现和平。由于是评论,文章的写作手法与一般的新闻有所不同,侧重于说明,而不是描述。

Understanding Sentences

　　① 你可以打你的如意算盘,把这一冲突放到你中东工作任务中次要的地位——远低于伊朗、叙利亚、阿富汗问题,以及伊斯兰政治上的民主化问题。
　　② 华盛顿自然的倾向便是利用陈旧的方法,把这些事情从紧急的议程上往后推:在加沙地带取得另一次埃及调停的停火,不管时间多短暂;向阿巴斯承诺,只要他不再到联合国申诉,政府将再次召开按照奥斯陆产生的模式的会谈来解决两国问题。
　　③ 现在,由于得到埃及穆斯林兄弟会政府和卡塔尔雄厚的资金支持,哈马斯比过去任何时候都感到更加自信,尽管它刚受到以色列的攻击。
　　④ 回顾过去,必须把它理解为是有关双方无法在难民回迁权利问题上和耶路撒冷天坛山问题上自圆其说的一种表现。

Exercises

I. Understanding Ideas in the News

1. According to the commentator, which of the following should be on the top of the list of the American administration?
   A. The democratizing of political Islam.
   B. The Israeli-Palestinian conflict.
   C. Recognition of Palestine as a quasi-state.

2. What tactics would the U. S. use for pushing these issues back off the immediate agenda?
   A. A two-state solution.
   B. Egyptian-mediate cease-fire in Gaza.
   C. Bombing the Gaza Strip.

3. Who are giving the Hamas in the Gaza Strip financial help?
   A. The Qataris.   B. The Egyptians.   C. The Israelis.

4. Why does the author think that negotiation is not a strategy for resolving the conflicts between Israel and Palestine?
   A. Because the issues are fundamental.
   B. Because the Palestinian Authority is close to bankrupt.
   C. Because there had no substantive negotiations.

5. Which of the following is suggested to be dealt with first by the Washington administration?
   A. The Temple Mount in Jerusalem.
   B. A negotiation between Hamas and Israel.
   C. The Israeli proposal of unilateral-withdrawal.

II. Language Points

derogate, contrive, bounce, shun, leverage   这些是新闻中用来讨论巴-以冲突的一些动词。

derogate：(贬损,贬低人、事) disparage (someone or something)   e. g. *It is typical of him to derogate the powers of reason.*

contrive：(安排,设计) to arrange a situation or event, or arrange for something to happen, using clever planning   e. g. *Couldn't you contrive a meeting between them?*

bounce back：(反弹) to start to be successful again after a difficult period, for example after experiencing failure, loss of confidence, illness or unhappiness   e. g. *Stock prices bounced back after a steep plunge earlier this week.*

shun：(避开) to avoid something   e. g. *She has shunned publicity since she retired from the theatre.*

leverage：(支撑,影响力) the power to influence a person or situation to achieve a particular outcome   e. g. *The company is highly leveraged and struggling with interest payments.*

III. Questions for Further Study

Why does the author say in this commentary that the Israeli-Palestinian conflict won't go away? Please find out some references about this conflict, and understand the history of this issue, so you may see what the author really means.

英语报刊知识介绍

英语报纸

世界各国都出版英语报纸，总量很多，单美国和英国的英语报纸就不下数千种，中国学生熟悉的主要有美国的《纽约时报》、《华盛顿邮报》、《华尔街日报》等，英国的《泰晤士报》、《每日电讯报》和《每日邮报》等。这些报刊上刊登的新闻及文字为我们学习英语提供了大量的、最新的材料。

英语报纸分日报和晚报，一般的日报都是在每天天一亮就开始和读者见面；而晚报则通常在下午出版。此外，还有大报和小报的区别。大报一般是以主流新闻为主的比较严肃的报纸，版面一般是对开；而小报则多报道日常生活中的事情，版面较小，文章精悍短小，多刊登大幅照片。

1. British newspapers on the newspaper stand for sale

2. The front page of a British tabloid *The Sun*, noticing the large font of the headline

Unit 3　The African Scene

Africa is the largest continent in the world, rich in natural resources and the history of human evolution. Many countries in Africa became independent after World War Ⅱ, and have been developing rapidly, especially since the end of the 20th century. African voices are more and more heard internationally now, which make us realize that it is not just the safari and game hunting in Africa. Because of historical reasons, English, French and Portuguese are widely used in Africa, esp. by the media, so newspapers, radio and television are mostly in English. This chapter includes three reports on political and military events in the northern and central African countries of Nigeria, Algeria and Central Africa, showing the recent situation in these areas.

非洲是地球上陆地面积最大的一个洲,每天在非洲大陆上所发生的一切,越来越受到世界的注意。自从第二次世界大战结束以后,许多非洲国家相继获得独立,一直到20世纪90年代。非洲国家在自身的建设上取得很大的成就,在国际事务中也发挥着越来越重要的作用。中国与非洲的外交、经贸关系也越来越密切。由于历史原因,大部分非洲国家广泛使用英语、法语或葡萄牙语,报刊、电台和电视也多用这几种语言,因此我们也可以阅读一些非洲国家的英文报刊文章,方便我们了解非洲的情况。本章包括了三篇关于北非、中非的新闻,分别是:尼日利亚一些地方的民众不满伊斯兰极端主义分子,希望政府军长期留下;西方国家对北非伊斯兰极端主义活跃的忧虑和他们面临的问题;关于中非共和国前总统在2012年垮台的报道和分析。

1. Boko Haram: Borno residents want permanent military presence

Lt. Gen Azubuike Ikejirika

African Herald Express
June 13, 2013

Residents of Kireona town in Marte Local Government Area of Borno State on Wednesday recounted their ordeal in the hands of the Boko Haram insurgents who built one of their camps in the area and terrorised the residents before the deployment of the Gen. Ihejirika-led Special Forces to liberate them. ①

Apparently heaving a sigh of relief from the terror unleashed on the community by the insurgents, they lamented the inhuman treatment meted out to them during the inglorious reign of Boko Haram in the area. ②

They, however, requested for a permanent military presence in the area as they expressed fears that the insurgents may return once the Special Forces completes their assignment and leave.

"We are afraid the Boko Haram terrorists may return if and when the military round off their mission to Marte; we hope the President will establish a military barracks in Kirenoa to seriously check activities of the Boko Haram sect.

"We are happy the President ordered the deployment of troops to Marte, though, initially we were afraid of the soldiers because of what happened in Baga recently but they have proved us wrong with their disposition towards us; we don't want them to leave again," a resident of the area, Malam Garba A. Garba, said.

Lamenting that women were forced into marriage by the terrorists, he noted that some young girls were also raped in the process, adding "and none of us could do any thing or complain because we fear for our lives." ③

He disclosed further that "The Boko Haram terrorists were seen dressed in military uniforms; they speak our local language," adding "They also raped some of our young girls while other girls were subjected into forced marriage."

He said some of the youths of the town were forcefully recruited by the sect who were always coming around to collect levies from the people.

However, the residents have also expressed fears that farming activities in the area may be adversely affected by the deployment of the Special Forces to the area with many farmers already complaining that they could not go to their farms as a result of heavy military presence in the area. ④

But the state governor, Alhaji Kashim Shettima, who said he had already taken the matter up with the military authority to allow the farmers, especially those working on the Chad Basin Development Authority farms, to go to their farms.

"We are all happy for the return of peace to Marte and its environs, the state government will not relent in its effort to ensure the protection of lives and properties," Shettima said during a visit to the area on Wednesday.

Shettima, who administered polio vaccines to children and gave out free drugs to nursing mothers during his visit to the area, also inspected the Marte General Hospital which has reached about 90 percent completion.

Meanwhile, the Secretary to the State Governor, Ambassador Baba Ahmed Jida, has commended the security operatives for their effort in combating the Boko Haram terrorists in the area. Jida, who hails from the town, also appealed to residents of the town to continue to cooperate with the Special Forces. (531 words)

Words and Expressions

recount	v.	叙述	recruit	v.	征募
ordeal	n.	痛苦的经历	sect	n.	教派
insurgent	n.	叛乱者,叛军	levy	v.	征税
deployment	n.	部署	adversely	ad.	不利地,有害地
unleash	v.	释放,放纵	relent	v.	发慈悲
lament	v.	悲叹,哀叹	polio vaccine		天花疫苗
mete out to		给予	commend	v.	称赞
inglorious	a.	可耻的	operative	n.	特务,特工
barrack	n.	军营	hail from		来自或发源于
disposition	n.	倾向,脾气			

Proper Nouns

Kireonat Marte　尼日利亚（Nigeria）北部博诺州玛特城的一个小镇

Borno State　博诺,尼日利亚东北部一个州

Boko Haram　博科·哈兰,一个伊斯兰圣战者的恐怖主义者组织,它控制了尼日利亚北部、喀麦隆北部等地

Lt. Gen Azubuike Ikejirika　尼日利亚阿比亚州政府首脑

Baga　博诺州的另一小镇

News Summary

非洲北面的尼日利亚是一个伊斯兰国家,原来是英国的殖民地。2002年以来,在穆罕默德·尤素夫的领导下,成立了博科·哈兰组织,这是一个类似伊斯兰极端主义组织jihad（圣战者）的组织,它活跃在尼日利亚北部的博诺州,屠杀当地的伊斯兰教徒。这个组织据说和"基地"（al-Qaeda）组织有联系。自2010年9月以来,该组织不断在博诺地区进行恐怖主义袭击,在他们占领的地方残杀百姓,制造恐怖气氛。这篇消息报道了去年6月份博诺州玛特城科里镇上的居民,在经历了博科·哈兰组织的恐怖统治之后表示希望政府军永久驻扎在那里,以免再次经受磨难。

Understanding Sentences

① 博诺州玛特城的科里奥纳镇上的居民在星期三讲述了他们在博科·哈兰叛军控制下所遭受的苦难,这些叛军在他们那里修建了一个营地,并威胁当地居民,直到衣吉利卡所领导的特别力量到来并解放了他们。

② 显然,他们刚刚摆脱叛军对社区所施加的恐怖,松了一口气,他们对于在博科·哈兰组织统治这个地区的那段可耻的日子里所遭受的非人道待遇感到悲哀。

③ 对于妇女被恐怖分子强迫结婚感到悲痛,他说,在这一过程中,一些女孩子也遭到强奸,他补充说,"我们没有人能做什么,或敢于抗议,因为我们担心自己的生命不保。"

④ 然而,居民们也表示,由于在这个地区部署特别部队,他们担心这里的农活会受到不利的影响,有很多农民抱怨说,由于这个地区有大量的军事力量存在,他们无法到农场干活。

Exercises

Ⅰ. **Understanding Ideas in the News**

1. What story did the people of Kireona town tell the reporter?
  A. Their sufferings under the Boko Haram insurgents.
  B. The camps built by the Boko Haram insurgents.
  C. The liberation by Gen. Ihejirika.
2. How were the local people treated during the Boko Haram rule of the area?
  A. Ingloriously.　　　B. Barbarously.　　　C. Cruelly.
3. What do the residents request of the government?
  A. To check activities of the Boko Haram sect.
  B. To stop the insurgents from returning.
  C. A permanent military presence in the area.
4. What concern did the local people express about the deployment of the Special Forces to the area?
  A. It might affect farming.
  B. It might affect the weather.
  C. Girls were subjected into forced marriage.
5. What did the state governor promise the people?
  A. To restore to normal agriculture activities.
  B. To relent its efforts.
  C. To give out polio vaccines.

Ⅱ. **Language Points**

unleash, mete, relent, recruit, lament 这些动词也是报刊英语常用的词语,简洁但能表达深刻的意思。

unleash:(释放) to release suddenly a strong, uncontrollable and usually destructive force　e.g. *Rachel's arrival on the scene had unleashed passions in him that he could scarcely control.*

mete out:(给予) to give or order a punishment or make someone receive cruel or unfair treatment　e.g. *Victorian school teachers regularly meted out physical punishment to their pupil.*

relent:(发慈悲) to act in a less severe way towards someone and allow something that you had refused to allow before　e.g. *Her parents eventually relented and let her go to the party.*

recruit: (征募) to persuade someone to work for a company or become a new member of an organization, especially the army   e.g. *Even young boys are now being recruited into the army.*

lament: (悲叹, 哀叹) to express sadness and regret about   e.g. *My grandmother, as usual, lamented the decline in moral standards in today's society.*

III. Questions for Further Study

This is a typical news report of the people of Kireona town complaining about the Boko Haram's terrorist rule of the area. The way of reporting is usual, and in the main part of the news report, some minor information is given after the main idea. When you read the news, try to understand the names of people and places, and get some background information from the reporting.

2. What are Western and African powers up against in Mali, Algeria?

Leaders around the world are vowing to strike back hard at Islamist militancy that is surging across North Africa. Here are some of the challenges they face.

French soldiers wait for a helicopter in Mali, one of several trouble spots in Africa drawing Western involvement.

By John Thorne, *Correspondent*
Christian Science Monitor
January 20, 2013

Today in Algeria, authorities are scouring a Saharan gas plant for bodies in the wake of a hostage crisis that ended in a shoot out between the Army and Islamist kidnappers. ①

Around the world, leaders are vowing to strike back hard at Islamist militancy that is surging across North Africa.

Meanwhile, in neighboring Mali, France is already leading a military intervention to dislodge Islamist fighters who seized the country's north last year. ② Paris has pledged to keep its troops there until those fighters are defeated and Mali is returned to stability.

So what are Western governments and their North African partners up against? It's a murky picture, but here are some outlines:

Is this a regional problem?

Yes. North Africa is home to various armed groups, from ideologically driven Islamists to criminal gangs. While their aims and loyalties don't always overlap, they have shown an increasing inclination to work together. Some have international appeal, with members reportedly hailing from a range of countries. And many operate across national borders, which count for little in the deep Sahara.

Could the problem get worse?

Yes. If unchecked, violence could intensify, at least in North African countries. Hardline Islamist ideology has gathered steam chiefly among poor young men left adrift amid youth unemployment and lack of development. Deepening conflict could also affect oil markets if installations in Algeria or Libya—both major hydrocarbons producers—come under threat.

Where does North African militancy come from?

Much Islamist militancy in North Africa traces its origins to 1990s Algeria, when the Army's decision to cancel elections that an Islamist party was expect to win tipped the country into a decade of civil strife. ③ Tens of thousands were killed in bombings, massacres, and disappearances, as government forces battled Islamist insurgents led by veterans of the Afghan war of the 1980s.

While Algeria is largely stable today, a militant Islamist faction called the Salafist Group for Call and Combat has continued attacks mainly on government forces. In 2007 the group formally changed its name to al-Qaeda in the Islamic Maghreb (AQIM) and remains North Africa's premier militant Islamist outfit.

Who's out there?

AQIM is North Africa's most powerful Islamist militant group, operating mainly in Algeria and northern Mali. While its exact structure isn't clear, it seems to consist of a northern wing based in Algeria's Kabylie region and Saharan bands based in northern Mali. ④

Also in Mali are Ansar al Din and the Movement for Unity and Jihad in West Africa (MUJAO). With AQIM, these groups have seized control of Mali's north. Their numbers are hard to gauge, but are believed to range in the hundreds to thousands.

Elsewhere in North Africa, small apparently independent groups—sometimes just a dozen or so people—have staged occasional bombings in recent years (Morocco) and gotten into firefights with police (Tunisia).

What do militants believe?

Most Islamist militants appear to share a brand of violent Salafism forged largely in the crucible of the 1980s Afghan war. Broadly, Salafis believe Islam should be followed to the letter in a quest to emulate the first generations of Muslims. That means rejecting centuries of Islamic thought and scholarship that most Muslims see as integral to their faith and worship. While many Salafis don't espouse violence, a minority—including North Africa's militants—do.

What do they want?

It's often hard to say exactly. In general, Islamist militants want to apply their religious beliefs, something that involves imposing their brand of Islam on other people. In northern Mali, militants have set up a harsh rule that includes amputating the hands of alleged thieves, banning music, and stoning people accused of adultery. However, some groups have also stated more specific political aims. AQIM, for example, has long said it wants to set up an Islamic state in Algeria.

Do they work together?

Sometimes. Northern Mali is one example, where Ansar al-Din, MUJAO, and AQIM are holding the north in concert with each other. Reports of black English-speakers among the ranks of the MUJAO also suggest that members of Boko Haram—Islamist militants from northern Nigeria—may at least be moonlighting as members of the Malian group. ⑤

More fundamentally, militant groups show solidarity. Last week's kidnappers in Algeria claimed their attack was retribution for the French-led intervention in Mali, and demanded it be stopped. While security analysts say the attack was probably planned before France took action, it still offered perpetrators a chance to give fellow Islamists a hand. (747 words)

Words and Expressions

scour	v.	搜寻,查找	gauge	v.	测量
wake	n.	余波	forge	v.	铸造,形成
militancy	n.	激进,好战	emulate	v.	仿效
surge	v.	涌出	crucible	n.	严酷的考验
dislodge	v.	驱逐	integral	a.	完整
murky	a.	模糊的	espouse	v.	支持,赞成
adrift	a.	漂浮的	amputate	v.	切除(手臂等)
tip	v.	使倾斜,使翻倒	in concert with		与……一致
strife	n.	冲突	retribution	n.	报偿

| outfit | n. 配备,装备 | perpetrator | n. 犯罪者 |

Proper Nouns

Sahara　撒哈拉沙漠
Salafist Group for Call and Combat　沙拉菲战斗组织,穆斯林逊尼派的一个组织
Salafism　沙拉菲主义,是穆斯林逊尼派的一个流派,形成于19世纪后半叶
al-Qaeda in the Islamic Maghreb（AQIM）　伊斯兰马格里布基地组织
Ansar al-Din　意思是"伊斯兰教的帮助者"或"信仰保卫者",北非一个伊斯兰好战者组织
the Movement for Unity and Jihad in West Africa(MUJAO)　西非团结和圣战运动

News Summary

这是美国《基督教科学箴言报》发表的关于北非伊斯兰激进派在几个国家活动的报道,文章采用了问答形式,便于读者抓住要点。文章开头提出了在阿尔及利亚和马里发生的两件事情,然后集中说明在北非的这些伊斯兰好战组织的来源、发生和发展,他们目前在北非这几个国家活动的情况,以及政府对他们采取的行动。随着利比亚原政权的垮台和去年发生在那里的对美国领事馆的爆炸袭击,北非的穆斯林好战分子组织已成为全球反恐的一部分,是美国打击的目标。

Understanding Sentences

① 今天,一起人质危机以政府军和伊斯兰分子绑架者之间互相开枪射击结束,阿尔及利亚当局正在撒哈拉一座煤气工厂搜寻留下的尸体。

② 与此同时,在邻国马里,法国已经采取了一场军事干预行动,驱赶那些去年占领了该国北部的伊斯兰主义战士。

③ 在北非,大部分伊斯兰主义激进行为起源于1990年底的阿尔及利亚,由于当时军方决定取消一个伊斯兰主义政党预计会胜出的选举,导致了该国为期十年的内战。

④ 虽然它(伊斯兰马格里布基地组织)准确的结构不清楚,它似乎由一个以阿尔及利亚的卡比列地区为基础的北部分支和一支以马里的北部为基地的撒哈拉队伍所组成。

⑤ 有关讲英语的黑人出现在西非团结和圣战运动领导层的报道也暗示,来自尼日利亚北部的伊斯兰激进分子组织博科哈兰的人至少临时充当马里队伍的战士。

Exercises

Ⅰ. Understanding Ideas in the News

1. What is the problem facing countries in north Africa?
   A. Military intervention.
   B. Hostage crisis.
   C. Islamist militancy.
2. Who have shown an increasing inclination to work together in North Africa?

A. France and Mali.

B. North African countries.

C. Islamists and criminal gangs.

3. What did the government forces of Algeria battle in the 1990s?

A. Islamist insurgents.

B. Veterans of the Afghan war.

C. AQIM.

4. Which organization is considered the most powerful Islamist militant group in North Africa?

A. MUJAO.　　　　　B. AQIM.　　　　　C. Ansar al Din.

5. What are the political aims of AQIM?

A. To believe in Salafism.

B. To impose their brand of Islam.

C. To set up an Islamic state.

Ⅱ. Language Points

military, militant & militancy, murky, adrift, integral 这些是新闻中使用的几个词语。

military：(军事的) relating to or belonging to the armed forces　e. g. *foreign military intervention*

militant：(好战的；斗士) active, determined and often willing to use force　e. g. *The group has taken a militant position on the abortion issue and is refusing to compromise.*

militancy：(激进，好战) the state of being militant

murky(模糊的)：describes a situation that is complicated and unpleasant, and about which many facts are unclear　e. g. *He became involved in the murky world of international drug-dealing.*

adrift(漂浮不定的)：If a person is adrift, they do not have a clear purpose in life and do not know what they want to do.　e. g. *Da Silva plays a bright, lonely student from New York, adrift in small-town Arizona.*

integral：(必需的，不可缺少的)：necessary and important as a part of, or contained within, a whole　e. g. *He's an integral part of the team and we can't do without him.*

Ⅲ. Questions for Further Study

This news report is in a unique form of question and answer after the lead paragraphs. It is for the convenience of reading, but also sum up the situation in some northern and western African countries so that the reader can have a picture of it. Analyze the reading to see how the questions are listed in some sort of order. The Islamic militants have different organizations in different African countries, such as the al-Qaeda in the Islamic Maghreb in Algeria; the Movement for Unity and Jihad in West Africa (such as Mali), and the Boko Haram in Nigeria. Find out more news reports related to these organizations and see what they have been doing in North Africa.

3. CAR: how Bozizé lost his piece of Africa

After 10 years in power, the statesman had few friends offering to help to fight off the rebels.

David Smith*
Mail &Guardian
28 Mar 2013 00:00

President François Bozizé's family and bodyguards were watching Cartoon Network when I went to meet him at the presidential palace in Bangui a few years ago.

At the time, there were allegations that he had ordered his troops, the Central African Republic army known as FACA, to adopt a scorched-earth policy in the northeast of the country, and I was part of a delegation from the Pan-African Parliament sent to investigate. Bozizé's eyes were half shut and he spoke like an audiotape being played at slow speed.

There had been damning reports from organisations including the International Crisis Group and Human Rights Watch claiming that Bozizé's soldiers had been killing, raping and looting in the area around Birao, a dry, isolated town sandwiched between Sudan's Darfur region and southeastern Chad. ①

I flew to Birao, much against the wishes of Bozizé's handlers, on a French military plane—the French were still giving Bozizé support back then, and were providing logistics to the FACA as they terrorised the locals. Birao was a burnt-out ruin and most

---

* David Smith is a director of Johannesburg-based Okapi Consulting. He lived in Bangui where he set up Radio Minurca (now Radio Ndeke Luka), the only independent radio station in the country.

of its residents had fled into the bush to escape government soldiers, many of whom were considerably younger than voting age. ②

Bozizé was hated in Birao, as he was in many other parts of the Central African Republic. The reasons for this were numerous. In the case of Birao, promises made by successive leaders over the decades, of which Bozizé was only the most recent, tended to be forgotten—schools had no teachers or books, hospitals had no doctors or medicine and roads linking the area to the rest of the country simply do not exist.

To be the president of the Central African Republic, whether one reaches that position through the ballot box or through the gun, for all intents and purposes means ruling over a small, decaying tropical city on the banks of the Oubangui River. ③ Presidential powers barely reach beyond the limits of Bangui.

During almost all of Bozizé's 10 years in office, large parts of the country were out of his control. Supporters of former president Ange-Félix Patassé, deposed by Bozizé in a military coup in 2003, together with other anti-government elements—in particular, Michel Djotodia—kept much of the country in a state of more or less permanent revolt.

Bozizé had been forcibly trying to remove Patassé from power since 2001, but in those days Patassé was able to rely on the support of troops loyal to Congolese rebel leader Jean-Pierre Bemba, who now awaits trial in The Hague for alleged war crimes in the Central African Republic.

Skirmishes in 2003 turned into large-scale rebellion in 2004 and Djotodia led an alliance of several rebel groups calling themselves the Union of Democratic Forces for Unity. His bush war finally yielded fruit last Saturday, when his most recent rebel alliance, Seleka, entered Bangui, and headed straight for the presidential palace, where Djotodia proclaimed himself president. ④

During his last year in office, Bozizé could count on very few friends in high places. The French were no longer interested in helping—their troops remained in Bangui only to protect French interests in the Central African Republic, which these days mean French nationals.

Historically, the former colonial power has had a heavy hand in the country, but its main economic interest there—the Areva uranium mine—was mothballed two years ago when the uranium price dropped in the wake of the Fukushima disaster. ⑤ Bozizé's other erstwhile close friend, Chadian president Idriss Déby, who supported the coup that brought Bozizé to power, did not offer to help fight off this latest menace. As the noose tightened, President Jacob Zuma seemed to be his only remaining friend.

There is much speculation about why this is the case and, chances are, many of the questions surrounding this odd friendship will emerge soon. Despite South Africa's offer to train the FACA, Bozizé always feared that he'd be relieved of power in much the same way as many of his predecessors had been, so he played the dangerous game of keeping his army weak just in case they should decide to turn on him. It was a losing wager. The end came swiftly.

By December last year, the writing was on the wall—Seleka forces had taken over much of the country before the president reluctantly agreed to participate in peace talks held in the Gabonese capital, Libreville. With little left under his control outside Bangui, Bozizé still displayed his arrogance by refusing to negotiate and turning up late at the talks. (757 words)

Words and Expressions

allegation	n.	断言	forcibly	ad.	强制地
scorched-earth		焦土政策	skirmish	n.	小冲突
investigate	v.	调查	mothball	v.	封存
damn	v.	谴责	erstwhile	ad.	以前,往昔
loot	v.	掠夺	menace	v. & n.	威胁
handler	n.	操纵者	noose	n.	套索
ballot box		投票箱	speculation	n.	思索
intent	n.	意图	predecessor	n.	前任
depose	v.	免责	wager	n.	赌注

Proper Nouns

Francois Bozize   博齐泽,中非共和国原总统,2013年3月份下台,被迫出走
Bangui   班吉,中非共和国首都
Pan-African Parliament   泛非洲议会
Birao   比劳,中非的一个地方
Darfur   达尔富尔
Libreville   利伯维尔(加蓬首都)
Oubangui River   乌班吉河
Ange-Felix Patasse   帕塔塞(被博齐泽发动政变推翻的前总统)
Michel Djotodia   杜托第亚(反对博齐泽的中非政治家)
Jean-Pierre Bemba   本巴(刚果共和国前反对派领袖)
The Hague   荷兰海牙
Seleka   中非的一个叛军组织,意思是"团结"
Fukushima   (日本)福岛

News Summary

这是一篇南非记者写的关于中非共和国前总统博齐泽的报道。据记者报道,南非派遣了军队到中非,结果有七名士兵不幸在一次行动中丧生,引发了南非国内的不满。记者曾经

拜访过博齐泽,也参加了对他的调查,所以对中非的局势和博齐泽垮台的原因比较了解,分析也比较中肯。中部非洲,包括西非的一些国家,政府、军队、部落、叛军之间矛盾激烈,还有原殖民者遗留的问题,导致战乱不停,政权更迭频繁,人民生活水平低下。目前,随着国际社会的关注,这些问题正引起人们的注意,阅读有关非洲的报道,可以让我们了解那里的形势和所发生的变化。

Understanding Sentences

① 已经有来自一些组织,包括国际危机组织和人权观察的报告,谴责博齐泽的士兵在比劳附近地区屠杀、强奸和抢掠民众。这个地区是位于苏丹达尔富尔和乍得东南部之间的一个干旱、孤立的小镇。

② 比劳成了一片烧焦的废墟,大部分居民已经逃到丛林里以不受政府军士兵的骚扰,许多士兵还不到法定的投票年龄。

③ 不管你是由投票选出的,还是用武力上台的,担任中非共和国的总统,几乎意味着只统治一座在乌班吉河岸边的破烂的小热带城市。

④ 上星期六,当他最近的叛军联盟——"团结"——攻进班吉的时候,他的丛林战争终于有了成果,他们直奔总统府,在那里杜托迪亚宣布就任总统。

⑤ 历史上,这个前殖民地宗主国(法国)曾经严厉控制过这个国家,但是它在那里的主要经济利益——阿海法铀矿——因两年前福岛核泄漏事故后铀价格下跌而关闭。

Exercises

Ⅰ. Understanding Ideas in the News

1. What was the reporter sent to investigate in Central Africa?

   A. Bozize's policy.

   B. Killing and looting by the army.

   C. The Pan-African Parliament.

2. How is Birao like when the reporter arrived there?

   A. It was burning.

   B. It was a deserted city.

   C. It was a poor city.

3. Why did the people in Birao hate their leaders?

   A. They would like to go to the North.

   B. People are very poor.

   C. None has kept his promises.

4. On whose support did Patasse rely before he was deposed by Bozize?

   A. Troops loyal to Jean-Pierre Bemba.

   B. Michel Djotodia and Seleka.

   C. Chadian president Idriss Deby.

5. Why did Bozize keep his army weak?

A. Because he ordered them to adopt a scorched-earth policy.

B. Because South Africa didn't train the FACA.

C. Because military coups d'état happen so often in Central Africa.

II. Language Points

intent, revolt, skirmish, noose, wager 这几个简单的双音节或单音节词所构成的短语表达了很深刻的意思。

for all intents：（基本上）in all the most important ways e.g. *For all intents and purposes, the project is completed.*

revolt：（反抗）If a large number of people revolt, they refuse to be controlled or ruled, and take often violent action against authority. e.g. *The people revolted against foreign rule and established their own government.*

skirmish：（小冲突）a fight between a small number of soldiers which is usually short and not planned, and which happens away from the main area of fighting in a war

noose：（套索）one end of a rope tied to form a circle which can be tightened round something e.g. *They put him on the back of a horse and looped a noose around his neck.*

wager：（赌注）an amount of money that you risk in the hope of winning more, a bet e.g. *She put a cash wager of 100 on the biggest horse race of the year.*

III. Questions for Further Study

Military Coups d'état are common in some central African countries where the government can change hands overnight. And that always happens in the case of a strong man who rules the nation like a dictator. From the news report piece together information given in the news to see how Bozize came to power, and how he ruled the country and gradually lost support from the people and from his friends. The lead begins with a descriptive paragraph which demonstrates how this dictation lived and ruled.

英语报刊知识介绍

英美报刊的形成和发展

十六世纪初期，英国出现了最早用于传播消息的出版物，到十七、十八世纪才逐渐有了每天固定出版的报纸。美国在还处于英国的殖民地时期也有了报纸，主要传播来自英国和欧洲的消息。独立以后，美国也有了自己的报纸。

进入二十世纪，随着技术的进步，报纸的编辑、排版、印刷和发行等方面都有很大的变化。二十世纪初的电台、二十世纪中的电视及计算机的发明、二十世纪末的互联网和无线电话及各种应用的出现，给报业带来很大的冲击，也引起报业自身的许多重大变化。

1. A copy of early British newspaper *The Oxford Gazette*

2. A copy of early British newspaper *The Derby Gazette*

Unit 4 Violence and Terrorist Attacks in the U. S.

Acts of violence and terrorism have been increasing worldwide, as has the destruction they cause. A gunman opens fire in a crowded restaurant. A bomb exploded in the basement of the World Trade Centre. The Oklahoma City federal building was destroyed by explosives and many working in the building died. These are serious cases of terrorism happening in the United States in the late 1990s. The most serious is the 9.11 terrorist attack at the beginning of the new century, which caused the World Trade Centres in New York to collapse and thousands of deaths. And bombing and suicidal attacks spread in the Middle East, north Africa, Western Asia, etc. What factors are contributing to this increase in terrorism and violence throughout the world? How should governments respond to terrorism? How should we strive to combat terrorism and other anti-social activities and make our world a harmonious place to live? Read the reports in this unit and discuss the issue of terrorism in class.

暴力事件和恐怖袭击自20世纪八九十年代以来在世界上愈演愈烈,其登峰造极之作可算2001年发生在美国纽约市的9·11事件。恐怖主义组织劫持了4架美国国内航班的客机,分别驾机撞向纽约世贸中心的两座高达100余层的大楼和美国国防部大楼的一角,导致大楼起火燃烧并迅速倒塌,几千人丧生。什么因素导致了这一事件的发生呢? 美国人把它归于拉登领导的基地组织,但是可能还有更深一层的原因值得我们去探索。本单元收集了两篇关于9·11事件的报道,可算是经典之作,第一篇是从正面报道了事件发生的经过,第二篇是从一个离现场比较远的旁观者的角度来报道事件的发生,"我看到有人从窗口落下来",这些都围绕同一事件从不同角度和细节来报道新闻,都值得我们好好阅读。第三篇是2013年5月刚在美国波士顿发生的一起爆炸事件,虽然规模较小,作案者也已经被抓获,但不少美国人对这样的恐怖事件,还是心有余悸的。

1. Terrorists hijack 4 airliners, destroy World Trade Center, hit Pentagon; hundreds dead

Bush promises retribution; military put on highest alert
By Michael Grunwald
From *Washington Post*
Wednesday September 12, 2001; Page A01

Terrorists unleashed an astonishing air assault on America's military and financial power centers yesterday morning, hijacking four commercial jets and then crashing them into the World Trade Center in New York, the Pentagon and the Pennsylvania countryside.[①]

Unit 4 Violence and Terrorist Attacks in the U. S.

There were no reliable estimates last night of how many people were killed in the most devastating terrorist operation in American history. The number was certainly in the hundreds and could be in the thousands.

It was the most dramatic attack on American soil since Pearl Harbor, and it created indelible scenes of carnage and chaos. The commandeered jets obliterated the World Trade Center's twin 110-story towers from their familiar perch above Manhattan's skyline and ripped a blazing swath through the Defense Department's imposing five-sided fortress, grounding the domestic air traffic system for the first time and plunging the entire nation into an unparalleled state of anxiety. ②

U. S. military forces at home and abroad were placed on their highest state of alert, and a loose network of Navy warships was deployed along both coasts for air defense.

The terrorists hijacked four California-bound planes from three airports on the Eastern Seaboard; the airliners were loaded with the maximum amount of fuel, suggesting a well-financed, well-coordinated plot. First, two planes slammed into the World Trade Center. Then an American Airlines plane out of Dulles International Airport ripped through the newly renovated walls of the Pentagon, perhaps the world's most secure office building. A fourth jet crashed 80 miles southeast of Pittsburgh, shortly after it was hijacked and turned in the direction of Washington.

None of the 266 people aboard the four planes survived. There were even more horrific but still untallied casualties in the World Trade Center and the Pentagon, which together provided office space for more than 70,000 people. At just one of the firms with offices in the World Trade Center, the Marsh & McLennan insurance brokerage, 1,200 of its 1,700 employees were unaccounted for last night. ③

The spectacular collapse of the Trade Center's historic twin towers and another less recognizable skyscraper during the rescue operations caused even more bloodshed. At least 300 New York firefighters and 85 police officers are presumed dead. The preliminary list of victims included the conservative commentator Barbara K. Olson, "Frasier" executive producer David Angell and two hockey scouts from the Los Angeles Kings.

No one claimed responsibility for the attacks, but federal officials said they suspect the involvement of Islamic extremists with links to fugitive terrorist Osama bin Laden, who has been implicated in the 1998 bombings of two U. S. embassies in Africa and several other attacks.④ Law enforcement sources said there is already evidence implicating bin Laden's militant network in the attack, and politicians from both parties predicted a major and immediate escalation in America's worldwide war against terrorism.

In a grim address to the nation last night, President Bush denounced the attacks as a failed attempt to frighten the United States, and promised to hunt down those responsible. "We will make no distinction," he said, "between the terrorists who committed these acts and those who harbor them."

Bush vowed that America would continue to function "without interruption", and federal offices and Congress are scheduled to be open today. But the New York Stock Exchange and Nasdaq Stock Market will remain closed, along with most businesses in lower Manhattan. And yesterday was a day of extraordinary interruptions — for the president, for federal Washington and for the country.

Bush was in a classroom in Florida yesterday morning when the attacks began and spent the day on the move for security reasons, flying to military bases in Louisiana and then Nebraska before returning to Washington in the evening. At one point at Barksdale Air Force Base in Louisiana, the president rode in a camouflaged, armored Humvee, guarded by machine gun-toting soldiers in fatigues.

Vice President Cheney and first lady Laura Bush were whisked away to undisclosed locations in the morning, and congressional leaders were temporarily moved to a secure facility 75 miles west of Washington. The White House, the Capitol, the Supreme Court, the State Department and the Treasury Department were evacuated, along with federal buildings nationwide and the United Nations in New York.

Private buildings also were shut down, from the Space Needle in Seattle to the Sears Tower in Chicago to Walt Disney World in Orlando. America's borders with Canada and Mexico were sealed. New York's mayoral primary was abruptly postponed. So was Major League Baseball's schedule for the night.

Wireless networks buckled under the barrage of cell phone calls. The besieged Internet search engine Google told Web surfers to try radio or TV instead. Amtrak train and Greyhound bus operations were also halted in the Northeast.

Last night, fires were still burning amid the rubble of the World Trade Center, and pools of highly flammable jet fuel continued to hinder rescue teams searching through waist-deep rubble.

The Federal Emergency Management Agency dispatched eight search-and-rescue

Unit 4 Violence and Terrorist Attacks in the U. S.

teams to New York and four teams to the Pentagon. The Department of Health and Human Services sent medical teams and mortuary teams, and activated a national medical emergency cadre of 7,000 volunteers for the first time.

The Empire State Building went dark as a symbol of national mourning. In Washington, Republicans and Democrats presented a united front in condemning the attacks; members of Congress delivered a spontaneous rendition of "God Bless America" after a news conference on the Capitol steps.

"We are outraged at this cowardly attack on the people of the United States," the leaders of Congress said in a bipartisan statement. "Our heartfelt prayers are with the victims and their families, and we stand strongly united behind the President as our commander-in-chief."

But amid all the sadness and all the outrage, there were questions about lax security and inadequate intelligence, as Americans tried to fathom how such a catastrophe could happen with no apparent warning. ⑤ On at least two of the airliners, according to federal officials, the hijackers were armed with nothing but knives. How did they get away with it? (1005 words)

Words and Expressions

hijack	*n. & v.*	劫持,劫机	spectacular	*a.*	惊人的;激动人心的
devastating	*a.*	破坏性的,毁灭性的	presume	*v.*	假设,认为
indelible	*a.*	不可磨灭的;难忘的	Islamic extremist		伊斯兰极端主义者
carnage	*n.*	残杀,流血	fugitive	*n.*	逃亡者
chaos	*n.*	混乱	implicate	*v.*	使牵连其中
commandeer	*v.*	征用;强征	escalation	*n.*	扩大,增加
obliterate	*v.*	使消失;除去	grim	*a.*	冷酷的,严厉的
perch	*n.*	栖木,有利的地位	denounce	*v.*	公开指责,谴责
rip	*v.*	撕裂	reverberate	*v.*	反响
blaze	*v.*	熊熊燃烧	bolster	*v.*	支持
swath	*n.*	狭长的条或片	dump	*v.*	低价投放(如货物、股票)
fortress	*n.*	堡垒,要塞			
plunge	*v.*	使投入,使陷入	frenzy	*n.*	狂暴,狂怒
unparallel	*a.*	从未有过的	array	*n.*	一大批
slam	*v.*	猛击,撞击	glee	*n.*	欢乐,高兴
renovate	*v.*	刷新,修复	lax	*a.*	松懈的,不严格的
tally	*v.*	点数,计算,记录	fathom	*v.*	理解
casualty	*n.*	伤亡	apparatus	*n.*	机构,机关
brokerage	*n.*	代理公司	camouflage	*v.*	伪装

News Summary

这是在9·11事件发生之后从正面直接、全面报道事件经过的第一篇新闻报道,刊登在9月12日的《华盛顿邮报》上。按照新闻报道的特点,导语段部分首先用概括的语言说明事件的经过和重大后果,然后新闻的主要部分详细描述事件经过和美国政府的第一反应,最后还提到了世界各国对事件的反应和人们的反思。整篇新闻报道思路清晰,主次分明,语言生动有力,同时也充分表达了作者的感情。

9·11事件的经过:在美国境内的恐怖主义分子按照事先的预谋,选择在9月11日发动这次袭击,因为911是美国应急电话的号码。他们分别劫持了4架民航客机,其中撞向纽约世贸中心双子座的两架飞机使大楼起火燃烧,最后引起大楼坍塌,来不及逃离大楼的人和冲上楼救火的消防员有数千人命丧火海之中。这篇新闻就是报道客机撞向大楼的情况的,尽管当时并不知道为什么会发生这样的惨剧。

Understanding Sentences

① 昨天上午,恐怖分子对美国军事和金融中心发动了一次意外的空中袭击,劫持了4架商业飞机并将它们撞向了纽约的世界贸易中心、五角大楼和宾夕法尼亚州的乡村。

② 被控制的飞机把世贸中心的两栋110层大楼从曼哈顿天际熟悉的位置上抹掉了,同时又把国防部那坚固的五角大楼的屋顶撕开一大块,第一次使国内航空系统处于瘫痪,使全国陷入前所未有的恐慌状态。

③ 仅以在世贸中心大楼里设有办公室的公司中一家为例,这家名为马斯和麦克蕾妮的保险公司有1 700名员工,昨晚就有1 200名失踪。

④ 暂时没有人宣称对这次袭击负责,但联邦政府官员表示,他们怀疑有与逃亡的恐怖主义者本·拉登有关联的伊斯兰极端分子介入,他被指控卷入了1998年非洲两所美国大使馆爆炸案和其他几次攻击。

⑤ 但是,在所有这些悲哀和愤怒中,美国人开始质问,为什么如此巨大的灾难竟然能发生在没有任何明显的警告的情况下,人们开始对松懈的保安工作和不足的情报工作提出疑问。

Exercises

Ⅰ. Understanding Ideas in the news

1. How serious was the terrorist attack regarded as expressed in the news?
   A. The most devastating and dramatic.
   B. The first one since Pearl Harbour.
   C. The greatest number of death.
2. What did the terrorists use as weapons to strike the targets?
   A. Great amounts of explosive.
   B. Military airplanes.
   C. Hijacked commercial airplanes.

3. What suggested that the attack was well-planned?

A. The commandeered planes hit the targets at the same time.

B. They hijacked airplanes loaded with maximum amount of fuel.

C. It happened on the date of September 11.

4. What is the estimated toll of death in the attack?

A. In thousands.　　　　B. 70 000.　　　　C. 1 200.

5. What made the American government suspect that Osama bin Laden was involved in the attack?

A. Osama bin Laden is linked to Islamic extremists.

B. America's worldwide war against terrorism would escalate.

C. Evidence showing that Osama bin Laden and his network has been and is involved.

II. Language Points

devastating, indelible, blazing, carnage, slam, rip 这些词在报道9·11事件中经常用到,突出了这次事件的严重性。

devastating:(破坏性的,毁灭性的) to destroy a place or thing completely or cause great damage

indelible:(不可磨灭的,难忘的) impossible to forget, or have a permanent influence or effect　　e.g. *In his twenty years working for the company, Joe Pearson made an indelible impression on it.*

blazing:(熊熊燃烧的) very fierce　　e.g. *They used to have some blazing rows over money.*

carnage:(残杀,流血) the violent killing of large numbers of people, especially in war　　e.g. *The Battle of the Somme was a scene of dreadful carnage.*

slam:(猛击,撞击) move against a hard surface with force and usually a loud noise　　e.g. *The wind made the door/window slam (shut).*

rip:(撕裂) to pull apart; to tear or be torn violently and quickly　　e.g. *His new trousers ripped when he bent down.*

III. Questions for Further Study

This is the first report on the attack of hijacked airplanes hitting the World Trade Center in New York, on September 11, 2001. Together with a picture of the burning tower, it made front page news of most newspapers worldwide. Notice that the reporter was writing in great hurry, and some of the information in this report was corrected later again and again, at least until the number of casualties was confirmed. Study the writing again and see how the reporter managed to get pieces of information for this report.

2. "I Saw Bodies Falling Out— Oh, God, Jumping, Falling"

By Barton Gellman, Staff Writer
From *Washington Post*
Wednesday, September 12, 2001

NEW YORK, Sept. 11 — Valerie Johnson stared, transfixed, at the inferno a thousand yards to her south and west. Tears streamed furrows through a film of ash on her face. Her mind tried to grasp what her eyes beheld: a blazing gash across the tower of wealth that symbolized New York for her all her life.① The fire marched downward, floor by floor, windows bursting out ahead of the flames.

Then Johnson screamed a guttural, wordless wail. A sound like nothing she ever heard — low as thunder, but louder and longer — pressed in on her chest for ten seconds or more, resounding through Centre Street at Foley Square.② The northern tower, the taller of the two, was gone. It was 10:29 a.m., an hour and three quarters after the first of two jetliners ripped through New York's twin emblems of global prestige.

"Oh God, oh God, my niece works in that building," Johnson breathed. "Oh God."

Where we stood there now came a roiling cloud — smoke and ash, ten stories tall, building speed as they reached the canyons of Manhattan's southern tip. Survivors streamed, choked and gagging, behind the cloud. Among them, stumbling blindly toward the fountain at Foley Square, were Elizabeth Belleau and Melissa Morales, strangers grasping hands with all their might as they ran. ③ Belleau plunged her head into the cooling waters and retched, coughing out ash and phlegm. The fountain enclosed a sculpture: "Triumph of the Human Spirit."

Belleau had been running for nearly two hours. Her morning commute on the BM-3 bus had stalled, then transformed to horror as the Brooklyn Battery Tunnel filled with smoke. The panicked driver abandoned the bus, and firefighters directed passengers to a makeshift triage station on Greenwich Street, just south of the burning towers.

"I saw bodies falling out of the World Trade Center — oh, God, jumping, falling, glass and smoke," Belleau said, heaving at the image. Then Tower One collapsed, and the world turned black. No sign of the triage station remained, nor of most of the emergency workers who guided her there. Belleau linked hands with five strangers, but lost them all. Later she found Morales, a voice in the dark.

It had taken a fistful of cash to a limousine driver, followed by a hitched ride on a Harley Davidson, to bring me this far south from upper Manhattan. ④ A walk further down through the financial district, bypassing police barricades, revealed a hellscape. Within minutes of the first collapse, ashes were ankle deep for block after city block. Nearer the spot where the towers had been, the ashes were knee deep and higher. Hundreds of small fires blazed.

Here and there stood survivors, in all the myriad displays of human shock.

Elaine Greenberg, a retired teacher, could not get over the broken vista, not at all as she felt certain it ought to be. "The Woolworth Building is the high building down there," she said, astonished.

Others could speak only of the jumpers, desperate beyond comprehension, leaping to certain death from the 80th, 90th, 100th floors.

"Look, mommy," 2-year-old William Watt had said, pointing to the tiny figures plunging down. Strangers grappled his 5-year-old sister aloft in her wheelchair and ran toward evacuation boats on the Hudson River. Monica Watt looked back, then held William tighter and turned her face away. She had no words to answer.

Jet A, the standard aviation fuel, is rated to produce 1,500 degrees Fahrenheit. Not much of a skyscraper's flesh and bones is supposed to burn, but the towers served for chimneys as floors collapsed into shafts. ⑤ "I don't know what it was like up there, but it must have been hell," said fire fighter Paul Curran of New York Fire Patrol 3, covered in a thick coat of gray ash outside a makeshift command post in the Gee Whiz restaurant at Greenwich and Warren streets. "There were a lot of jumpers. I saw bodies hit the upper level concrete of the second floor overhang of Tower One. Others were falling into West Street."

Tower One collapsed atop the broken bodies. Then it buried the staging post where Curran prepared to enter the lobby for a staircase, heading up. "We all just ran", he said. "We couldn't do nothing but save ourselves. I got under a parked car with my respirator on. I was in total darkness for at least five minutes."

Dozens of Curran's comrades, some said hundreds, had already plunged inside the burning tower.

"You know what haunts me?" said Peter Genova, of GC Services Capital, who escaped down the fire stairs. "There had to be 200 firemen that passed us [going up] on our way down. God only knows how many were up there when it collapsed." (788 words)

Words and Expressions

transfix	v.	使大吃一惊		phlegm	n.	黏液,痰,黏液质
inferno	n.	大火,火海		stall	v.	(使)停止,迟延
furrow	n.	犁沟,皱纹		panicked	a.	恐慌的,惊慌失措的
blaze	v.	燃烧,照耀		triage	n.	伤员鉴别分类
gash	n.	裂口		hellscape	n.	地狱般的场面
guttural	a.	喉咙的,喉音的		myriad	n.	无数,无数的人或物
wail	n.	悲叹,哀号		vista	n.	街景,展望
emblem	n.	象征,徽章,符号		grapple	v.	紧紧地抓住
prestige	n.	声望,威望,威信		aloft	a.	在高处,在上
roil	v.	使……混浊		shaft	n.	轴,杆状物
choke	v.	窒息,使呼吸困难		respirator	n.	呼吸器
gag	v.	塞物于……口中,使窒息		makeshift	a.	权宜之计的,凑合的
retch	v.	作呕,恶心				

News Summary

这是一篇报道细节的新闻,与报道9·11事件的主要新闻同时刊登在第一版上,给读者提供一些生动的、具体的信息。这类新闻报道的主要特点是以具体的描写或采访人物的谈话为主。因此,本报道以采访对象的一句话"我看到身体掉下来——啊,天哪,跳下来,落下来"为标题,突出报道了现场附近的人们在飞机撞上世贸中心大楼时不顾一切地从高楼上跳下来的情景,给读者留下深刻的印象。接着,文章又报道了大楼坍塌的情景,把恐怖袭击之后所造成的严重后果、人员伤亡和财产损失等具体报道出来。

Understanding Sentences

① 她脑子里尽量在捕捉刚才看到的一幕——一阵强烈的火光在她一生中都认为是纽约象征的财富大楼上划过。

② 一阵她从未听过的声音——像雷声般低沉,但越来越响——在她胸口震撼了十来秒钟,在佛来广场的中央大街上回荡。

③ 在这些跌跌撞撞地朝着佛来广场中间的喷池跑去的人中,有伊丽莎白贝楼和蒙丽莎莫雷斯——两只手紧紧握在一起拼命奔跑的两个陌生人。

Unit 4 Violence and Terrorist Attacks in the U.S.

④ 我给了出租车司机一摞钞票,接着又搭上一辆哈里摩托车,才从曼哈顿北边赶到南边这里(靠近世贸中心)。

⑤ 一座摩天大楼的框架结构和填充材料中并没有多少能够燃烧,但随着楼层的一层层倒塌,形成风井,大楼就好像烟囱一样。

Exercises

Ⅰ. **Understanding Ideas in the News**

1. What did Valerie Johnson see on the World Trade Center?
A. A inferno a thousand yards to her south and west.
B. A fire coming out from the World Trade Center.
C. The towers that symbolized New York.
2. What did the collapse of the northern tower create?
A. A blazing in the sky.
B. A crowd of people running down.
C. A thick cloud of smoke and ash.
3. What happened when Elizabeth Belleau's bus arrived at Brooklyn Battery Tunnel?
A. The tower was hit by an aeroplane.
B. There was a fire at the Tunnel.
C. Tower One collapses.
4. What gave the people around the two buildings the deepest impression?
A. People stumbling blindly toward the fountain.
B. People who are shocked by what had happened.
C. People jumping out from the burning buildings.
5. Which of the following groups of people had the most casualties in the incident?
A. Children.　　　　B. Fire fighters.　　　C. Teachers.

Ⅱ. **Language Points**

inferno, blazing gash, roiling cloud, broken vista, hellscape, desperate beyond comprehension 这些词语生动地描述了世贸中心被恐怖分子所劫持的飞机撞击后,大火燃烧和爆炸时的情景。

inferno:(大火,火海) a very large uncontrolled fire   e.g. *The building was an inferno by the time the fire service arrived.*

gash:(裂口) a long deep cut, especially in the skin

roiling:(使……混浊) make (a liquid) turbid or muddy by disturbing the sediment   e.g. *winds roil these waters*

vista:(街景,展望) a view, especially a splendid view from a high position   e.g. *After a hard climb, we were rewarded by a picture-postcard vista of rolling hills under a deep blue summer sky.*

hellscape:(地狱般的场面) used to form nouns referring to a wide view of a place, often one represented in a picture, like the hell

III. Questions for Further Study

This news report tries to present the scene of the two towers after they were hit by the hijacked aircrafts. It begins by quoting some witnesses who happened to be around and noticed to aircrafts bumping into the towers. Most of the description is from the outside, because at that time, people couldn't know what was it like inside. Analyze the news story to see how many quotes are used, what details are presented with the quotes, and what they want to support in the news.

3. 2nd bombing suspect caught after frenzied hunt paralyzes Boston

The F. B. I. wanted poster for Dzhokhar A. Tsarnaev.

By KATHARINE Q. SEELYE, WILLIAM K. RASHBAUM and MICHAEL COOPER
The New York Times
April 19, 2013

BOSTON — The teenage suspect in the Boston Marathon bombings, whose flight from the police after a furious gunfight overnight prompted an intense manhunt that virtually shut down the Boston area all day, was taken into custody Friday night after the police found him in nearby Watertown, Mass., officials said. ①

The suspect, Dzhokhar A. Tsarnaev, 19, was found hiding in a boat just outside the area where the police had been conducting door-to-door searches all day, the Boston police commissioner, Edward Davis, said at a news conference Friday night.

"A man had gone out of his house after being inside the house all day, abiding by our request to stay inside," Mr. Davis said, referring to the advice officials gave to residents to remain behind locked doors. "He walked outside and saw blood on a boat in the backyard. He then opened the tarp on the top of the boat, and he looked in and saw a man covered with blood. He retreated and called us."

"Over the course of the next hour or so we exchanged gunfire with the suspect, who

Unit 4 Violence and Terrorist Attacks in the U. S.

was inside the boat, and ultimately the hostage rescue team of the F. B. I. made an entry into the boat and removed the suspect, who was still alive," Mr. Davis said. ② He said the suspect was in "serious condition" and had apparently been wounded in the gunfight that left his brother dead.

A federal law enforcement official said he would not be read his Miranda rights, because the authorities would be invoking the public safety exception in order to question him extensively about other potential explosive devices or accomplices and to try to gain intelligence. ③

The Boston Police Department announced on Twitter: "Suspect in custody. Officers sweeping the area," and Mayor Thomas M. Menino posted: "We got him."

President Obama praised the law enforcement officials who took the suspect into custody in a statement from the White House shortly after 10 p. m., saying, "We've closed an important chapter in this tragedy."

The president said that he had directed federal law enforcement officials to continue to investigate, and he urged people not to rush to judgment about the motivations behind the attacks.

The discovery of Mr. Tsarnaev came just over 26 hours after the F. B. I. circulated pictures of him and his brother and called them suspects in Monday's bombings, which killed three people and wounded more than 170. Events unfolded quickly — and lethally — after that. Law enforcement officials said that within hours of the pictures' release, the two shot and killed a campus police officer at the Massachusetts Institute of Technology, carjacked a sport utility vehicle, and led police on a chase, tossing several pipe bombs from their vehicle. ④

Then the men got into a pitched gun battle with the police in Watertown in which more than 200 rounds were fired and a transit police officer was critically wounded. When the shootout ended, one of the suspects, Tamerlan Tsarnaev, 26, a former boxer, had been shot and fatally wounded. He was wearing explosives, several law enforcement officials said. But Dzhokhar Tsarnaev (joe-HARR tsar-NAH-yev) managed to escape — running over his older brother as he sped away, the officials said.

His disappearance, and fears that he could be armed with more explosives, set off an intense manhunt. SWAT teams and Humvees rolled through residential streets. Military helicopters hovered overhead. Bomb squads were called to several locations. And Boston, New England's largest city, was essentially shut down.

Transit service was suspended all day. Classes at Harvard, M. I. T., Boston University and other area colleges were canceled. Amtrak halted service into Boston. The Red Sox game at Fenway Park was postponed, as was a concert at Symphony Hall. Gov. Deval Patrick of Massachusetts urged residents to stay behind locked doors all day — not lifting the request until shortly after 6 p. m., when transit service in the shaken, seemingly deserted region was finally restored.

As the hundreds of police officers fanned out across New England looking for Dzhokhar Tsarnaev, investigators tried to piece together a fuller picture of the two brothers, to determine more about the bombing at the Boston Marathon.⑤ (681 words)

Words and Expressions

prompt	v.	引起,激起	circulate	v.	散发
manhunt	n.	搜捕	lethally	ad.	致死地,能致命地
custody	n.	拘留,监禁	carjack	n.	劫持汽车
commissioner	n.	专员,长官	chase	v.	追赶
abide by		遵守	pitch	n.	对阵战
tarp	n.	防水布,油布	squad	n.	班
invoke	v.	援引,援用	toss	v.	扔
accomplice	n.	从犯,帮凶			

Proper Nouns

Boston Marathon 波士顿马拉松赛跑

Miranda rights 米兰德权利,源自美国1966年的一起法律诉讼,指向嫌疑犯宣读其权利

Humvee 悍马(一种大马力汽车)

Amtrak 美国火车公司

News Summary

美国波士顿马拉松赛是每年五月份在波士顿举行的一项全球性比赛,2013年5月,当比赛选手就要到达在市区的终点时,看台附近发生了两次爆炸,有四名观众不幸身亡。爆炸使现场陷入一片混乱,比赛也只好草草收场,嫌犯趁乱逃离现场。美国民众对这起爆炸的凶犯及其动机众说纷纭,一时间,在美国本土又发生伊斯兰恐怖主义袭击的说法成为人们谈论的话题。当天晚上,两名涉嫌制造爆炸的青年逃到附近的麻省理工学院,打死一名校警,劫持一辆汽车又逃往纽约。在警察的追捕之下,其中一名被打死,另一名逃到波士顿郊外的沃特镇,躲在一只游艇里,第二天被人发现。据官方公布,这两名嫌疑犯是兄弟俩,十几年前随父母从俄罗斯移居美国。

Understanding Sentences

① 据官方消息,波士顿马拉松比赛爆炸事件中的在逃青少年嫌疑犯前晚从和警察进行的激烈枪击战中逃脱,引发了第二天警察进行几乎关闭全城的大搜捕,嫌犯已经于星期五晚在附近的沃特镇被抓获。

② 戴维斯先生说:"在紧接着的一个多小时里,我们和躲在小艇里的嫌犯进行了激烈枪战,最后,联邦调查局人质解救队登上小艇,把还活着的嫌犯抓获。"

③ 一名联邦执法官员说,将不会对他宣读米兰德权利,因为当局打算引用公共安全的例外,对他进行彻底盘问,以了解是否还有其他的爆炸装置或从犯,从而获取更多的情报。

Unit 4 Violence and Terrorist Attacks in the U. S.

④ 执法官员说,在嫌犯的照片发布几个小时之内,他们两人在麻省理工学院校园杀害了一名校园保安队员,劫持了一辆跑车,引发警察追赶,并在这一过程中从他们的车上向警察扔炸弹。

⑤ 随着数百名警察分布在新英格兰地区搜捕多佐卡塔纳耶夫,调查人员正试图获得这两兄弟的更完整材料,以弄清波士顿马拉松爆炸事件的更多相关材料。

Exercises

Ⅰ. **Understanding Ideas in the News**

1. Where was the teenage suspect in the Boston Marathon bombing finally caught?
   A. In nearby Watertown.　　　　B. In the water.
   C. In a house.

2. How was the suspect found?
   A. By a police commissioner.　　B. By a local resident.
   C. By the hostage rescue team.

3. What reason would police use for questioning the suspect after taking him into custody?
   A. Public safety exception.　　　B. Boston Marathon bombing.
   C. Intense manhunt.

4. What did the president urge people not to do?
   A. To remain behind locked doors.
   B. To judge about the motivation behind the bombing.
   C. To question him extensively.

5. What made the police decide to hunt for the second suspect who managed to escape after the gunfire with police?
   A. He had been shot and fatally wounded.
   B. He ran through residential streets.
   C. He could be armed with more explosives.

Ⅱ. **Language Points**

suspect, custody, manhunt, accomplice, lethal, pitched battle 这些词语是新闻中用于描述爆炸发生之后波士顿警察展开抓捕行动的。

suspect: (疑犯) a person believed to have committed a crime or done something wrong　e.g. *Police have issued a photograph of the suspect.*

custody: (关押) the state of being kept in prison, especially while waiting to go to court for trial　e.g. *You will be remanded in custody until your trial.*

manhunt: ((对逃犯等的)搜捕,追捕) to search so as to capture the convict

accomplice: (从犯) a person who helps someone else to commit a crime or to do something morally wrong

lethal: (致命的) able to cause or causing death; extremely dangerous　e.g. *Three*

59

minutes after the fire started, the house was full of lethal fumes.

pitched：（对阵战）a large fight, or a battle in which both sides stay in the same place

III. Questions for Further Study

This news report is about the capture of the second suspect who set a bomb at the Boston Marathon in 2013. The way information is organized and source of information is given is worth noticing here. A press conference will be held, especially when the event is of public concern and more authentic information is needed. The reporter usually attends the press release and use the materials from the conference for writing his report. Notice how all these are well managed in this news report.

英语报刊知识介绍

英语新闻期刊

英语新闻期刊一般指报道时事的周刊。新闻期刊上的文章一般比报纸上的新闻深入，会比较全面、深入地介绍重大事件的发生及背景等，而不限于简单地报道新闻。这是由于期刊的出版周期比较长，记者和编辑可以花比较多时间来采访、调查和组织新闻稿，并对文字做更多的修改润饰。

美国出版的各种期刊超过一万份，发行量和影响力最大的有六十多种；英国也有很多的新闻期刊。美国的《时代周刊》和《新闻周刊》是最主要的新闻期刊，此外还有像《纽约人》一类的集新闻、随笔和评论一身的文学期刊。英国也有《经济学家》、《旁观者》等一类的新闻期刊。

新闻期刊的报道方式对其他媒体也有影响，如广播电台和电视台都有"深度报道"类型节目。对于同一新闻来讲，这些和纸质的期刊一起构成了全方位、多媒体的新闻报道。

Unit 4　Violence and Terrorist Attacks in the U. S.

1. The cover of an issue of *The New Yorker*

2. The cover of an issue of *The Time*

Unit 5 American Election 2012

Democracy is the core value of the Western world and voting is widely used in deciding on everything that concerns people's life. Most western countries now elect their head of state or the executive in cycles of four or five years. Every four years, the Americans go to vote for their president, which is extensively covered by the media nowadays. As they follow the set procedures, reporters can make use of the previous coverage, only to change the names and places. In the last edition of this book, we selected some reports on transition of the presidency from Bill Clinton to Barack Obama, the first black president in American history. This edition includes some reports on Obama's running for a second term, which he did manage to succeed.

选举是西方民主制度的核心观念,目前大多数的西方国家,每隔几年就要选举他们的国家元首或首相,如美国每四年选举一次总统,英国每五年选举一次首相。因此,选举是他们政治生活中的一件大事,媒体都给予大量的报道。由于两百多年来的不断完善和改进,美国的选举已经有一套相对固定的程序,媒体报道的时候也就"有样可依"——有些经典的报道经常成为初入门记者的必读范文。本书的上一版,我们选了几篇关于克林顿怎样输给奥巴马的报道,那是美国历史上首次产生了一位黑人总统。本次修订也选了几篇关于奥巴马怎样获得连任的报道。

1. With debates over, candidates race to clinch vital states

President Obama kept up attacks on Mitt Romney in Delray Beach, Fla., on Tuesday, a drive that Mr. Romney called desperate.

By MICHAEL D. SHEAR and HELENE COOPER
The New York Times
Published: October 23, 2012

DAYTON, Ohio —President Obama started making his closing argument for a second term on Tuesday, beginning a furious two-week effort to beat back a late surge by Mitt Romney and hang on to battleground states where voters are already casting ballots in large numbers. ①

At the beginning of what the campaign described as a round-the-clock blitz, and on the day after his final debate, Mr. Obama tried to address what polling has shown is a consistent question among voters: What kind of agenda does he have for a second term? He released a 20-page booklet encapsulating previously announced policies and contrasting his positions to those of Mr. Romney.

The document contains no new proposals, and was derided by a spokesman for Mr. Romney as a "glossy panic button". But along with a new television advertisement that began running in nine battleground states, the president's aides predicted it would help counter the Romney assault plan for the next two weeks that aims to convince voters that Mr. Obama has no plans to fix the ailing economy. ②

Mr. Romney and his campaign spent Tuesday pounding away at points Mr. Obama made during the debate on Monday night, including accusing the president of apologizing for the United States and cutting military spending excessively. Mr. Romney flew from Florida to Nevada, where he mocked Mr. Obama's attacks on him as desperate moves by a losing candidate.

"You know, the truth is that attacks on me are not an agenda," Mr. Romney said to a crowd of about 6,000 people in Henderson, Nev. "His is a status quo candidacy. His is a message of going forward with the same policies of the last four years, and that's why his campaign is slipping, and that's why ours is gaining so much steam."

In the president's minute-long ad, and in appearances at the start of a frenetic week, Mr. Obama stepped up his effort to convince the nation that he had brought it back from the brink of economic collapse and that Mr. Romney would embrace the policies that caused the problems. ③ Looking directly into the camera, the president asks voters to "read my plan, compare it to Governor Romney's and decide which is better for you".

But even as he sought to strike a positive note at the start of a three-day swing that is taking him through Ohio, Iowa, Colorado, Nevada, Florida and Virginia, Mr. Obama also enthusiastically stepped up his attacks. The Republican candidate, the president said at a rally in Florida, wants to "turn back the clock 50 years for immigrants and gays and women" and is pursuing a foreign policy that is "all over the map".

Appearing later with Vice President Joseph R. Biden Jr. at a raucous rally before 9,500 people in Dayton, the president went into a spirited assault, using his new favorite attack word — "Romnesia" — to highlight his rival's position on the auto bailout, which the White House says was vital to saving jobs in Ohio and throughout the Midwest.

"Last night, Governor Romney looked me right in the eye, tried to pretend he never said, 'Let Detroit go bankrupt.' " Mr. Obama said, one of many instances all day when he suggested Mr. Romney was not being honest about his positions as he seeks to appeal to a general-election audience after a Republican primary campaign in which he emphasized conservative stances.

With some polls suggesting that Mr. Romney is closing the gap, Mr. Obama's top strategists described twin approaches: to make final appeals to independents, moderates, women and minorities as they offer lacerating assessments of Mr. Romney's qualifications and credibility.④

Still, Mr. Obama's schedule and the tenor of his campaign appearances made clear that his primary mission now was to energize his own supporters and get them to vote, preferably right away. In Florida, where he appeared in the morning, and later in Ohio, the constant refrain at his rallies was "Vote! Vote! Vote!" Early voting begins in Florida on Saturday and is already under way in Ohio. The terrain that Mr. Obama and Mr. Romney are covering this week illustrates a battleground within a battleground. The campaigns are advertising in nine states — stretching from North Carolina to Nevada — but are spending most of their most crucial resource — their time — in the Midwest.

Mr. Romney is scheduled to zip back and forth on Wednesday, Thursday and Friday between Ohio and Iowa. Winning those states is the most efficient way for him to block Mr. Obama from returning to the White House or for Mr. Obama to lock down a path to 270 electoral votes.

In a sign of the closeness of the race, a "super PAC" supporting Mr. Romney, Restore Our Future, reserved television time in Maine, traditionally a Democratic state. Maine allocates its electoral votes by Congressional district, and Mr. Romney's supporters hope they may be able to pick off the single electoral vote available from the state's more conservative Second District.

In the final two weeks Mr. Romney has the challenge of maintaining a strategy of presenting himself as more reasonable and pragmatic than the image the White House built of him over the summer: that of an out-of-touch, job-killing plutocrat. But to the degree that strategy involves emphasizing more moderate positions than he stressed during the Republican primary campaign, it creates the potential for him to face renewed questions among conservatives on his ideological commitment.⑤ (899 words)

Words and Expressions

furious	a.	猛烈的	pound away at		抨击
status quo		现状,维持现状	frenetic	a.	狂热的,发狂似的
battleground	n.	战场,争夺激烈的地方	raucous	a.	吵闹的,乱哄哄的
clinch	vt.	确定获胜	stance	n.	态度,立场,观点
surge	v.	激增	lacerate	v.	伤害(感情等)

blitz	n.	闪电战，闪击战
encapsulate	v.	简要描述，概括
deride	v.	表示轻蔑，嘲笑
assault	v.	猛烈的口头攻击

tenor	n.	大意，要领
terrain	n.	领域，范围
plutocrat	n.	富豪，财阀，有钱人（用于贬义）

Proper Nouns

Romnesia （用 Romney 的名字加上后缀-sia 造出的词）朗尼西亚，即朗尼的观点

super PAC （美国选举法中规定的一种筹款委员会，是传统的"政治行动委员会" Political-Action Committee 的变种，它可以接受任何人不受限制的政治捐款，并把它用于竞选的宣传等）

Restore Our Future 重拾未来（是"super PAC"所指的机构）

News Summary

四年一次的美国总统选举，或称"大选"，基本上是按照已形成的"套路"进行的，而各种媒体的报道也是紧跟每一阶段的发展和两党候选人的口号、言论进行的。这篇新闻，就是报道在接连举行了两次总统候选人之间的电视辩论之后，两名候选人各自提出了自己的政纲和口号，并分别到竞争激烈、选情"胶着"的几个大州去参加政党集会以争取选民的活动情况。美国的总统选举并不是完全由选民直接投票来决定的，而是每个州按人口拥有一定的"选举人票"，如一名候选人在某个州的选民直接投票中获得超过半数的票，这个州的"选举人票"就都投向他。新闻开头要点非常突出和清楚，分别说明了两位候选人的观点、对对手攻击的要点和自己提出的口号。

Understanding Sentences

① 奥巴马总统星期二开始为连任而发表最后的演讲，从而开始了为期两周的急速行动，以回击密特·朗尼刚对他做出的大量攻击，守住争夺激烈的几个州，那里的选民已开始投票。

② 但是，总统的助手们估计，随着新一轮的电视广告开始在争夺激烈的九个州播出，它有助于反击朗尼在接下来两周的攻击计划；该计划的目标是争取选民相信奥巴马没有拯救经济的打算。

③ 在总统的一分钟长的广告中，在紧张的一周开始时的露面中，奥巴马先生尽力让全国人民相信，是他把美国从经济崩溃的边缘拉了回来，而朗尼先生却要拥抱那些导致这些问题的政策。

④ 有些民意调查认为朗尼先生正在缩小这个差距，奥巴马先生的首席策划随即提出了双重策略：最后努力争取那些独立人士、中间派、妇女和少数族裔的支持，因为这些人散布对朗尼先生的资格和可信度的不利言论。

⑤ 但是，由于该策略涉及强调比他在民主党代表大会上所重申的更温和的立场，这也使他可能面对来自保守派的关于他的思想观念的新问题。

Exercises

I. Understanding Ideas in the News

1. What will Obama and Romney do after the presidential debates are over?

   A. To argue furiously for a second term.

   B. To release a 20-page booklet.

   C. To address gatherings in nine vital states.

2. What is described as a "glossy panic button"?

   A. A 20-page booklet.

   B. A furious two-week effort.

   C. A round-the-clock blitz.

3. How did Romney reply to Obama's attack on him?

   A. He pounded away at points he made during the debate on Monday.

   B. He mocked him by attacking Obama's candidacy.

   C. He accused him of apologizing for the United States.

4. On which issue did Obama keep criticizing Romney?

   A. The auto bailout.

   B. The policies that caused the problems.

   C. Immigrants and gays.

5. What is the primary mission of Obama's campaign in the final weeks?

   A. To make final appeals to the undecided.

   B. To urge his supporters to vote.

   C. To close the gap.

II. Language Points

furious, frenetic, raucous, consistent, constant 这几个词用于报道奥巴马和朗尼的竞选到了最后两周的激烈程度。

furious：(猛烈的) using a lot of effort or strength   e.g. *There is a furious struggle going on between the two presidential candidates.*

frenetic：(狂热的,发狂似的) involving a lot of movement or activity; extremely active, excited or uncontrolled   e.g. *After weeks of frenetic activity, the job was finally finished.*

raucous：(吵闹的,乱哄哄的) loud and unpleasant   e.g. *I heard the raucous call of the crows.*

consistent：(一致的) always behaving or happening in a similar, especially positive, way   e.g. *There has been a consistent improvement in her attitude.*

constant：(不变的,持续的) happening a lot or all the time   e.g. *He's in constant trouble with the police.*

III. Questions for Further Study

This news report is mostly about what the two candidates will be doing in the last two weeks of the campaign—to appeal to the voters in the "vital" states, i. e. states that have a lot of electorate votes. In order to win, they usually employ two strategies: make their objectives clear, and attack the opponent. Notice how the reporter introduces each candidate's objectives, and what differences there are, if any. Also the reporter covers their schedules in the last two weeks. The whole structure is effectively organized, and ideas are expressed clearly in language.

2. Heated fight for presidency goes to voters

Tribune wire reports
8:49 a. m. CST, November 6, 2012

WASHINGTON (AP) — Two fierce competitors who've given their all, President Barack Obama and Republican Mitt Romney now yield center stage to voters Tuesday for an Election Day choice that will frame the contours of government and the nation for years to come.

After a grinding presidential campaign that packed suspense to the finish, Americans head into polling places in sleepy hollows, bustling cities and superstorm-ravaged beach towns deeply divided. All sides are awaiting, in particular, a verdict from the nine battleground states whose votes will determine which man can piece together the 270 electoral votes needed for victory. ①

Obama has more options for getting there. So Romney decided to make a late dash to Cleveland and Pittsburgh on Tuesday while running mate Paul Ryan threw in stops in Cleveland and Richmond, Va. Obama opted to make a dozen radio and satellite TV interviews from his hometown of Chicago to keep his closing arguments fresh in voters' minds.

"I feel optimistic but only cautiously optimistic," Obama said on "The Steve Harvey

Morning Show". "Because until people actually show up at the polls and cast their ballot, the rest of this stuff is all just speculation."

Romney, asked on WTAM radio in Cleveland whether he agrees that voters always get it right in the end. "I won't guarantee that they'll get it right, but I think they will," Romney replied.

The GOP nominee then drove to a community center five minutes from his Belmont, Mass., home and cast his ballot with wife Ann at his side. The couple went from the polling site to the airport for his under-the-wire campaign swing.

Vice President Joe Biden and his wife, Jill Biden, were among the first voters Tuesday in at a polling place in Greenville, Del., Biden's home state. Smiling broadly, Biden waited in line with the other voters and greeted them with a handshake. Outside he sent a message to people across the country who may encounter crowded polling places. "I encourage you to stand in line as long as you have to," he told television cameras.

Both sides cast the Election Day choice as one with far-reaching repercussions for a nation still recovering from the biggest economic downturn since the Great Depression and at odds over how big a role government should play in solving the country's problems. ②

"It's a choice between two different visions for America," Obama declared in Madison, Wis., on Monday asking voters to let him complete work on the economic turnaround that began in his first term. "It's a choice between returning to the top-down policies that crashed our economy, or a future that's built on providing opportunity to everybody and growing a strong middle class."

Romney argued that Obama had his chance and blew it.

"The president thinks more government is the answer," he said in Sanford, Fla. "No, Mr. President, more jobs, that's the answer for America."

With both sides keeping up the onslaught of political ads in battleground states right into Election Day, on one thing, at least, there was broad agreement: "I am ready for it to be over," said nurse Jennifer Walker in Columbus, Ohio.

It wasn't just the presidency at stake Tuesday: Every House seat, a third of the Senate and 11 governorships were on the line, along with state ballot proposals on topics ranging from gay marriage and casino gambling to repealing the death penalty and legalizing marijuana. ③ Democrats were defending their majority in the Senate, and Republicans doing likewise in the House, raising the prospect of continued partisan wrangling in the years ahead no matter who might be president.

If past elections are any guide, a small but significant percentage of voters won't decide which presidential candidate they're voting for until Tuesday. ④ Four percent of voters reported making up their minds on Election Day in 2008, and the figure was 5 percent four years earlier, according to exit polls. In Washington Lee High School in Arlington, Va., hundreds of voters were in line shortly after the polls opened at 6 a.m.

and had to wait over an hour to cast their ballot.

By contrast, Election Day came early for more than a third of Americans, who chose to cast ballots days or even weeks in advance.

An estimated 46 million ballots, or 35 percent of the 133 million expected to be cast, were projected to be early ballots, according to Michael McDonald, an early voting expert at George Mason University who tallies voting statistics for the United States Elections Project. None of those ballots were being counted until Tuesday.

The two candidates and their running mates, propelled by adrenalin, throat lozenges and a determination to look back with no regrets, stormed through eight battleground states and logged more than 6,000 flight miles Monday on their final full day of campaigning, a political marathon featuring urgency, humor and celebrity. ⑤

Obama's final campaign rally, Monday night in Des Moines, Iowa, was filled with nostalgia. A single tear streamed down Obama's face during his remarks, though it was hard to tell whether it was from emotion or the bitter cold.

Team Obama's closing lineup included Bruce Springsteen, rapper Jay-Z, singers Mariah Carey, Ricky Martin and John Mellencamp, the NBA's Derek Fisher and actors Samuel L. Jackson and Chris Rock. Springsteen, who hitched a ride aboard Air Force One for part of the day, even composed an anthem for the president, rhyming "Obama" with "pajamas".

"Not the best I've ever written," the rocker confessed.

Obama, making his last run for office at the still-young age of 51, was tickled to have Springsteen along as his traveling campaign, telling the crowd in Madison, "I get to fly around with him on the last day that I will ever campaign — so that's not a bad way to end things."

Team Romney's closing events offered a slimmer celebrity quotient, including Kid Rock and country rock performers The Marshall Tucker Band. But the GOP nominee didn't seem to mind.

After a warm welcome at a rally in Fairfax, Va., Romney, 65, told cheering supporters: "I'm looking around to see if we have the Beatles here or something to have brought you. But it looks like you came just for the campaign and I appreciate it." (1046 words)

Words and Expressions

yield	vt.	让给；放弃	at stake		在争论中，危急
contour	n.	轮廓；外形	repeal	v.	撤销（法律）废止
grinding	a.	难熬的；折磨人的	partisan	a.	党派的
repercussion	n.	后果，反响	wrangle	v.	争吵，争论；争辩
verdict	n.	结果，决定	adrenalin	n.	肾上腺素

| speculation | n. | 推测 | throat lozenge | 润喉片 |
| onslaught | n. | 猛攻，攻击 | | |

Proper Nouns

Election Day　选举日，在美国是 11 月的第一个星期二
electoral votes　　选举人票，美国各州按照人口比例得到的选举总统的票数
the Great Depression　指 20 世纪 30 年代美国发生的经济危机
Bruce Springsteen　　布鲁斯·斯布林思丁，美国摇滚乐手

News Summary

　　这是一份美联社发出的通稿，又被《芝加哥论坛报》刊登在其网站上。由于涉及是否能最早报道选举结果，所以具有很强的时间性。报道一开始就点题，指出经过激烈的竞选活动以后，选举已经进入投票，结果很快就可见分晓。由于奥巴马是在任总统，具有一定优势，所以朗尼及其搭档在投票的当天还从克里芙兰到匹兹堡做最后的努力，而奥巴马也没有放松，星期一还飞到爱荷华州的达莫斯做最后的演讲，而且，双方都带了不少的明星助阵。

Understanding Sentences

　　① 经过了一次把悬念推至最后时刻的、十分胶着的总统竞选，美国各地的选民，从朦胧的乡村、沸腾的城市到刚经受超强热带风暴袭击的海滨小城，持着完全不同的态度进入投票站。双方尤其期待的是来自九个关键州的投票结果，这些结果将决定哪个人能得到当选总统所必需的 270 张选举人票。

　　② 双方在选举日都投下了一票，做出他们的选择。这一票，对于一个正在从经济大萧条时代以来最大的经济危机中复苏的国家来说，对于一个在政府解决这些问题时应该起多大的作用方面意见并不统一的国家来说，将具有深远的意义。

　　③ 星期二这天要决定的，不只是总统职位。众议院的每个席位、三分之一的参议院职位、十一个州的州长都要在这一天选出，此外还有公民投票决定的提案，从同性恋结婚和赌场，到取消死刑和使大麻合法化。

　　④ 假如以往的选举结果值得借鉴的话，少数但能起决定作用的选民要直到星期二才会决定他们的这一票投给两个总统候选人中的哪一位。

　　⑤ 这两位候选人和他们的竞选搭档，带着高涨的激情、润喉片和以后回顾的时候不会感到遗憾的决心，在整个竞选活动的最后一个星期一，又飞行了六千多英里，闪电式地到访八个关键州进行竞选——这是一场紧迫的、幽默的，且有明星助阵的政治马拉松。

Exercises

Ⅰ. Understanding Ideas in the News

　　1. What is the significance of the vote on Tuesday?

　　A. It will determine the government and its policy.

　　B. It will decide whether Obama will be re-elected.

C. It is a deeply divided campaign.
2. Where did Romney cast his vote?
A. Cleveland.
B. Pittsburgh.
C. Belmont, Mass.
3. How did Obama spend his last day of campaign?
A. Campaigning in Des Moines, Iowa.
B. Speaking in Madison, Wis.
C. Making radio and satellite TV interviews.
4. What is Obama's view of the different visions for America?
A. A matter of who'll be the president of the U. S.
B. What is the solution to economic recovery.
C. Whether America needs a big government.
5. What do we learn from past elections?
A. A small percentage of people only make up their minds at the last moment.
B. Early ballots can be cast for 133 million people.
C. People have to wait over an hour to cast their ballots.

II. Language Points

grinding campaign, cautiously optimistic, onslaught of political ads, partisan wrangling, celebrity quotient 这些词语组成巧妙的搭配,可以表达深刻的含义,使新闻更加生动。

grind:(碾(碎),折磨) to make something into small pieces or a powder by pressing between hard surfaces   e. g. *to grind coffee*

cautiously:(慎重地) a feeling that you can be generally hopeful about a situation even though you do not expect complete success or improvement

onslaught:(猛攻,攻击) a very powerful attack   e. g. *It is unlikely that his forces could withstand an allied onslaught for very long.*

wrangle:(争论,争吵) an argument, especially one which continues for a long period of time

quotient:(应得的份额) a particular degree or amount of something   e. g. *This is a car with a high head-turning quotient* (= a lot of people turn to look at it).

III. Questions for Further Study

This news report is about almost the last stage of the campaign, when people in some states have started to vote. As the result is yet to come out, there is still speculation, and the candidates are still campaigning. Read this news article carefully, and find out how the reporter quotes the two candidates to show their different points of views on issues in the campaign, and how this is linked to reporting facts about their campaign travels, especially during the last hours when people have started to vote.

3. Will we be better off in 2016?

By ADAM DAVIDSON
The New York Times
October 23, 2012

Now that the campaign is almost over, it's clear that this presidential cycle was all about the economy. Just not the economy we're actually entering. This thought crossed my mind during the second presidential debate as Mitt Romney declared that, if elected, he would label China as a currency manipulator. It was a rehearsed entreaty meant to appeal to thousands of frustrated manufacturing workers and their bosses in Rust Belt states. ① But it mainly confirmed how far we are from understanding our place in the new global economy.

Not that long ago, the U.S. had that global economy all to itself. From the 1950s to the 1980s, it was the world's dominant producer and consumer. In countries spanning Europe to Latin America, and throughout Asia, success was determined by how well they could siphon off a bit of this incredible growth. ② Things began to change in the 1970s, however, when Japan and Germany started making cars and factory equipment and electronic gadgets that beat their American competitors. And for the next 30 years, the U.S. struggled to adjust to increasingly competitive Asian and Latin American producers. But as long as it remained the world's largest consumer market, the U.S. maintained lots of leverage. The government persuaded Pakistan to join the global war on terror, for instance, partly by promising its sock manufacturers duty-free access to its market.

It's useful to consider the framework of Ian Bremmer, president of the Eurasia Group, a political consultancy. American power during the past half century, Bremmer says, has been based on a strong military and an enormous market — one that can reward and punish. ③ And while the former has maintained its standing, the rest of the world is becoming much less fixated on the latter. ④ Romney and Barack Obama can promise to punish China all they want (Obama, in fact, made an identical point in

2008), but their statements merely suggest either that they don't realize America's economic power has diminished or (more likely) that they're just too afraid to say it out loud.[5] And that's too bad. Those Rust Belt voters would be better served, Bremmer says, if the next president could persuade American businesses to stop complaining about China and instead focus on making goods that its consumers want to buy. For decades, Chinese businesses studied the American market. Now it's time to play catch-up.

As this political cycle comes to a close, it's clear that the U.S. has entered a new economic chapter. By the next election, the upheaval of the past few years will have (hopefully) settled, and we'll be looking at a clearer vision of our future. I asked several leading experts to project what the U.S. will look like by 2016, and there was a consensus. Instead of a sudden bounce back, Harvard's Jeffry Frieden told me, there will be steady but far-too-slow growth. Unemployment will be at around 6.4 percent, according to Nigel Gault of IHS Global Insight, an economic forecaster. More significant, by 2016, Frieden and Bremmer noted, the U.S. will be adjusting to an economy in which inequality is a structural fixture. There will be millions who are unable to get work, and tens of millions more who will have to adapt to lower income. Meanwhile, those with college and advanced degrees will experience a country that has rebounded. Their incomes will grow.

China's economy probably won't eclipse the U.S. economy until some time in the 2020s, but by 2016, far fewer Americans will believe that the U.S. can stop China from manipulating its currency or doing whatever else it wants. By then Americans will probably have experienced its economic might firsthand. Brent Iadarola, a director at the industry-research firm Frost & Sullivan, told me that the new global economy will look like our current mobile-phone market. Nearly every American adult has a cellphone, but only 40 percent of them have an iPhone, Android or other smartphone. As such, the industry is expecting rapid growth in the next few years. By 2016, though, the U.S. market should be saturated, and smartphone manufacturers will have to add a lot of new features just to get a small number of people to upgrade. There won't be large growth or large profits in the U.S. The major companies — and the secondary economy of case makers and app designers — will be focused on the tastes of emerging markets in Asia, Eastern Europe, Latin America and Africa.

It's also going to be much clearer to American workers in various industries that many of their best opportunities are overseas. Pharmaceutical companies are encouraged by the U.S. market in the next few years partly because so many baby boomers are reaching their peak medicine-consuming years. Once that market begins to disappear, though, Big Pharma will most likely pursue the billions of middle-aged people in quickly advancing poor countries. (They'll have their work cut out for them competing against generic and local companies, but the potential is extraordinary.) According to the IMS Institute for Healthcare Informatics, 41 percent of all drugs sold throughout the world in

2006 were sold to Americans. Only 14 percent of drugs were sold to all of the emerging markets combined. By 2016, IMS expects that patients in those markets will buy the same value of drugs as Americans.

I heard this basic outline again and again — from cars to entertainment and even to agriculture. Mark Evans, editor of the trade journal Fertilizer International, told me that even in the crop-fertilizer industry "the baton is being passed". Which is the best way to think of the shift our economy will take. It's not that the U.S. economy will shrink. Rather, the U.S. economy is becoming boring while other markets are offering huge opportunity. An empire may not be abruptly ending, but the days of politicians talking dismissively about China's monetary policy sure are.⑥ (980 words)

Words and Expressions

entreaty	n.	乞求,恳求	saturate	v.	饱和
siphon off	v.	吮吸;(喻)挪用,盗用	generic	a.	一般的,普通的
leverage	n.	(喻)(为取得某种结果而施加的)影响力	eclipse	v.	遮掩,使失色
			baton	n.	指挥棒
fixate	v.	使痴迷,使固着于	dismissive	a.	轻视的,轻蔑的
consensus	n.	一致的看法	frustrate	v.	挫败,使感到灰心
upheaval	n.	动乱,大变动	pharmaceutical	a.	制药(学)上的

Proper Nouns

the Rust Belt 铁锈带(指美国中、东部几个州,因原有工业萎缩导致经济衰退、人口减少和城镇荒芜)

the Eurasia Group 欧亚集团(世界上最大的政治风险咨询机构,成立于1998年)

IHS Global Insight 美国一家经济信息服务公司(IHS: Information Handling Service)

Frost & Sullivan 美国一家咨询公司,提供市场分析等服务

Android 安卓(一种智能手机的操作系统)

IMS Institute for Healthcare Informatics 制药业和保健用品业的信息服务公司

News Summary

这是一篇发表在《纽约时报》杂志上的表达观点的文章,有点类似于社论。有些报纸每周末出版一期"杂志",装订成一本,内容多是读者比较关注的话题,再加上大量的照片,如时装表演等。这篇文章主要想说明,在四年一度的大选快要进入尾声的时候,回顾一下两位候选人之间所进行的辩论和他们各自的竞选口号,可以看出本次大选的争议主要是围绕着经济问题,而实质是美国人对他们今天的经济地位认识不足,看不到(或是不承认)美国已经失去了全球经济霸主的地位。作者接着引用了一些学者和机构的分析,预测到2016年下一次选举时,美国的经济或者会有稍微的好转。

Understanding Sentences

① 那是一个经过反复排练的句子,用来打动在"铁锈带"州的千千万万感到沮丧的制造业工人和他们的老板。

② 在跨越欧洲和拉丁美洲的国家中,以及整个亚洲的国家中,成功取决于他们怎样能从这不可思议的增长中咬下一口。

③ 贝宁姆说,半个世纪以来,美国的力量一直是建立在一支强大的军队和一个巨大的市场的基础上———一种既能够给予回报,也能够给予惩罚的力量。

④ 虽然前者还保持着它的地位(指军事力量),世界上其他地方正在变得不再那么依附于后者(指巨大的市场)了。

⑤ 朗尼和奥巴马可以随心所欲地承诺打击中国(事实上,奥巴马在 2008 年曾有过相似的说法),但是他们的声明仅能说明,他们要么并没有认识到美国的经济力量已经减弱,要么(更有可能)他们过分害怕,不敢大声说出。

⑥ 一个强大的帝国也许不至于突然消失,但是,那些政治家们可以对中国货币政策采取不屑一顾态度的日子肯定要过去的。

Exercises

Ⅰ. **Understanding Ideas in the News**

1. What does the author think about Romney's statement — if elected, he would label China as a currency manipulator?

    A. Romney is strongly anti-China.

    B. Americans don't realize the problems in their economy.

    C. It is rehearsed to appeal to workers and their bosses.

2. When did the world economy begin to change?

    A. In the 1970s.

    B. From the 1950s to the 1980s.

    C. In the 21st century.

3. What will the American economic look like in 2016?

    A. There will be a steady and slow growth.

    B. There will be an upheaval.

    C. Many people will be unemployed.

4. What is expected of the smartphone manufacturers in 2016?

    A. They will have to manufacture more Android phones.

    B. They will make large profits in the U.S.

    C. They will have to add a lot of new features.

5. What industry is used as an example to illustrate the American economy in 2016?

    A. Information technology.

    B. Pharmaceutical.

    C. Smart phones.

Ⅱ. Language Points

frustrate, siphon off, leverage, fixate, bounce 这些词语是作者在描述美国经济情况时使用的,它们生动而准确地说明了现在美国面临的处境。

frustrate:(挫败,使感到灰心)to make someone feel annoyed or discouraged because they cannot achieve what they want   e. g. *It frustrates me that I'm not able to put any of my ideas into practice.*

siphon off:((喻)挪用,盗用)to dishonestly take money from an organization or other supply, and use it for a purpose for which it was not intended   e. g. *He lost his job when it was discovered that he had been siphoning off money from the company for his own use.*

leverage:((喻)影响力)power to influence people and get the results you want   e. g. *If the United Nations had more troops in the area, it would have greater leverage.*

fixate:(使痴迷)unable to stop thinking about something   e. g *a nation fixated on the past*

bounce:(反弹)to (cause to) move up or away after hitting a surface   e. g. *The ball bounced off the post and into the net.*

Ⅲ. Questions for Further Study

This magazine article is a commentary in nature. It begins with a quote by the Republic candidate Mitt Romney, which bring up the topic of the American economy. Then the reporter quotes some experts on the economy, esp. the economic situation at the next election in 2016. Although the reporter's attitude is not very optimistic, there is a little hope for a better future, and the issues of debate in this election will most likely be over. See how the reporter organizes the information around the main idea of this article.

英语报刊知识介绍

新闻通讯社和新闻通稿

新闻通讯社指专门搜集和供应新闻稿件、图片和资料的新闻发表机构。它是集中采写新闻的主要机构,也是新闻流通和发布的重要渠道,被称为"消息总汇"、"提供新闻的大动脉"。

世界各国几乎都有各自的官方新闻通讯社,以发表官方的权威新闻。此外,也有不少的商业性新闻通讯社,其中一些以提供金融、期货及股市方面的新闻为主,称为商业新闻社。现在还有"新闻专线",能在网络上向所有媒体提供快速及时的新闻传输。

英美最大的新闻通讯社有:美联社(Associated Press)、合众国际社(United Press International)和路透社(Reuters Ltd.)。此外还有有线新闻(CNN)、英国广播公司(BBC)等电台、电视新闻媒体。

Unit 5　American Election 2012

1. The Reuter's website

2. The CNN's website

Unit 6 Social News—the U. S.

Social news covers a wider range of news reports on events happening in our daily lives, and is best grouped under geographical regions. Except news on election and government, there are various topics that may be included in this category, such as: a news report on a decision of the local municipality, a natural disaster that just hit the local community, a case of murder or robbery, and many others about the life of the people in a certain place. This chapter includes a report on the disaster caused by a tropical storm, a report on the gun shooting on campus, and a report on the gun-control policy in the United States. Such news normally appear in the "national" section of a newspaper.

"社会新闻"主要报道社会上发生的各种各样的事情。这类新闻的特点在于它跟人们的生活密切相关,如当地政府出台某项政策法规,发生在当地的自然灾害,抢劫、谋杀等犯罪案件,以及其他形形色色的消息。由于地区和国家不同,地方的概念可以是一个大都市,如美国的纽约和中国的北京,也可以是一个小城镇。在美国主要的报纸上,这类新闻通常出现在"国内"这一栏目中。本章收集了三篇发生在美国的社会新闻:一篇关于2012年强热带风暴"仙迪"袭击美国东海岸所造成的灾害;一篇关于校园枪击事件;另一篇关于人们对待枪支管制的态度。

1. Storm barrels through region, leaving destructive path

A resident of Little Ferry, N. J., biked to charge his cell phone.

By JAMES BARRON
The New York Times
October 29, 2012

Hurricane Sandy battered the mid-Atlantic region on Monday, its powerful gusts and storm surges causing once-in-a-generation flooding in coastal communities, knocking down trees and power lines and leaving more than five million people — including a large swath of Manhattan — in the rain-soaked dark. ① At least seven deaths in the New York region were tied to the storm.

The mammoth and merciless storm made landfall near Atlantic City around 8 p. m. , with maximum sustained winds of about 80 miles per hour, the National Hurricane Center said. That was shortly after the center had reclassified the storm as a post-tropical cyclone, a scientific renaming that had no bearing on the powerful winds, driving rains and life-threatening storm surge expected to accompany its push onto land.

The storm had unexpectedly picked up speed as it roared over the Atlantic Ocean on a slate-gray day and went on to paralyze life for millions of people in more than a half-dozen states, with extensive evacuations that turned shorefront neighborhoods into ghost towns. ② Even the superintendent of the Statue of Liberty left to ride out the storm at his mother's house in New Jersey; he said the statue itself was "high and dry", but his house in the shadow of the torch was not.

The wind-driven rain lashed sea walls and protective barriers in places like Atlantic City, where the Boardwalk was damaged as water forced its way inland. ③ Foam was spitting, and the sand gave in to the waves along the beach at Sandy Hook, N. J. , at the entrance to New York Harbor. Water was thigh-high on the streets in Sea Bright, N. J. , a three-mile sand-sliver of a town where the ocean joined the Shrewsbury River.

"It's the worst I've seen," said David Arnold, watching the storm from his longtime home in Long Branch, N. J. "The ocean is in the road, there are trees down everywhere. I've never seen it this bad."

In New York, Gov. Andrew M. Cuomo's office said late Monday night that at least five deaths in the state were attributable to the storm. At least three of those involved falling trees. About 7 p. m. , a tree fell on a house in Queens, killing a 30-year-old man, the city police said. About the same time, two boys, ages 11 and 13, were killed in North Salem in Westchester County, when a tree fell on the house they were in, according to the State Police.

In Morris County, N. J. , a man and a woman were killed when a tree fell on their car Monday evening, The Associated Press reported.

In Manhattan, NYU Langone Medical Center's backup power system failed Monday evening, forcing the evacuation of patients to other facilities.

In a Queens beach community, nearly 200 firefighters were battling a huge blaze early on Tuesday morning that tore through more than 50 tightly-packed homes in an area where heavy flooding slowed responders. ④

Earlier, a construction crane atop one of the tallest buildings in the city came loose and dangled 80 stories over West 57th Street, across the street from Carnegie Hall.

Soon power was going out and water was rushing in. Waves topped the sea wall in the financial district in Manhattan, sending cars floating downstream. West Street, along the western edge of Lower Manhattan, looked like a river. The Brooklyn-Battery Tunnel, known officially as the Hugh L. Carey Tunnel in memory of a former governor, flooded "from end to end", the Metropolitan Transportation Authority said, hours after Gov. Andrew M. Cuomo of New York ordered it closed to traffic. Officials said water also seeped into seven subway tunnels under the East River.

By early evening, the storm knocked out power to hundreds of thousands of homes, stores and office buildings. Consolidated Edison said that as of 1:30 a.m. Tuesday, 634,000 customers in New York City and Westchester County were without power. Con Edison, fearing damage to its electrical equipment, shut down power pre-emptively in sections of Lower Manhattan on Monday evening, and then, at 8:30 p.m., an unplanned failure, probably caused by flooding in substations, knocked out power to most of Manhattan below Midtown, about 250,000 customers.⑤ Later, an explosion at a Con Ed substation on East 14th Street knocked out power to another 250,000 customers.

In New Jersey, more than two million customers were without power as of 1:30 a.m. Tuesday, and in Connecticut nearly 500,000.

President Obama, who returned to the White House and met with top advisers, said Monday that the storm would disrupt the rhythms of daily life in the states it hit. "Transportation is going to be tied up for a long time," he said, adding that besides flooding, there would probably be widespread power failures. He said utility companies had lined up crews to begin making repairs. But he cautioned that it could be slow going.

"The fact is, a lot of these emergency crews are not going to get into position to start restoring power until some of these winds die down," the president said. He added, "That may take several days."

Forecasters attributed the power of the storm to a convergence of weather systems. As the hurricane swirled north in the Atlantic and then pivoted toward land, a wintry storm was heading toward it from the west, and cold air was blowing south from the Arctic.⑥ The hurricane left more than 60 people dead in the Caribbean before it began crawling toward the Northeast. (899 words)

Words and Expressions

barrel	v.	高速行驶；飞奔	lash	v.	冲击
batter	v.	连续猛击	attributable	a.	可归于……的
gust	n.	一阵强风，一阵狂风	blaze	n.	大火，烈火
swath	n.	狭长的条或片	seep	n. & v.	（油水）渗出地表的地方；渗出
mammoth	a.	巨大的，庞大的			
pre-emptively	ad.	抢先地，先发制人地	cyclone	n.	（气象）旋风；龙卷风

slate-gray		石板色,蓝灰色	convergence	n.	汇集;相交
evacuation	n.	撤离;疏散;撤退;转移	swirl	v.	打旋;旋动
dangle	v.	摇摆	pivot	v.	使绕枢轴转动
sustained	a.	持久的			

Proper Nouns

Consolidate Edison, commonly known as Con Edison   总部在纽约的一家能源公司

News Summary

  这是一篇关于自然灾害的新闻报道,它的第一要素当然是时间性。飓风在10月28日(星期一)袭击了美国东部的六个州,包括纽约市,第二天,有关新闻就见诸报端。第二要素是信息量。由于恶劣的天气条件,一些通常传递信息的媒介也许失去作用,因此,更多的人依赖报纸获取信息。人们关心的问题主要是自然灾害的性质和它所造成的后果,尤其是所引起的人员伤亡情况。这篇新闻的导语段就清楚交代了飓风所造成的损坏,主要是吹倒了许多大树和电线杆,导致供电中断,以及带来洪水和其他损失,最后就是人员伤亡。然后,新闻开始比较详细地介绍主要地点的情况。第三个特点是语言表达,既简洁又不失生动,这与新闻报道中常用的一些词语,特别是短而有力的词语有关。同时,同一概念又可以有多种表达,使文字不会枯燥无味。

Understanding Sentences

  ① 飓风"仙迪"在星期一横扫中大西洋地区,强大的阵风及暴风雨袭击引发了沿岸地区罕见的大洪水,许多大树和电线杆被吹倒,超过五百万人,包括曼哈顿区的大片地区,处在大雨浸泡的黑暗中。

  ② 狂风暴雨从灰蒙蒙的天空中呼啸着扑向大西洋,其速度越来越快,使超过六个州数以百万计的人们的生活陷于瘫痪,人们大量从沿海社区撤离,使那里成为空荡荡的一片"鬼城"。

  ③ 狂风裹着大雨,冲击着像大西洋城的海岸防线和防护堤,海水冲毁了木板铺成的小道,涌进里面。

  ④ 在皇后区一个海滩社区,星期二早晨,约二百名消防队员正在扑灭一场吞没了五十多间连成一片的房子的大火,那里很深的水妨碍了人们进行抢救。

  ⑤ 由于担心飓风会给电力设施带来损坏,爱迪生公司星期一晚上关闭了下曼哈顿各地的电力供应;接着,晚上8:30时,预料之外的一次事故,可能由供电站浸水引起,使曼哈顿自中区起大部地区电力供应均中断,影响了约二十五万用户。

  ⑥ 气象预报人员把这次风暴的强度归咎于不同气象系统的汇集:随着飓风在大西洋上往北吹去,然后朝陆地旋转,一个冬季风暴正从西边朝它移动,同时来自北极的冷空气强烈地往南吹。

Exercises

I. Understanding Ideas in the News

1. What damages did Hurricane Sandy cause?
   A. Powerful gusts and storm surges.
   B. Flooding, power failure and death.
   C. Driving rains and life-threatening storm surge.
2. Where did this mammoth and merciless storm hit first?
   A. Atlantic City.　　　B. New York City.　　　C. New Jersey City.
3. What is the main cause of the deaths reported in New York city?
   A. Flooding.　　　B. Falling trees.　　　C. Power failure.
4. How was the subway system in Manhattan affected by the storm?
   A. A huge blaze tore through more than 50 homes.
   B. Waves topped the sea walls.
   C. Water seeped into seven subway tunnels.
5. What did forecasters attribute the power of the storm to?
   A. A wintry storm.
   B. Cold air blowing from the Arctic.
   C. A convergence of weather systems.

II. Language Points

barrel, batter, paralyze, lash, pivot 这些是新闻中用来描述强热带风暴的行径和危害的动词。

barrel：（高速移动）to drive or move at high speed

batter：（连续猛击）to strike repeatedly so as to bruise, shatter, or break; to beat continuously or violently

paralyze：（使瘫痪）to make powerless, helpless, inactive, or ineffective; to halt the normal activity of (a factory, community, etc.)

lash：（冲击）to hit with a lot of force　e.g. *The sound of the rain lashing against the windows was deafening.*

pivot：（使绕枢轴转动）to swing round a central point

III. Questions for Further Study

Study and analyze the structure of this news report to understand how a report on disaster is normally organized, and consists of what major elements. The lead paragraph summarizes the damages caused by the tropical storm. Then the reporter describes the forming of the storm and as it moved and hit land, the serious damages caused by the storm. In doing so, lots of descriptive words, esp. those associated with natural disasters are used. The reporter also tries the best to find reliable sources for the damages, and uses them in the report.

Unit 6   Social News—the U. S.

2. Nation reels after gunman massacres 20 children at school in Connecticut

Connecticut State Police stood guard outside Sandy Hook Elementary School on Saturday morning.

By JAMES BARRON
The New York Times
December 14, 2012

A 20-year-old man wearing combat gear and armed with semiautomatic pistols and a semiautomatic rifle killed 26 people — 20 of them children — in an attack in an elementary school in central Connecticut on Friday. Witnesses and officials described a horrific scene as the gunman, with brutal efficiency, chose his victims in two classrooms while other students dove under desks and hid in closets. ①

Hundreds of terrified parents arrived as their sobbing children were led out of the Sandy Hook Elementary School in a wooded corner of Newtown, Conn. By then, all of the victims had been shot and most were dead, and the gunman, identified as Adam Lanza, had committed suicide. The children killed were said to be 5 to 10 years old.

A 28th person, found dead in a house in the town, was also believed to have been shot by Mr. Lanza. That victim, one law enforcement official said, was Mr. Lanza's mother, Nancy Lanza, who was initially reported to be a teacher at the school. ② She apparently owned the guns he used.

Although reports at the time indicated that the principal of the school let Mr. Lanza in because she recognized him, his mother did not work at the school, and he shot his way in, defeating a security system requiring visitors to be buzzed in. ③ Moments later, the principal was shot dead when she went to investigate the sound of gunshots. The school psychologist was also among those who died.

The rampage, coming less than two weeks before Christmas, was the nation's second-deadliest school shooting, exceeded only by the 2007 Virginia Tech massacre, in which a gunman killed 32 people and then himself.

Law enforcement officials said Mr. Lanza had grown up in Newtown, and he was remembered by high school classmates as smart, introverted and nervous. They said he had gone out of his way not to attract attention when he was younger.

The gunman was chillingly accurate. A spokesman for the State Police said he left only one wounded survivor at the school. All the others hit by the barrage of bullets from the guns Mr. Lanza carried died, suggesting that they were shot at point-blank range. ④ One law enforcement official said the shootings occurred in two classrooms in a section of the single-story Sandy Hook Elementary School.

Some who were there said the shooting occurred during morning announcements, and the initial shots could be heard over the school's public address system. The bodies of those killed were still in the school as of 10 p. m. Friday.

The New York City medical examiner's office sent a "portable morgue" to Newtown to help with the aftermath of the shootings, a spokeswoman, Ellen Borakove, confirmed late Friday.

Law enforcement officials offered no hint of what had motivated Mr. Lanza. It was also unclear, one investigator said, why Mr. Lanza — after shooting his mother to death inside her home — drove her car to the school and slaughtered the children. "I don't think anyone knows the answers to those questions at this point," the official said. As for a possible motive, he added, "we don't know much for sure."

F. B. I. agents interviewed his brother, Ryan Lanza, in Hoboken, N. J. His father, Peter Lanza, who was divorced from Nancy Lanza, was also questioned, one official said.

Newtown, a postcard-perfect New England town where everyone seems to know everyone else and where there had lately been holiday tree lightings with apple cider and hot chocolate, was plunged into mourning. ⑤ Stunned residents attended four memorial services in the town on Friday evening as detectives continued the search for clues, and an explanation.

Maureen Kerins, a hospital nurse who lives close to the school, learned of the shooting from television and hurried to the school to see if she could help.

"I stood outside waiting to go in, but a police officer came out and said they didn't need any nurses," she said, "so I knew it wasn't good."

In the cold light of Friday morning, faces told the story outside the stricken school. There were the frightened faces of children who were crying as they were led out in a line. There were the grim faces of women. There were the relieved-looking faces of a couple and their little girl.

The shootings set off a tide of anguish nationwide. In Illinois and Georgia, flags were lowered to half-staff in memory of the victims. And at the White House, President

Unit 6　Social News—the U. S.

Obama struggled to read a statement in the White House briefing room. More than once, he dabbed his eyes.

"Our hearts are broken," Mr. Obama said, adding that his first reaction was not as a president, but as a parent.

"I know there is not a parent in America who does not feel the same overwhelming grief that I do," he said.

He called the victims "beautiful little kids".

"They had their entire lives ahead of them: birthdays, graduations, weddings, kids of their own," he said. Then the president reached up to the corner of one eye.

Mr. Obama called for "meaningful action" to stop such shootings, but he did not spell out details. In his nearly four years in office, he has not pressed for expanded gun control. But he did allude on Friday to a desire to have politicians put aside their differences to deal with ways to prevent future shootings.（891 words）

Words and Expressions

reel	v.	晕眩,茫然,不知所措	dive	v.	潜水,跳下
horrific	a.	令人恐惧的, 可怕的	point-blank	a.	（子弹）近距离直射的
buzz	v.	用蜂鸣器发信号	morgue	n.	停尸室
rampage	n.	暴怒的行为	stricken	a.	（表情）非常悲痛的
introvert	n. & v.	性格内向的人；使内向，使内省	dab	v.	（用吸水物）轻拍,轻擦
			allude	v.	暗示,间接提到；暗指
barrage	n.	一阵急速的扫射	combat gear		战斗服

News Summary

由于美国的枪支管制比较松,因此很多人都拥有枪支,导致枪杀事件时有发生,尤其是群死群伤的这类事件,通常在人群密集的地方发生,如在学校里。这篇新闻报道的事发生在2012年圣诞节前两周,一名20岁的青年闯进一所小学,在两个教室里对着小学生开枪,一共杀死了26人,枪手最后自杀。新闻叙述很有条理,从总结性的导语句开始,记者回顾了事件发生的大致过程、警察处理的过程、学生和家长的反应,以及当地群众的态度。在叙述的过程中,记者不断插入来自权威部门的消息和引用接受采访的群众的话。

Understanding Sentences

① 目击者和警官描述了这样一幅令人发指的恐怖场面:凶徒闯进两间教室,冷酷而准确地枪杀那些受害者,其他学生纷纷躲在桌子下或钻进壁柜里。

② 一位警官说,这位受害者是凶手兰扎的母亲南希·兰扎,最初的报道说她是该校的一名教师。

③ 虽然当时有报道说是学校的校长让兰扎进了校园,因为她认识他,但实际情况是他母亲并不在学校工作,是他开枪打坏了需要刷卡进入学校的保安系统,闯了进去。

④ 被兰扎的枪射出的一阵急速的子弹击中的所有其他人都死了,说明他们都是被近距

离击中的。

⑤ 新城是新英格兰一个如风景明信片般美丽的小镇,镇上的人几乎都互相认识,前几天他们还一边喝着苹果汁和热朱古力一边装饰圣诞树,现在却沉浸在哀伤之中。

Exercises

Ⅰ. Understanding Ideas in the News

1. How many victims were killed by the gunman?
A. 26.   B. 28.   C. 20.

2. Where did the killing happen?
A. An elementary school.
B. In Connecticut State.
C. Sandy Hook Elementary School in Newtown.

3. How did the gunman get into the school?
A. He broke the security system by shooting.
B. The principal of the school let him in.
C. He drove a car to the school.

4. What suggests that the gunman shoot the students with accuracy?
A. He shot at point-blank range.
B. He was a smart student when young.
C. He left only one wounded survivor at the school.

5. Why did President Obama dab his eyes when reading a statement?
A. He was feeling uncomfortable.
B. He was sad for the children killed.
C. He called for "meaningful action" to stop such shootings.

Ⅱ. Language Points

brutal efficiency, chillingly accurate, rampage, barrage, slaughter 这些词或短语用来描述枪手的行为,尤其是前两个词组深刻地表达了枪手的冷酷无情。

brutal:(残忍的) cruel, violent and completely without feelings   e. g. *He had presided over a brutal regime in which thousands of people had "disappeared".*

chilling:(冷酷的) in a frightening way or manner

rampage:(暴怒的行为) violent and usually wild behaviour

barrage:(一阵急速的扫射) continuous firing of large guns

slaughter:(屠杀,残杀) the killing of many people cruelly and unfairly, especially in a war   e. g. *Hardly anyone in the town escaped the slaughter when the rebels were defeated.*

Ⅲ. Questions for Further Study

This is a typical news report on the shooting at schools. The first paragraph presents a rough idea of what happened and how many were killed or injured. Then in the main part of the news, more information is given that is related to the event, such as parents' hurrying back to school; his mother found death, and mention of how he could enter the school. Try to understand the style of this writing and see what has been agreed up, and how the host country deal with the event.

3. Some give up their guns as others rally against tighter laws

Dallas sees dueling gun buybacks: A church collects firearms to be destroyed while a rival group helps unwanted weapons find new owners.

Derek Ringley shows a pistol being auctioned at an event organized to compete with First Presbyterian Church of Dallas' gun buyback.

By Molly Hennessy-Fiske
Los Angeles Times
January 19, 2013, 9:15 p.m.

DALLAS — On one side of Young Street, volunteers from First Presbyterian Church of Dallas attempted to persuade gun owners to turn in their firearms. They would receive $50 to $200 — from donors — and know that their guns would be destroyed.

Across the downtown street, members of the Right Group — formed to compete with the church event — set up in a rented vacant lot to urge visitors to resell their firearms rather than destroy them. ①They had signs reading "We pay more" and "Gun rescue".

The dueling buybacks came on a day when thousands attended peaceful Guns Across America rallies at state capitals nationwide to oppose tighter gun laws.② Separately, a Republican consulting firm had promoted Saturday as Gun Appreciation Day, three days after President Obama laid out a slew of proposals designed to restrict gun access in the wake of last month's Newtown, Conn., school shooting.

Among the hundreds who gathered in Sacramento in front of the Capitol was Christina Marotti, 33, of East Sacramento, who brought her daughters, ages 2 and 4. One had a sign saying, "My mom [hearts] guns." The other's said, "Arm my teacher."

"Wherever you take away the right to have guns, the crime rate increases," Marotti said. "As a mother, that scares me."

Some customers at the bustling Los Angeles Gun Club, a popular downtown shooting range, were unaware of the Gun Appreciation Day campaign.

"Yay for the 2nd Amendment, especially in the times we're in now," said Jonathan Wright, who was celebrating his upcoming 24th birthday with a group of friends.

Alex Katz, 25, who said he visited ranges a couple of times a month and described himself as pro-gun control, found the "appreciation day" concept "a little tasteless right now".

In Dallas, the church made the first buyback purchase: $50 for an old pistol from a pair of local women.

Scott Mankoff, 43, of Dallas waded through the rival group's crowd of about 100 — then headed to the church.

Mankoff, a retired artist, opposes new gun laws but came to turn in a spare .22 rifle to be destroyed because of the Newtown shootings.

"It's not about the money — it's about getting it off the street," he said.

For others, it was more about the money.

They showed up to sell .22 rifles, .40-and .45-caliber handguns, a Ruger M-77 rifle, a Chinese SKS rifle, some for $400. One 19-year-old showed up trying to sell his customized AR-15, worth about $1,000, knowing gun prices spiked after the Newtown shootings.③

James Brown, 41, of Dallas initially went to the church buyback but got tired of waiting in the long line with his 13-year-old son.

When they crossed the street, they were applauded and led to the back of a pickup truck, where Brown's Rossi Ranch Hand .45 was auctioned for $300 and his .25 handgun for $200.

"I prefer to keep it in the family. If it's a good gun, and people can use it, why not sell it?" he said.

Brown said he didn't blame guns for the tragedy at Newtown.

"A gun can be your best friend. You get thugs on the street and you can protect your family," he said.

The church, a long-established landmark with a congregation of 1,600 that includes the mayor, has staged buybacks in the past, but it had never faced a counter-buyback. Some organizers were irritated to see people drawn to the other lot. The pastor's wife, Carol Adams, started toting a sign of her own and alerting police when she thought those across the street were becoming too aggressive. ④

Inside the garage, church volunteer Mike Haney, 65, an attorney, gun owner and hunter who supports new gun control legislation, handled the buys as the pace picked up.

"We have to stop the gun violence, the unspeakable tragedy in Connecticut," Haney said, calling it "startling" and "surprising" that "we as a country can't agree that something can be done."

"I don't know that anything we do here today will address that," Haney said as he filled out a receipt for a handgun someone had brought in a Baby Gap bag.

Across the street, organizer Collin Baker said he didn't oppose all new gun laws.

Baker, 30, of Fort Worth, who works at a car dealership and also as a firearms instructor, said he wouldn't oppose expanding federal background checks to close the "gun show loophole". ⑤ However, Baker also owns an AR-15 automatic-style rifle, whose strength and refinement he likens to a fast sports car, and he opposes a federal assault-rifle ban.

"The people who want to get rid of guns should sell them to responsible gun owners like myself," he said, dismissing the church buyback as "obscene" and "wasteful".

By afternoon, Baker had presided over a slew of sales, holding rifles and handguns aloft during bids, but he was still worried.

"The morning went to us, but I think the afternoon went to them," he said as he watched a line of determined sellers heading into the church garage.

By day's end, Baker's group had seen 40 to 50 guns resold, and it plans to hold similar events in the future. "You guys helped make this a success," he told the crowd.

Across the street, church volunteers had bought enough rifles to fill two large garbage cans. Handguns were stacked on three chairs. In total, they had bought 109 guns, which the Rev. Bruce Buchanan said would be loaded into a truck and ground up at a later date. He hopes the church's success leads other groups to sponsor similar buybacks.

"I think it's the mood of the country," Haney said. (935 words)

Words and Expressions

duel	v.	决斗	thug	n.	恶棍,暴徒;罪犯
slew	n.	许多,大量	tote	v.	携带,手持
bustling	a.	繁忙的；熙熙攘攘的	startling	a.	令人吃惊的,非常惊人的
wade	v.	涉过,蹚过(有水处)	rally	v.	集合,集结(军队)
spike	v.	突然猛增	loophole	n.	(法律的)漏洞
mood	n.	心情,状态			

Proper Nouns

First Presbyterian Church　第一长老会
The Gun Appreciation Day　主张拥有枪支的人的一个节日
Rossi Ranch Hand .45　0.45口径罗西手枪
Ruger M-77　罗格M77步枪

News Summary

这是与前一篇新闻相呼应的报道。由于持枪杀人,特别是集中枪杀学生的事件频繁发生,美国人开始对枪支控制进行激烈的讨论,许多人敦促政府修改枪支法,更严格审查持枪人的材料。有些人发起回购枪支以销毁的活动。但是也有些人认为拥有枪支是公民的权利,主张不需要的人出售他们手上的枪支。本文就是与此相关的一篇报道:在德克萨斯州的达拉斯,持有两种不同意见的人同时在街上宣传和吸引群众,希望人们能把枪支交给他们处理,以换取一定的现金。文章的主要特点是引用了一些受采访的人的话,表达完全不同的观点。

Understanding Sentences

① 在这条市区街道的另一边,一个为与教堂的活动叫板而成立的名为"权利小组"的组织成员在一块租来的空地上搭起架子,鼓动人们重新出售他们的枪支,而不是把它们销毁。

② 这场收购枪支的对台戏发生在数以千计的民众在全国各州的首府举行"美国枪支"的和平集会、反对更加严格的枪支法的当天。

③ 一名19岁的青年带着他经过改造的、价值约一千美元的AR-15步枪来这里出售,他知道在新城的枪杀事件发生以后,枪支的价格突然升得很厉害。

④ 牧师的妻子卡罗·亚当斯开始扛起一块她自己做的招牌游走,当她认为马路对面的那些人的挑衅太过分的时候,就通知了警察。

⑤ 来自沃思堡的三十岁的贝克尔从事汽车销售工作,同时也是武器教练,说他不会反对扩大联邦政府对购枪者的背景审查,以堵塞持枪法的漏洞。

Exercises

Ⅰ. Understanding Ideas in the News

1. What did the Church group persuade people to do?
   A. To sell their guns.　　　　　　　　B. To donate their guns.
   C. To turn in guns to be destroyed.

2. What's the slogan used by the Right Group?
   A. "We resell guns."　　B. "We pay more."　　C. "We destroy guns."

3. Which of the following is a pro-control organization or group?
   A. First Presbyterian Church.　　　　B. Guns Across America.
   C. Gun Appreciation Day.

4. What is the argument for people's right to own guns?

A. It is stated in the 2nd Amendment.

B. It can reduce crime rates.

C. They didn't blame guns for the tragedy at Newtown.

5. Why do some people want to sell their guns to the Right Group?

A. They knew gun prices spiked.

B. They got tired of waiting in the long line.

C. They expected to get more money.

II. Language Points

duel, slew, spike, startling, obscene 这几个词用来描写人们对加强枪支控制的态度。

duel：(决斗) to fight a duel or be involved in a conflict   e.g. *In the 19th century, men often dueled over small matters.*

slew：(许多,大量) a large amount or number   e.g. *Mr. Savino has been charged with three murders as well as a whole slew of other crimes.*

spike：(突然猛增) suddenly increase

startling：(令人吃惊的) surprising and sometimes worrying   e.g. *He made some startling admissions about his past.*

obscene：(不公正的) morally wrong, often describing something that is morally wrong because it is too large   e.g. *The salaries some company directors earn are obscene.*

III. Questions for Further Study

This news report is about how people react to the shooting on campus. The event reported happened in Dallas. As a church group is buying back guns, an opposite group is also buying, but then selling them to other people. The reading compares the slogans by the two groups and their achievements. Find out more arguments from the pro-gun and pro-control groups, make a list of the main points for comparison, and present your own reasoning.

英语报刊知识介绍

英语报纸的编辑与版面

记者在参加新闻发布会、现场采访或收集材料之后就开始写作。他们写好的新闻稿送到报社办公室。这时候,稿件编辑对新闻的导语、内容及其他写作上的问题等一一进行审阅和修改,然后版面编辑从文稿是否符合通讯社的规范、语法表达有没有错误、词语拼写有没有错误等方面进行审核,再加上标题和必要的插图,安排好版面位置等,最后才送到执行编辑那里。这是报社一般的编辑流程。

英语报刊的版面有不同的设计,这是根据报纸的性质和法人的喜好,通过编排美工等人员实现的,主要的目的就是要使报纸第一眼看上去有吸引力。有一种说法是,编辑首先在每一版上留出广告的位置,然后再安排文章和照片的位置、标题的字体字号等,最后才是把新闻放进去。重要的新闻通常都放在第一版,但由于空间限制,很多时候只能把文章的大部分放在后面各版。

1. A glimpse of a newspaper editing room

2. Hot off the press—the printing machine turns off copies of newspaper

Unit 7 National News—the UK

"National news" in the major newspapers is section that carries news happening in the country. In the UK, there are many newspapers, such as *The Daily Telegraph*, *The Guardian*, *Daily Express*, etc., that report extensively about happening in the country. Topics range from politics, government, and other major events. This chapter includes three reports on the politics and the government: a defense of Cameron on his post as Prime Minister; a story about the MP's expense records, and a report on people's responses to the death of a former Prime Minister, Mrs. Thatcher.

"国内新闻"是主要英语报纸的一大组成部分,通常刊登有关国内事件的报道。英国有很多报纸,如《每日电讯报》、《卫报》、《每日快报》等,都大量报道英国国内的事件。国内新闻的话题范围很广,从政治、政府到其他重大事件,无所不包。本章包括了关于英国政治的三篇报道:一篇是为现任英国首相、保守党政治家卡梅隆辩护的;一篇是关于国会议员报销费用的,还有一篇是在英国前首相撒切尔逝世以后,记者采访民众对她的印象和态度的。

1. David Cameron's critics are wrong. He's on the verge of something great

A revolution is under way in health, welfare and education that may change Britain forever.

A great and noble undertaking: MPs applaud as David Cameron delivers his keynote speech at the Conservative Party conference in Birmingham. (Photo: Reuters)

By Peter Oborne
The Daily Telegraph
8:43 p.m. BST, 03 Apr., 2013

Under the new electoral timetable, Parliament must be dissolved on March 30, 2015, ahead of a general election on May 7. So when MPs reassemble after the Easter recess, there will be less than two years to go. Naturally, minds are focusing on the future—to the extent that, for many, it is tempting to speak of the Coalition in the past tense. ①

For Lib Dems, that means pondering a rewarding new alliance with Labour, while for a large and noisy body of Conservative MPs, it means ditching David Cameron. It has become fashionable to assert that after seven years he has served long enough as party leader. ② Indeed, there is a powerful body of backbench opinion which holds that the Prime Minister is not really a Conservative at all, and that the sooner he goes the better.

Benedict Brogan accurately recorded this mood on this page last week: "His party operates as if he is already a lame duck. A verdict on the Cameron years is setting like concrete around his feet. His premiership is marked by disappointments, changes of direction, a falling out with his MPs and his party, and an overarching sense of promise unfulfilled." ③

The purpose of my article today is to make the case for Mr. Cameron. First of all, I will highlight the very significant achievements of the Coalition he leads. Then I will examine the motives, calibre and moral character of his critics, before scrutinising the prospects and strategy of the Opposition. Finally, I will demonstrate that, though not without serious faults, Mr. Cameron is leading a Government with a reasonable claim to be one of the great reforming administrations. I will not make my argument by responding to the cheap jibes and poisonous insults aimed at the Prime Minister by his would-be assassins. ④ Instead, I will concentrate on genuine, substantive, lasting achievement.

Let's consider the reforms unleashed over the past week alone. On Monday, George Osborne scrapped the Financial Services Authority, the catastrophic Gordon Brown innovation whose incompetence was partly responsible for the 2008 crash. This is a sensible move that returns regulatory oversight to the Bank of England, from which it should never have been removed.

On the same day, Andrew Lansley's NHS reforms, which have removed commissioning powers from bureaucrats and returned them to doctors, took effect. This is a thoroughly welcome change, based on solid Conservative principles, which puts decisions in the hands of the people who should make them.

Meanwhile, Michael Gove has been fighting an utterly crucial battle against the teaching unions, who are determined to resist—through desperate means—his plans to enforce high standards in British schools. At stake are the life chances of millions of children and, in the long term, this country's future as an advanced industrial economy. ⑤ Nothing could be more important or worthwhile.

Next week, this Coalition government becomes yet more audacious, as Iain Duncan Smith's historic reconstruction of the post-war welfare state gets into full swing with a barrage of reforms aimed at restoring the original vision and integrity of its great founder, William Beveridge.

On Monday, the disability living allowance—for so long a charter for deceit and recipe for state-sponsored idleness—will be replaced by a far more humane and realistic system.⑥ A week later, the first councils will start to cap welfare benefits at the average salary of ￡26,000 a week. Already, claimants have been told that the state will no longer pay for their spare bedroom. Finally, at the end of the month, a pilot scheme will begin for Mr. Duncan Smith's noblest idea of all, Universal Credit. The intention is to remove the financial disincentive to work, which was deliberately entrenched by Labour at the heart of our benefits system. Mr. Duncan Smith's plan is fantastically risky, because it involves the installation of a new national computer system, but the risk is worth it.

It is very important to understand that all these announcements are the exact opposite of the "eye-catching initiatives" which Tony Blair used to demand from his ministers. They have all been thought through meticulously, planned while the Conservatives were in Opposition, and only implemented—with extreme care, over a long period of time—once in power.

This is mature, grown-up government of the highest calibre. Put all these changes together, and it is evidence that this Government is potentially as ambitious as the great Attlee administration of 1945-1951, or the Thatcher government 30 years later. It is simultaneously trying to mend our broken NHS, education and welfare systems. If it succeeds in only one of these ambitions, the Coalition will have been worthwhile.⑦ If it succeeds in two, it will be remembered as one of the great reforming peacetime administrations. Even if it largely fails (perhaps the most likely outcome), it will still have made a heroic and admirable effort to change Britain for the better. (822 words)

Words and Expressions

electoral	a.	选举的		commission	n.	委员会
dissolve	v.	解散,结束		audacious	a.	大胆的
ditch	v.	抛弃,扔掉		scrap	n.	碎片
backbench	n.	后排座位		integrity	n.	正直
lame duck		即将去职的官员		recipe	n.	处方
overarching	a.	上面做出拱形的		claimant	n.	原告
calibre	n.	口径,标准		disincentive	a.	妨碍活动的
scrutinise	v.	仔细检查		entrench	v.	固守,牢固树立
jibe	n.	嘲笑		meticulously	ad.	小心翼翼地
unleash	v.	释放		coalition	n.	(尤指组成政府的政党、州的)临时结合,联合,联盟
on the verge of		在……边缘				

Proper Nouns

Lib Dems（short for Liberal Democrats） 自由民主党人

Gordon Brown 布朗,英国工党政治家,2007—2010 年任英国首相

the great Attlee administration of 1945-1951 Clement Attlee,英国工党政治家,1945—1951 年任英国首相

Tony Blare 英国工党政治家,前英国首相（1999—2008）

News Summary

进入二十一世纪以来,英国工党连续执政,但政绩平平,很多困扰英国社会的问题并没有得到改善。2010 年,布朗下台,新的联合政府成立,大卫·卡梅隆就任首相。但是,反对派不断地攻击卡梅隆政府所做的一些改革。本文一开始提出,按照选举时间表,再过两年就要进行大选,但人们已经普遍认为,卡梅隆的联合政府即将结束。作者在第四段明确说明,他是要为卡梅隆辩护的,而且也从卡梅隆所做的一些改革入手,说明他是正确的。

Understanding Sentences

① 自然地,人们的想法集中在未来——对很多人来说,他们倾向于认为联合政府将成为过去时。

② 已经成为一种时髦说法的是,经过这七年的执政,他担任党魁的时间已经太长了。

③ 他担任首相时期所做的一切令人失望,他经常改变方向,与国会议员及他的政党不和,已经给人越来越多没有信守承诺的感觉。

④ 我不打算对那些来自他的批评者的、瞄准首相个人的廉价嘲笑和恶意侮辱做出回应,并以此作为我意见的开始。

⑤ 有危险的是数以百万计的儿童的生存机会,以及,长远来说,我们作为一个先进工业国国家的前途。

⑥ 星期一,这种残疾生活补贴将被一种更加具有人文关怀和实际意义的系统所取代,它不再是欺骗的特许状,也不会导致政府补贴懒汉的情况出现。

⑦ 即使联合政府仅仅只是在这些计划其中之一上取得成功,它也就值得存在。

Exercises

I. Understanding Ideas in the News

1. What are many MPs thinking about two years before the next general election?

   A. David Cameron will be re-elected.

   B. The Coalition will be over.

   C. They will come back after the Easter recess.

2. What do the Conservatives think of David Cameron?

   A. He is the leader of the Conservative Party.

   B. He is not a Conservative in fact.

   C. He is a lame duck.

3. What will the writer do first in defense of David Cameron?
A. He will list the achievements by the Coalition.
B. He will study the strategy used by the Opposition.
C. He will show that the Coalition led by him is right.

4. What is the intention of the proposed reform of the welfare system?
A. To encourage people to work.
B. To give the unemployed financial help.
C. To create more job opportunities.

5. How are all these announcements different from those by Tony Blair?
A. They are quite different.
B. They are "eye-catching".
C. They are exactly the opposite.

II. Language Points

dissolve, ditch, jibe, assassin, audacious 这些词语用来描述英国的选举和反对派对首相的攻击等。它们是新闻英语中的常用语,具有很强的表达力。

dissolve:(解散,结束) to end an official organization or a legal arrangement e. g. *Parliament has been dissolved. Their marriage was dissolved in* 2014.

ditch:(抛弃,扔掉) to get rid of something or someone that is no longer wanted e. g. *The getaway car had been ditched a couple of kilometres away from the scene of the robbery.*

jibe:(嘲笑) an insulting remark that is intended to make someone look stupid e. g. *Unlike many other politicians, he refuses to indulge in cheap jibes at other people's expenses.*

assassin:(暗杀者,刺客) someone who kills a famous or important person usually for political reasons or in exchange for money e. g. *John Lennon's assassin was Mark Chapman.*

audacious:(大胆的) showing a willingness to take risks or offend people e. g. *He described the plan as ambitious and audacious.*

III. Questions for Further Study

This news report is in defense of the new Prime Minister, David Cameron. In the beginning, the writer mentions the attack on Cameron from the opposition, and also from within the Conservative Party. In the fourth paragraph, he sets the outline of the article, and also the way he will write for Cameron. Due to limit of space, the second and third parts are not included here. Analyze how the writer defends Cameron: what he mentions, and how.

2. MPs to escape expenses investigations after paperwork destroyed by Parliament

House of Commons authorities have destroyed all evidence of MPs expenses' claims prior to 2010, meaning end of official investigations into scandal.

Maria Miller was forced out the Cabinet in 2014 over expenses claims dating back to 2005. (Photo: Andrew Parsons)

By Matthew Holehouse, Political Correspondent
The Telegraph
9:30 p.m. GMT, 02 Nov., 2014

MPs accused of abusing the unreformed expenses system will escape official investigation after the House of Commons authorities destroyed all record of their claims, the Telegraph can reveal.

John Bercow, the Speaker, faces accusations he has presided over a fresh cover-up of MPs' expenses after tens of thousands of pieces of paperwork relating to claims made before 2010 under the scandal-hit regime were shredded. ①

Members of the public who have written to Kathryn Hudson, the standards watchdog, to raise concerns about their MP's claims have been told there can be no investigation due to lack of evidence.

Under the House of Commons' "Authorised Records Disposal Practice", which is overseen by Mr. Bercow's committee, records of MPs' expenses claims are destroyed after three years. The move is necessary to comply with data protection laws, a Commons spokesman said.

However, under that same set of guidelines, the pay, discipline and sickness records of Commons staff are kept until their 100th birthday. Health and safety records are kept for up to 40 years, while thousands of other classes of official documents on the day-to-day running of the House are stored indefinitely in the Parliamentary Archive. ②

It means that the Telegraph, which exposed the scandal that rocked Parliament in 2009 after obtaining a leaked CD, holds the only unredacted record of claims made under the unreformed system. That leak followed a High Court battle by the Commons authorities to prevent the release of the information.

It also means that "cold case" investigations like that into Maria Miller, the former Culture Secretary, by the expenses watchdog are now unlikely.

In April Mrs. Miller was forced to resign from the Cabinet and apologise to the Commons after Mrs. Hudson was ruled she had wrongly claimed thousands of pounds in mortgage payments between 2005 and 2009 on a home occupied by her parents. ③ The case was first uncovered by the Telegraph in 2012.

The policy came to light after Tory activists asked Mrs. Hudson to investigate accommodation claims worth £103,000 made by Andrew Turner, their local Conservative MP, between 2004 and 2010.

David Pugh, Alan Stovell and Gary Taylor, members of the Isle of Wight Conservative Association, alleged Mr. Turner had improperly designated the five-bedroom island home he shares with his partner as his "second home", while telling the fees office that a one-bedroom flat in London was his main home.

Mr. Turner last night insisted his claims were audited and found in compliance with the rules at the time.

Mrs. Hudson, the Parliamentary Commissioner for Standards, told Mr. Pugh the allegation was "serious", but refused to investigate, citing "availability of evidence".

"All records relating to expenses claims before 2010 have now been destroyed. No unredacted information is now available here nor any notes of conversations or advice given to Mr. Turner which might establish the facts," she wrote. Half of the period in dispute fell outside the seven-year time limit for investigation, she added.

Mr. Pugh told Mrs. Hudson the decision to destroy the paperwork was "extremely concerning".

"This is, in our view, sadly indicative of a wider culture within the Westminster and Whitehall establishment of an inclination to destroy information and evidence which may give rise to future difficult questions about MPs and those in positions of power," he wrote. ④

A House of Commons spokesman said the policy on destroying MPs' expenses records was "long-standing", but it was originally set by the Members Estimate Committee, which is now chaired by Mr. Bercow.

However, committee minutes seen by this newspaper show that in March 2010, in the wake of the MPs expenses scandal, Mr. Bercow's committee called for the policy to be suspended and all expenses records to be saved.⑤

Then, in February 2012, the committee discussed and agreed to implement the "existing policy on the retention and disposal of records" relating to expenses.

MPs at that meeting, which took place in the Speaker's House, included Sir George Young, the Conservative Leader of the House; Angela Eagle, his Labour shadow; and John Thurso, the senior Liberal Democrats.

Only expenses records where inquiries into wrongdoing have already been opened have been retained.

John Mann, the Labour MP for Bassetlaw, said members have been kept in the dark about the policy. He will tabled a question, asking Mr. Bercow to explain himself in the Commons.

"It sounds like MPs trying to protect MPs again. It will make the public very suspicious of what the motive is. The old gentlemen's club is resurrecting itself."

Sir Alistair Graham, the former chairman of the Committee on Standards in Public Life, said historians have been denied the chance to study Parliament's "worst hour".

"It is scandalous that anybody has destroyed the records for that period. Who knows what anybody's motivation was?"

"The people concerned should know better. There was a strong public interest in retaining this information so that people have access to it, and I'm really very surprised." (820 words)

Words and Expressions

abuse	v.	滥用	accusation	n.	指控
shred	v.	撕碎,切碎	authorise	v.	授权
comply	v.	顺从,答应,遵守	redact	v.	编辑,编写
mortgage	n.	抵押	designate	v.	指定,指派
audit	v.	审计,稽核,查账	compliance	n.	依从,顺从
retention	n.	保持力	disposal	n.	处理
resurrect	v.	使复活;复兴	retain	v.	保留,保存

Proper Nouns

Isle of Wight 怀特岛,英格兰最大的岛屿
The Daily Telegraph 《每日电讯报》英国一份报纸
Westminster 西斯敏特,伦敦中部一个区
Whitehall 西斯敏特区的一条街道,也是英国政府中枢的所在地

News Summary

玛利亚·米勒是英国保守党的一名国会议员,从2012年至2014年曾经担任过文化部长和妇女及平等部部长,由于一笔九万英镑的报销单受到舆论的压力,被迫在2014年4月

辞职。这则新闻是报道国会下议院通过决议,可以销毁国会议员的报销单据,而不是按照以前的决定必须保留一定时间。因此,题头还配了一幅玛利亚和首相卡梅隆合影的照片。

Understanding Sentences

① 国会发言人约翰·贝尔考面临着指控,说他主导了新一轮的对国会议员报销费用的掩盖行为,数以万计的文件被销毁,这些文件都与2010年之前当时已经丑闻缠身的政府提出的报销申请有关。

② 健康和安全记录一般保留40年以上,而数以千计的其他有关国会下议院日常运作的官方文件则被无限期存放在国会档案馆里。

③ 四月份,在哈得逊夫人被认定她在2005年至2009年之间不适当地替她父母所居住的房子的分期付款报销了数万英镑之后,米勒夫人被迫辞去内阁的职位,并向众议院道歉。

④ 他写道,"我们认为,可怕的是,这表现了政府机构之内有意销毁那些将来可能给国会议员和掌握权力的人带来麻烦的信息和证据的一种普遍做法。"

⑤ 然而,本报所掌握的委员会记录显示,在2010年3月,紧接着有关国会议员报销费用的丑闻之后,贝尔考先生的委员会要求暂停执行该项政策,并保存所有的报销记录。

Exercises

Ⅰ. Understanding Ideas in the News

1. Under the House of Commons "Authorized Records Disposal Practice", records of claims are kept for _____.

　　A. three years　　　　B. ten years　　　　C. a hundred years

2. Who heads the committee that oversees the practice?

　　A. Kathryn Hudson.　　B. John Bercow.　　C. Maria Miller.

3. What does the passing of the practice mean to the MPs?

　　A. MPs will have to comply with data protection laws.

　　B. There are two different sets of guidelines.

　　C. MPs accused of abusing the system will escape official investigation.

4. What is Mr. Andrew Turner accused of?

　　A. He had made accommodation claims worth ₤103,000 for his parents.

　　B. He had made accommodation claims worth ₤103,000 for himself.

　　C. He had claimed thousands of pounds in mortgage payments.

5. What makes the public concerned about the practice?

　　A. There will be the issue of "availability of evidence".

　　B. It sounds like MPs trying to protect MPs again.

　　C. The policy on destroying MPs' expenses records was long-standing.

Ⅱ. Language Points

audit, authorize, designate, dispose, retain 这几个动词是新闻中用来描述英国国会

下院对议员报销费用的单证的处理情况的。

audit：（审计，稽核，查账）to make an official examination of the accounts of a business

authorize：（授权）to give official permission for something to happen, or to give someone official permission to do something   e. g. *Who authorized this expenditure?*

designate：（指定，指派）to choose someone officially to do a particular job   e. g. *Traditionally, the president designates his or her successor.*

dispose of：（处理）to get rid of someone or something or deal with something so that the matter is finished   e. g. *How did they dispose of the body?*

retain：（保留,保存）to keep or continue to have something   e. g. *She has lost her battle to retain control of the company.*

III. Questions for Further Study

This news report has almost all the characteristics of a newspaper news. After the headline, there is a news summary sentence, which lets the reader capture the main idea of the news. Then the photo of Cameron and Maria gives the reading some hints about the content, and the caption also highlights the content of the news. See how all these components of a news story work together to get the message through to the reader at the fastest speed; analyze and discuss it.

3. Thatcher's death has Britain peering back through time

Driving around the UK to assess Thatcher's legacy is by turns fascinating, sad, bittersweet, and surprisingly moving.

John Harris
The Guardian
Friday, 12 April, 2013, 19:04 BST

The south Wales town of Merthyr Tydfil feels like somewhere haunted by ghosts: not just of the coal industry that once underwrote hundreds of local livelihoods, or the renowned Hoover factory that closed four years ago—but of a way of collective being that slipped away during the 1980s. ①

"It's a dead-end place now," says 78-year-old Jean Stanton, waiting outside the local Salvation Army shop where she does voluntary work.

"It used to be booming. Lovely. But that's all gone."

At the mention of Margaret Thatcher, some of Merthyr's younger residents talk about fragments of this week's news—the cost of her funeral, mainly—and the odd second-hand memory of her time in office. ②

But for older people, the recollections remain vivid and the wounds are apparently still raw. With them, such frippery as what David Beckham has said by way of tribute or whether Radio 1 will play Ding Dong! The Witch Is Dead count for nothing. Instead, when I ask for opinions about Thatcher's life and death, people talk about events that happened 30 years ago as if they had only just drawn to a close—particularly when it comes to the miners' strike of 1984-1985, the bitter end of which spelled the start of her most turbocharged phase. ③

After two days on the road, this much is clear: driving around the UK to assess Thatcher's legacy is, by turns, fascinating, sad, bittersweet and surprisingly moving. ④ Usually, trying to start conversations about mainstream politics—let alone the events of three decades ago—can be unproductive and frustrating. But this week, there's a sense of scores of Britons peering back through time, and thinking about then, and now. And in the midst of so many chats about recent history, mundane aspects of the modern British expanse—the ubiquitous Tesco, derelict factories, even the M25—suddenly assume a symbolic potency. ⑤

A few miles from Merthyr is the site of the old Merthyr Vale colliery, a byword for the unimaginable horror of the 1966 Aberfan disaster and one of the incidents that, two decades later, arguably pointed to the miners' eventual defeat. On 30 November,1984, a taxi driver named David Wilkie was driving a miner who had returned to work to the pit when his car was hit by a concrete post, dropped from a bridge by two strikers. Thatcher said she was enraged "at what this has done to the family of a person only doing his duty and taking someone to work who wanted to go to work"; for the National Union of Mineworkers, it represented a further blow to morale and confirmation that things were spiralling out of control.

Outside Tesco, I meet Malcolm Thomas, 73, a retired electrician, and Bert Lang, 67, who once worked at the Merthyr Vale pit. Like other locals, they wearily mention Arthur Scargill's serial failures as the leader of the NUM and debates that can still flare up about the way he led the miners through something that felt close to a kind of civil war. ⑥

The killing of David Wilkie, says Thomas, "put a dent in the union's end—it was a stupid thing to do." The strike, he tells me, "is still embedded in us down here. It's still something to talk about every day. Someone will always fetch it up: 'What would have happened if it had gone the other way?'"

For other people, though, all that means next to nothing. Tamzin Cross, 16, lives in nearby Aberdare: she is unemployed and used to scores of job applications not even prompting a reply. What, I wonder, does she know about the woman staring from the front pages of all those newspapers? "I know she was the prime minister of Britain," she tells me. "And she was quite unfair to the lower classes."

It may be some token of how much Merthyr has changed that when I ask her if she knows what a trade union is, I draw a blank. "I don't know," she says. "I should know, probably."

Ninety minutes down the M4 in Bristol, 200 residents of the Easton area spent Monday evening staging a celebration of Thatcher's passing that ended with a small-scale riot. When I stop to canvass opinions in the nearby enclave of Stokes Croft—the scene, famously, of violence sparked by the opening of a branch of Tesco—mention of this causes at least two on-street arguments. "Disgusting," says one man. "If people wanted to have a party, then fair enough," reckons another. At one point, I find myself deep in a conversation about that byword for the pre-Thatcher UK, British Leyland. Here, though, what's most interesting is a sense of what happened to one strain of left politics in the wake of the 1980s' endless setbacks: what was once known as socialism reinvented not as a grand political project, but a matter of local culture and personal preference. ⑦

Outside the Magpie, a former charity shop now squatted by artists and activists, a 33-year-old local who calls himself Tom Roots says: "She was an icon of a lot of things we don't like: an embodiment of what we want to move away from. And I don't think she'd have liked us." Does the Stokes Croft life represent some kind of alternative to Thatcher's immovable legacy? "It's very different. This is social living. It's not about amassing lots of money and shutting yourself away from other people."

Back on the M25, I meet Scott Parker, 40, from Bishop's Waltham in Hampshire, who is on his way to Salisbury Plain to lay telephone cables for the army. One mention of Thatcher and he's away: another person, it seems, happy to take the opportunity to look back 30 years. "She gave everyone the chance to own their own home," he says. "She got us out of that trade union stuff, where we was being held to ransom. And I don't think today's politician would have the arseholes, basically, to do that. Like or loathe her, she told you the truth. Today's ones [politicians] just tell you what they think you want to hear."

I cast my mind back to Merthyr Tydfil, and wonder: does he feel sorry for any of the places that had it rough during the 1980s? "Yeah," he says. Then a pause. "Yeah." Another pause. "But it's hard, isn't it?' cos today's politicians would still have done what she done, if you know what I mean. But you knew where you were with her. You might have been at the bottom of the pile, but you knew where you stood." (1105 words)

Words and Expressions

frippery	n.	（语言等的）浮夸，低俗	tribute	n.	称赞
turbocharged	a.	增压的	peer	v.	凝视,盯着
mundane	a.	平凡的,平淡的	ubiquitous	a.	普遍存在的
derelict	a.	被抛弃的	potency	n.	力量,权力
colliery	n.	煤矿	byword	n.	代名词
Ding Dong		（口语）傻瓜	wearily	ad.	疲倦地,无聊地
spiral	v.	使螺旋形上升	dent	n.	凹, 凹痕
canvass	v.	细查,讨论	ransom	n.	劫持,绑架
arsehole	n.	屁眼儿			

Proper Nouns

Salvation Army （基督教）救世军,一个基督教组织和国际慈善机构
Tesco   英国一家跨国超市
the M25   英国伦敦附近一条高速公路的编号
the 1966 Aberfan disaster   1966 年发生在 Merthyl Tydfil 附近的一次严重煤矿事故
the NUM   全国矿工协会
Stokes Croft   英国布里斯托的一条路
British Leyland   英国于 1968 年成立的汽车制造商

News Summary

玛格丽特·撒切尔是第 49 任英国首相,于 1979—1990 年在任,是至今为止英国唯一一位女首相。她于 2013 年 4 月 8 日逝世。这则新闻不是简单地报道她逝世消息的新闻,而是记者沿着威尔士南部矿山小镇所进行的采访。从采访报道中可以看出,尽管撒切尔夫人在执政期间曾经采取许多措施发展经济、增加就业和改善民生,她辞职以后,英国社会又发生了很大变化,年轻一代对不久以前的过去已经逐渐淡忘,对曾经的政治家及其政绩的评价也褒贬兼有,而不是单方面的评论。

Understanding Sentences

① 威尔士南部小镇蒙特·泰菲尔好像一个幽灵出没的地方:不仅是由于曾经支持当地数百个家庭生计的煤炭工业日渐萧条,或是四年前刚关闭了有名的胡佛工厂,而主要是由于

二十世纪八十年代的某种生活方式消失了。

② 当提到玛格丽特·撒切尔的时候,蒙特的一些年轻人谈到了本周新闻中的一些片断,主要是她的葬礼的费用,还有那些听说的关于她执政时期的一些故事。

③ 相反,当我问到他们对撒切尔的一生及逝世的看法时,人们谈到了三十年前所发生的事情,犹如它们刚刚过去一样,尤其是发生在1984—1985年之间的煤矿工人罢工,那次罢工的悲剧结局开始了她执政时期承受最大压力的阶段。

④ 经过两天来的一路采访,有一点是清楚的:开着车在英国各地跑,了解人们对撒切尔的评价,得到的反馈五味杂陈——有魅力的、可悲的、又苦又甜的,或者令人意外地感动的。

⑤ 而且,在许多关于最近的历史、关于现代大英帝国的扩张的方方面面的交谈中,如那到处都是的塔斯科连锁店、废弃的工厂,甚至是25号公路,突然间,这些东西承受了一种象征性的力量。

⑥ 像其他当地人一样,他们不大愿意提起作为全国矿工协会负责人的阿瑟·斯卡吉尔的一系列过失和那些随时可能爆发的关于他带领矿工进行那场非常接近某种形式内战的方法的辩论。

⑦ 然而,这里最使人感兴趣的是,在遭受了二十世纪八十年代的许多挫折之后,人们对左派政治的努力所发生的一切的看法:再提起什么是过去曾经的社会主义时,不是作为一个重大政治项目,而是一种当地文化和个人喜爱。

Exercises

I. Understanding Ideas in the News

1. How did the younger generation at Merthyr respond to the news about the death of Thatcher?

A. They complained about the cost of her funeral.

B. The remembered her time in office.

C. They talked about what they heard from the news.

2. What was the feeling of the older people about Thatcher?

A. They still felt the wounds in those days.

B. They paid tribute to her time in office.

C. They would like to play Ding Dong.

3. What is the reporter's feeling in interviewing people about politics in this week?

A. Unproductive and frustrating.

B. Peering back and thinking.

C. Fascinating, sad, bittersweet and moving.

4. What incident caused the miners' eventual defeat in the 1996 Aberfan disaster?

A. The killing of a worker.

B. The killing of David Wilkie.

C. The killing of a striker.

5. What do Tesco and British Leyland represent to the people about Thatcher's era?
A. Bywords of the pre-Thatcher UK.
B. Symbols of Thatcher's success.
C. Icons of things people don't like.

Ⅱ. Language Points

frippery, byword, tribute, potency, dent 这些词用于谈论有关对撒切尔的评价。

frippery：((语言等的)浮夸，低俗) a silly decoration or other useless object e.g. *fashion fripperies*

byword：(代名词) a person or thing that is very closely connected with a particular quality e.g. *Their shops are a byword for good value.*

tribute：(称赞) something that you say, write or give which shows your respect and admiration for someone, especially on a formal occasion e.g. *Tributes have been pouring in from all over the world for the famous actor who died yesterday.*

potency：(力量,权力) strength, influence or effectiveness e.g. *This new drug's potency is not yet known. He owed his popular support to the potency of his propaganda machine.*

dent：(凹，凹痕) a small hollow mark in the surface of something, caused by pressure or being hit e.g. *a dent in the door of a car*

Ⅲ. Questions for Further Study

This news report puts together the interviews the reporter had with the local people of Merthyr Tydfil on their reaction to the news of Thatcher's death in 2013. Analyze this piece of news report in details according to the places where the reporter traveled to, the people he interviewed, and the different opinions of Thatcher's legacy.

英语报刊知识介绍

新闻的特性和新闻英语

新闻具有三个基本特性：①时效性；②地域性；③重要性。根据这几方面，又可以把新闻分成硬新闻和软新闻。硬新闻一般指国际、国内的重大事件，从政权交叠到战争，从新法令、法规到自然灾害，对人们生活影响大的、影响范围广的都属于这一类。一般的生活知识、娱乐新闻和旅游文章等就是软新闻。从报道新闻的媒体来说，又有文字新闻、声音新闻和电视（视频）新闻等的区分。报刊新闻主要是通过文字的形式来传递新闻。

新闻英语就是适应新闻的特性而产生的一种英语文体。文字英语新闻是一种独立的文体，其内容和结构都与所发生的新闻密切相关，重点突出但文字松散，一个句子常包含好几方面的信息，但一段常只由一个句子构成，表达上简明生动，相对常用单音节词及比较容易上口的词，有时候也会出现一些"创造"出来的新词语。

1. Newspaper clip from *The New York Times*, news of Bin Laden killed by U. S. forces

2. Front page of *The Wall Street Journal*

Unit 8　Social News—South Africa

Social news refers to news about the happenings in a specific location or community. It may include a wide variety of event: government legislations, police brutality, demonstration, memorial service, court trials, murder cases, natural disasters, etc. It is often grouped under the section name of national or local. Traditionally, social news was spread through the newspaper, radio and television, but as a result of technology development, people now can access news through various new media, such as the cell phone, Internet, and many Internet-based applications. This chapter contains reports about police chasing suspects of a burglar, police shooting the miners on strike, and people wishing a recovery to the health of Nelson Mandela, all happening in South Africa.

社会新闻一般指某一地区或社区所发生的事件，它可以包括很广泛的内容：政府通过新的法规法令、警察施暴、示威、追思、法庭审判、谋杀案件，以及自然灾害等。它经常出现在冠以"地方"或"国内"的栏目之下。传统的传播方法是报纸、电台和电视，但由于技术的发展，现在人们获取社会新闻的渠道变得多样化了，如手机、互联网以及各种基于互联网的应用。本章收集了一篇关于警察追捕逃犯的报道、一篇关于警察对罢工的矿工开枪的报道，以及一篇人们祈求曼德拉早日康复的报道，都是发生在南非的。

1. Bloody gunfight

Cops and thugs face off in suburban search-and-chase.

Shain Germaner
The Star

July 10, 2012   Tuesday

Robbers went head-to-head with the police yesterday, and came off second best in a vicious gun battle and chase that had Lenasia residents locking their doors. ①

Police shot dead one thug and the other turned his gun on himself when he was cornered in somebody's yard. The gangsters injured one cop. The third one was arrested.

It all started when the brazen and nonchalant thugs were trying to walk away through a homeowner's garage after completing their "job". ②

The man realised something was amiss when he didn't recognise the people on his property, but didn't think it was a robbery, with it being only about 8.15am.

But that all changed when the Swan Street, Lenasia Extension 1, householder noticed a man actually in his garage.

He screamed at the intruder to get out and rushed to a nearby panic button, and pressed it.

He hoped that the sound would scare him, but the gangster remained very casual.

Then the householder noticed that three men had been in his house, and were trying to leave through the garage.

And, rather than running off, he said the intruders simply wandered away down the road.

The householder, who did not want to be named, alerted the suburban security company Rainbow Security.

It joined forces with the police tactical response team, and the hunt was on.

The thugs panicked and tried to hide in houses two streets away.

It wasn't their day.

They ran through a nearby mosque to make their way to Lark Street, where they split up.

Two of the intruders ran in opposite directions down Lark Street and opened fire on the pursuing officers.

One cop was wounded.

Then Faizel Akoob heard footsteps on his roof, and three gunshots rang out.

He ran to tell his family to lock the kitchen door, and when he looked out of a window into his courtyard, he saw a police officer with an assault rifle and the body of a man, with blood pooling underneath him. ③

Meanwhile, the other thug was cornered in another yard in the area.

Under pressure, he didn't waste time. He pointed his 9mm pistol at his head and pulled the trigger.

A police helicopter hovered overhead and patrols went from home to home looking for other suspects.

One suspect was arrested in a domestic worker's bathroom, apparently after wrapping his gun in plastic and trying to hide it in the cistern.④

He put up a huge fight in an attempt to resist arrest, but all he had to show for it was some spectacular bruises.

Lieutenant-Colonel Katlego Mogale said the police officer who was shot several times is in a serious but stable condition in hospital.

Akoob said he was simply glad that "no one inside was hurt", and that his family was safe. (466 words)

Words and Expressions

thug	n.	暴徒，凶手	vicious	a.	恶意的，恶毒的
gangster	n.	歹徒，土匪，强盗	brazen	a.	厚颜无耻的
nonchalant	a.	冷淡的，不在乎的	alert	v.	使……处于戒备
mosque	n.	清真寺	cistern	n.	水塔，蓄水池
bruise	n.	瘀伤，擦伤			

News Summary

这是一篇关于警察和在作案之后企图逃跑的三名入屋盗窃者遭遇的报道。警察开枪打死了其中一名，另一名见走投无路开枪自杀，最后一名在藏身之地束手就擒。这篇新闻用简单的语言和结构，交代了事件发生的经过和结局，文字不长，但交代得清楚，读者一看就明白，而且应该知道的细节也一目了然。这是典型的关于突发事件的新闻报道。

Understanding Sentences

① 昨天，警察面对几名企图逃跑的抢劫者，在一场紧张的开枪和追逐中胜出，事件使得里纳西亚区的居民纷纷闭门上锁。

② 这一切从那几个老练的、故作镇定的暴徒企图在干完"工作"以后试图从一家人的车库离开开始。

③ 他跑回去告诉家人把厨房的门关好的时候，从窗户向院子里望去，看到一名手里握着一把手枪的警察和倒在地上的一名歹徒，鲜血从他的身体下面涌出。

④ 其中一名疑犯在工人房的浴室里被抓获，显然他想用塑料纸把手枪包起来，藏进水箱里。

Exercises

Ⅰ. **Understanding Ideas in the News**

1. What happened in Lenasia?

A. Three gangsters broke into a house and stole something.

B. Residents in Lenasia locked their doors for the whole day.

C. Police encountered three suspects trying to walk away from a garage.

2. How many gangsters did the police kill in the chase?
   A. One.　　　　　　B. Two.　　　　　　C. Three.
3. What made the householder realize that something was amiss?
   A. He screamed at the intruder in his garage.
   B. He saw strangers in the neighborhood early in the morning.
   C. He rushed to a nearby panic button and pressed it.
4. How did the gangsters behave at the beginning?
   A. They were quite panic.
   B. They made their way to Lark Street.
   C. They remained very casual.
5. What happened to the suspect who was finally arrested?
   A. He was beaten black and blue by the police.
   B. He appeared to have been injured during the fight.
   C. He pointed his 9mm pistol at his head and pulled the trigger.

II. Language Points

thug, gangster, intruder, suspect, nonchalant 这几个词用来指那几名入屋盗窃者，分别用在不同场合。

thug：(暴徒，凶手) a man who acts violently, especially to commit a crime　e.g. *Some thugs smashed his window.*

gangster：(歹徒) a member of an organized group of violent criminals

intruder：(入侵者) someone who enters a place without permission in order to commit a crime　e.g. *Intruders had entered the house through a back window.*

suspect：(嫌疑犯) a person believed to have committed a crime or done something wrong, or something believed to have caused something bad　e.g. *Police have issued a photograph of the suspect.*

nonchalant：(冷淡的，不在乎的) behaving in a calm manner, often in a way which suggests lack of interest or care　e.g. *a nonchalant manner/shrug*

III. Questions for Further Study

Study the structure of this news report in details: first divide it into sections, then analyze how the most important information is conveyed in the lead paragraphs so that readers can get the main idea quickly. See how the details are presented in the rest of the news. Search the Internet and find another similar report, and analyze it to the whole class.

2. Marikana: 900 bullets

Experts put on alert to process crime scene eight hours in advance.

Unit 8　Social News—South Africa

GRUESOME: Crime scene expert Captain Apollo Mohlaki testified yesterday police had fired not less than 400 live rounds and 500 rubber bullets at striking Marikana miners. (Picture: Phill Magakoe)

Poloko Tau
The Star
Thursday, November 1, 2012

The police had fired at least 900 bullets on the day 34 striking Lonmin employees were killed in Marikana in August.

This was stated yesterday at the Farlam Commission of Inquiry in Rustenburg by the police's legal representative, advocate Ishmael Semenya.

He said evidence at the commission would show that the police had fired "not less than" 400 live rounds and 500 rubber bullets between the scene at the Kraal and the small hill on August 16. ①

Semenya was cross-examining police crime scene expert Captain Apollo Mohlaki, who attended to the second crime scene at the koppie, where more than 10 bodies were found.

The police captain said 61 spent bullet cases had been found among exhibits recovered at the koppie.

Earlier in his evidence, Mohlaki said a team of crime scene experts had been put on standby and told to wait to be called to process a crime scene about eight hours before the Marikana killings. ②

Mohlaki said he and four others had waited in a holding area less than 2 km from the area where the massacre took place.

Mohlaki told the inquiry that he had expected to go and take pictures of traditional

113

weapons that would have been confiscated from the about 300 striking Lonmin miners on August 16.

"I was informed that an agreement had been reached that the people gathered at the koppie were going to disarm and withdraw, and then we'd be called in to document weapons [surrendered to the police]," he said. ③

Human rights lawyer advocate George Bizos, who represents the Legal Resources Centre and the Bench Marks foundation, asked if Mohlaki had expected trouble.

"I didn't expect anything to go wrong when told they'll give their traditional weapons to the police and withdraw," Mohlaki said.

The crime scene expert was surprised when shown the scene with bullet-riddled bodies.

"I asked myself, what happened now?" Mohlaki said.

He said he was told by a General Naidoo that "this is the crime scene".

He was asked to move from the first scene at a kraal to the second, up at the koppie, where more men lay dead or injured.

Mohlaki said he had not been aware that there had been more shooting there.

He said he had found the police and paramedics milling around, with the injured demonstrators being attended to nearby and those arrested lying on the ground. ④

Police crime scene markings at the koppie were found defaced a few days after the killings.

Mohlaki had previously told the commission during the inspection in loco that he did not know who had defaced his bright-green alphabetical markings.

The commission chairman, retired Judge Ian Farlam, asked yesterday for the bodies to be identified by their names so they could be linked to their autopsy reports.

Mohlaki said traditional weapons, including axes, iron rods with sharp points, spears and knobkieries, were among the things found around the bodies at the koppie. ⑤

The crime scene expert said some bodies, had been found between large rocks and added that rifle casings were also found in the area.

He said he had marked with an F a pistol loaded with 15 bullets.

Mohlaki said he had also recorded two other firearms that were not fully loaded that were found in possession of the arrested men.

Judge Fariam asked if pistol F had been used at all.

"Unless it has been reloaded, [then] it hasn't been fired at all?" he asked.

"It's possible: you can shoot and reload. I have, however, had them sent to ballistics people who were to ascertain [if those firearms had been used]," Mohlaki said.

In their opening statement, the police told the inquiry that they returned fire towards the koppie, from where they believed they were being shot at.

The pistol marked F was found between the bodies of Thabiso Mosebetsane and Mafolisi Mabiya.

Mohlaki said the body of one of those who had died, Nkosinathi Xalabile, was found on the edge of a large rock next to a tree. He said a rifle cartridge was found lying about 3 m from Xalabile's body.

The commission adjourned until Monday. (684 words)

Words and Expressions

gruesome	a.	可怕的	koppie	n.	（南非）小山
exhibit	n.	展品	confiscate	v.	没收
bullet-riddled		布满子弹孔的	kraal	n.	牛栏,小村庄
paramedic	n.	护理人员	deface	v.	毁容,损伤外观
loco	n.	火车头	autopsy	n.	（为查明死因而做的）尸体解剖,验尸
knobkierie (knobkerrie)		圆头棍（南非祖鲁族人使用的一种武器）	ballistics	n.	弹道学

Proper Nouns

Lonmin 位于南非 Bushveld 的一家英国公司,生产铂金 platinum。

Marikana 位于南非西北省的一个矿山小镇,2012 年 8 月 16 日,南非警察向罢工的工人开枪,造成 34 人死亡。

Farlam Commission of Inquiry 以南非最高上诉法院退休法官 Ian Gordon Farlam 为首的一个调查委员会。

Rustenburg 南非西北省的城市,位于 Magaliesberg 山麓。

News Summary

此则新闻是南非主要英语报纸《星报》在"马里坎那事件"不久之后报道对该事件调查进展情况的文章之一,主要内容就是调查委员会对负责清理现场的警官莫拉其的盘问,以弄清楚警察是在什么情况下开枪的。它的写作手法与上一篇大致相同:导语段给出基本结论之后,再逐步展开询问的结果。2012 年 8 月 16 日,南非警察面对聚集在马里坎那一个小山头上的几千名罢工工人,在几米之外的近距离对聚集的工人开枪,导致 34 人死亡,78 人受伤。而这是"种族隔离"政权结束,新政权建立以来警察对人民采取的最大一次暴力行动。

Understanding Sentences

① 他说,来自调查委员会的证据表明,在八月十六日当天,警察在村庄和小山之间的现场发射了"至少 400 发"实弹和 500 发橡皮子弹。

② 莫拉其此前的证据中说,在马里坎那开枪事件发生大约八小时之前,一组犯罪现场侦破专家已经处于待命状态,并被告知他们必须等候在那里,准备去收拾一处犯罪现场。

③ "我得到的消息是,此前已经达成协议,聚集在小山坡上的人将交出武器并撤退,然

后我们将被召集起来清点和登记(上交给警察的)武器,"他说。

④ 他说他已经发现警察和护理人员在周围四处走动,受伤的示威者就在附近接受救治,而被逮捕的人则躺在地上。

⑤ 莫拉其说,在躺在山坡上的死尸身上发现的武器包括斧头、带有尖端的铁棍、矛和圆头棍等常规武器。

Exercises

Ⅰ. **Understanding Ideas in the News**

1. What did Ishmael Semenya say about the shooting at Marikana?
   A. The police had fired not less than 900 bullets.
   B. The police had prepared for opening fire at the workers.
   C. The police had called some experts to the scene.

2. What was Captain Apollo Mohlaki told to do at first?
   A. To open fire at the striking Lonmin miners.
   B. To process a crime scene at the Kraal and the koppie.
   C. To document the traditional weapons confiscated.

3. How did Mohlaki feel when shown the scene with bullet-riddled bodies?
   A. He was surprised.   B. He was moved.   C. He was puzzled.

4. Why did the commission chairman ask for the bodies to be identified by their names?
   A. They would count the number of death.
   B. They would identify the bodies with the autopsy reports.
   C. They would bury the bodies one by one.

5. What did Mohlaki find at that scene that could have supported police's claim that they were being shot at?
   A. He proved that pistol F had not been used at all.
   B. He found police markings defaced a few days after the killings.
   C. He found some loaded pistols nearby some bodies of the death.

Ⅱ. **Language Points**

koppie, kraal, knobkierie 这几个词均来自南非荷兰语(Afrikaans),但也在南非英语中广泛使用。

koppie:(小山) from Dutch kopje, "kop" means "head", so the word means "a little head".

kraal:(牛栏,小村庄) from Portuguese curral, meaning "pen for cattle, enclosure"; an enclosure for animals, esp. in southern Africa; also means: a village of southern African natives

knobkierie:(圆头棍) a short wooden club with a knob at one end used as a missile or in close attack, esp. by Zulus of southern African natives. It also comes from

Afrikaans "knopkirie".

III. Questions for Further Study

This news report is mainly about the cross examination of police crime scene expert Captain Apollo Mohlaki. Find out how Mohlaki's witness is presented after the lead paragraph: how many main indirect and direct quotes are used, what information is exposed through each of them, and what implication each may have.

3. Nelson Mandela's condition "unchanged", officials say

Jacob Zuma's office issues statement after two-day silence created a vacuum filled with relatives' comments and media speculation

Nelson Mandela on the front page of a South African newspaper. *The Star* newspaper quoted a senior government official saying Mandela was "holding on to his life, but it's bad". (Photograph: Siphiwe Sibeko/Reuters)

David Smith in Johannesburg
guardian. co. uk, Monday
10 June, 2013, 11:26 BST

Officials in South Africa have broken their two-day silence over Nelson Mandela's health to say there is no change in his condition.

The 94-year-old former president was admitted to hospital in the early hours of Saturday with a recurring lung infection. He was described at the time as in a "serious but stable" condition, but the official silence since then has created a vacuum filled with off-the-cuff comments by relatives and speculation in the media. ①

On Monday, the office of President Jacob Zuma said: "Former president Nelson Mandela remains in hospital, and his condition is unchanged. Madiba [his clan name] was admitted on Saturday, 8 June 2013, for treatment in a Pretoria hospital for a lung infection."

The statement added: "President Jacob Zuma reiterates his call for South Africa to pray for Madiba and the family during this time."

It is the third time Mandela has been admitted to hospital this year. His wife, Graça Machel, cancelled a speaking engagement in London to be at his bedside in Pretoria.

On Sunday he was visited by a handful of family members. Mandela's daughter Zindzi said: "I've seen my father and he's well. He's a fighter." Meanwhile, his grandson and political heir apparent, Mandla Mandela, was reportedly seen watching a football match near his home in Eastern Cape province.②

But on Monday, South Africa's *Star* newspaper quoted a senior government official as saying Mandela was "not well", adding: "It's scary. He's still holding on to his life, but it's bad."③

"The family doesn't want visitors because of his condition. They told the hospital not to allow anyone in because they are a distraction."

The Star also cited sources saying the government's logistical plan for Mandela's death—known as the "M Plan"—had been reactivated after his admission to hospital.

Jackson Mthembu, national spokesman for the governing African National Congress (ANC), welcomed the move to restrict visitors to family members. He was quoted by eNews Channel Africa as saying: "The Mandelas are well within their rights to afford Madiba privacy while he recovers."

Zuma's spokesman, Mac Maharaj, used the words "intensive care" in connection with Mandela. "I see the rumours in the media; I want to say that there is no such blockages anywhere," he told the BBC. "The reality is that the normal procedures when a patient is under intensive care are applying from the medical side."④

"Therefore there are limitations on visitors and you know that when a person is in intensive care the doctors only allow some very close people to be there—it is not the way it is being presented in the media."

Mandela's frail condition has put millions of South Africans on edge. Prayers for the recovery of their first black president were held in churches across the country on Sunday. Messages of goodwill have come from the White House and Downing Street.

On Monday the South African Democratic Teachers' Union (SADTU) became the latest organisation to wish Mandela well. "SADTU's more than 260,000 members join millions in South Africa and the rest of the world in keeping our most revered icon Madiba and his family in our thoughts and prayers," it said. "We wish Madiba a speedy recovery."

But Andrew Mlangeni, an old friend of the statesman, told South Africa's Sunday Times that he had been taken to hospital "too many times" and there was a possibility he would not recover. "The family must release him so that God may have his own way," Mlangeni said.

Mthembu added: "The African National Congress dismisses the reported claim that the Mandela family has barred senior party leaders and government officials from visiting the hospital. We have spoken to the family about this report and they deny that they issued such an instruction or spoke to the media on barring the ANC and government from visiting Madiba.⑤

"What we know is that given the pressure associated with the admission of President Mandela there are general restrictions that permit only relevant people to have access. As the ANC we have deferred this responsibility to President Zuma to liaise with the family and the hospital."

He continued: "We call on all media houses and journalists to treat Madiba's health as a serious matter and stop making unwarranted speculations. We request the media to give the Madiba the privacy and respect they deserve at this time." (724 words)

Words and Expressions

recur	v.	复发，重现，再来	vacuum	n.	真空
off-the-cuff	a.	未预备的，即席的	speculation	n.	猜测
reiterate	v.	反复地说，重申	heir apparent		有确定继承权的人
scary	a.	引起惊慌的	distraction	n.	分心，分心的事物
logistical	a.	后勤的	blockage	n.	封锁，妨碍
frail	a.	虚弱的，脆弱的	revered	a.	受尊敬的
defer	v.	推迟，延期	unwarranted	a.	无保证的，未获承认的

Proper Nouns

Mandla Mandela 门德勒·曼德拉，南非已故黑人政治家、前总统曼德拉的长孙，曼德拉的政治继承人，东开普省黑人部落姆贝左的酋长

African National Congress 非洲国民议会，也称"非国大"，现南非执政党。

News Summary

纳尔逊曼德拉是南非黑人，出生于东开普省的特兰斯卡（Mvezo, Transkei）。他一生为反对南非种族隔离而奋斗，曾被当时的南非政府关押在罗本岛上长达27年，1994—1999年间担任南非总统，是第一个由全民代议制民主选举出来的南非总统。他任内致力于废除种族隔离制度和实现种族和解，消除贫困和不公。2013年6月，年近94岁的曼德拉因肺部感染，开始住进医院，这引发了人们对他健康情况的猜测，纷纷祈求他能渡过难关，但不幸的是，他于12月5日病逝。本文主要就是介绍他首次住院以后，广大人民对他的祝福和对他健康情况的祈祷。

Understanding Sentences

① 当时，他被描述为处于"严重但稳定的"状态，但是，自那时以来官方的沉默产生了一个大量报道他的亲戚所做的各种即席评论和媒体猜测的空间。

② 与此同时,有消息说他的长孙、政治继承人门德勒·曼德拉在东开普省他的家附近观看一场足球比赛。

③ 但是星期一时,南非的《星报》引用了一位高级政府官员的话,说曼德拉的情况"不妙了",还说,"很可怕。他还活着,但气若游丝。"

④ "事实上是,从医学角度来说,当病人处于深度护理时所应该执行的程序都用上了。"

⑤ 我们已经和(曼德拉)家人谈到了有关的报道,他们否认发布过这样的指令,或对媒体谈起有关禁止非国大和政府官员探望曼德拉的事情。

Exercises

Ⅰ. **Understanding Ideas in the News**

1. What is the condition of Mandela as described by officials?

    A. Lung infection.

    B. Serious but stable.

    C. Repeatedly ill.

2. What caused a vacuum for comments and speculation?

    A. No official announcement was made public about his conditions.

    B. He had been admitted into the hospital for two days.

    C. His wife cancelled a speaking engagement in London.

3. What made people think that Mandela's health was seriously endangered?

    A. The fact that he was admitted into hospital for three times.

    B. Words made by government officials who had visited him.

    C. His family didn't want visitors because of fear of distraction.

4. Why did doctors limit access to Mandela by the ANC and government officials?

    A. Because his condition was frail.

    B. Because he had lung infection.

    C. Because he was under intensive care.

5. What were people doing for Mandela at the moment?

    A. They were praying for his speedy recovery.

    B. They were visiting him in the hospital.

    C. They were talking to government officials.

Ⅱ. **Language Points**

frail, scary, apparent, unwarranted 都是新闻中用来描写人们的态度、反应的形容词。

frail:(虚弱的,脆弱的) weak or unhealthy, or easily damaged, broken or harmed

e.g. *I last saw him just last week and thought how old and frail he looked.*

scary:(引起惊慌的) frightening   e.g. *a scary movie/story*

apparent:(显然的) able to be seen or understood   e.g. *Her unhappiness was apparent to everyone.*

unwarranted:(无保证的,未获承认的) lacking a good reason and therefore annoying or unfair   e. g. *People need to be protected against such unwarranted intrusions into their private lives by journalist.*

Ⅲ. **Questions for Further Study**

Read this news report again, and summarize the main idea of the news. See how this main idea is expressed in the lead paragraphs, and how the idea that Mandela is seriously ill is conveyed in the news. How does the report present the point that Mandela's family didn't limit visits by government officials?

英语报刊知识介绍

英语新闻的结构和要素

一般英语新闻都采用"倒金字塔"结构,也就是说,新闻文章的开头一般用一个导语句说明新闻的主要内容,接着可能有几段补充一些无法包括在导语段里的内容。导语部分以后是新闻的主体,按照从重要到次要的顺序出现,中间可以回顾事件的过程和发展。在这一部分,记者也可能插入一些有关的背景知识,引用各种来源的说法,一般并不按照时间顺序。文章的最后并没有总结性的叙述,而是顺便提及相关的、但不很重要的事情。

倒金字塔结构是绝大多数客观报道的写作规则,被广泛应用到严肃刊物的写作中,同时也是最为常见和最为短小的新闻写作叙事结构。这种新闻报道,一般一个自然段只写一个事实,而且记者不发议论,只交代事实。本书所收集的英语新闻大部分就是这种结构,我们把它称为"新闻英语"。

1. A news report

Man shot in head blows the bullet out his nose

By KAREN FERNAU
Phoenix Gazette

CHANDLER, Ariz. — A man who had been shot in the head during a traffic dispute blew the bullet out of his nose in a hospital emergency room.

The victim, a 25-year-old Chandler man, was riding in a car when he was shot above the right temple by an angry driver at 1:25 a.m. Sunday.

While at Desert Samaritan Medical Center in Mesa, the victim's nose began bleeding, and he expelled a .22-caliber bullet.

"One of our officers who went with him to the emergency room handed him a towel, and (he) blew the bullet out," said Sgt. Steve Spraggins, a police spokesman.

"It was a freak kind of accident in which the bullet did not hit the brain, but apparently lodged in his sinus cavity."

The man's fiancee, who was driving when the victim was hit, asked that the couple's names not be printed because the man suspected of shooting her boyfriend has been released from jail.

2. Front page of *International New York Times*, showing the headline of three news reports

英美报刊选读 | Selected Reading from American and British Newspapers and Magazines (2nd Edition)

Unit 9 Social News—Life and Lawsuits

This category of news reports groups wide varieties of news based on genre and location. Everything that happens in a certain community can be "social news", according to its news value. From earthquake to a new law in town, or a criminal case to road or sea accidents, events are covered by reporters almost everywhere in the world, so long as there is a local or community newspaper. This chapter collects three reports, one on a rape case happened in India, the other on a lawsuit of a ship sunk in Cape Town, South Africa, and the last on the killing of his girl friend by a celebrity.

这一类的新闻报道可以根据内容和发生的地点分为很多种类的新闻。任何社区里所发生的任何事情,依据其新闻价值,都可以是"社会新闻"。从地震到市政府通过一条新的法律,从一件刑事犯罪到一宗交通事故,所有事件都通过记者在很多地方的报纸上发表。本章收集了三篇此类新闻,一篇是发生在印度的一宗导致受害人死亡的强奸案,另一篇是一名英国人为她父亲在发生于开普敦的一起沉船事故中死去提起诉讼,最后一篇是关于南非一位体育明星杀害他女朋友的报道。

1. Victim's friend tells of brutal gang attack

Francis Elliott
The Times
Middle East and Asia edition
Wednesday, January 9, 2013

Naked and gashed, his leg broken, Awindra Pandey waved for help opposite the strip of neon-lit hotels that mark the turn-off to Delhi airport. Beside him lay his female friend, Jyoti Singh Pandey, barely conscious, bleeding from severe injuries.

For 20 minutes rickshaws, motorcycles, cars, buses and lorries streamed past: it was 10 p. m. on a Sunday and no one, it seemed, wanted to get involved in someone else's nightmare.

Three weeks on, the gang rape and murdered of a 23-year-old physiotherapy student is a horror that will not stop haunting India.① Jyoti's friend, who tried valiantly but in vain to protect her, is determined that it should not. Mr. Pandey, a 28-year-old software engineer, gave a full, harrowing—and damning—account of the crime and its aftermath in an interview with *The Times* yesterday. Eyes red-rimmed with exhaustion, his leg in a brace, Mr. Pandey urged on the protesters who have taken to the streets of Delhi and several other cities and says he wants his friend's ordeal "to wake up India".②

Even after the police eventually arrived, he says, they squabbled among themselves over who should take the case.

"She was asking for water and complaining of pain in her stomach." But the policemen, he says, didn't want to help her into a police van as they waited for the ambulance. "She was bleeding heavily. They asked me to put her in the van."

When at last a sheet was fetched from one of the hotels, the police asked Mr. Pandey to wrap it around her—he believes the officers didn't want to get blood on their uniforms. When the ambulance came, they took the pair to a government hospital, driving past better-equipped private clinics.

Ten hours earlier Mr. Pandey's phone had rung as he lay dozing in his Delhi flat. "It was a Sunday at about 1:30 p. m. and she called. 'OK, so what are we going to do today?'" Her brisk tone, he says, was typical. "She was very dynamic, very ambitious."

They had met two years before through a mutual friend (despite the shared surname they are not related). After spending four years at her studies the trainee physiotherapist had come to Delhi for an internship. She had dreams of studying for a master's degree in the US or Britain.

The pair weren't dating, he says. They had just started hanging out together during her time in the capital. They chose to meet at Saket Citywalk, a complex of shops and cinemas in the southern suburbs. Jyoti, who was 5 ft 3in, was wearing a brown and black long woolen pullover, had streaked her hair and was wearing heels.③ From the film listing they chose *Life of Pi*. By the time it had finished ("she liked it very much") it was 8:30 p. m. and time to get back.

But Dwarka, the distant suburb where she was staying with her parents, was a fare no rickshaw driver would take and they could only coax one to take them half-way. In an impossibly painful irony it was a call on her mobile phone from her mother, urging her to come home quickly, that led to the pair's one, terrible mistake.④ Mr. Pandey hadn't liked the look of the minibus with its tinted windows and curtains, but she told him not to worry.⑤

"I told her that she shouldn't take this type of bus if she was alone." She said she wasn't alone—and that her mother wanted her home.

It took less than five minutes for the insults to start flying from some of the other "passengers".

The police allege that all those on the bus, including the driver, were members of a criminal gang. All six are accused of rape and murder, although one will be tried in a juvenile court.

Mr. Pandey confronted and briefly bested three, but then the gang produced iron rods. It was these that inflicted some of the rape victim's worst injuries. ⑥

"She was crying, 'Help, help, help', but they started to hit me in the head and on the leg and arms. I fell on the floor of the bus. After 15 or 20 minutes, I heard one of the people say, 'OK, she's died.'

"They came and took all of my clothes, my watch and all my things, and decided to throw us from the bus." Dragging himself to his feet despite a broken leg Mr. Pandey tried to flag down help.

"I waved my hand to take help, but people were watching but didn't stop. I tried so many cars, autos, bikes but no one helped me."

Recovering from his injuries at his father's home in Gorakhpur, in Uttar Pradesh, he has had the cold comfort of knowing that, awful as it is, the case is holding a mirror up to some of his country's most unpleasant features. (812 words)

Words and Expressions

gash	v.	砍伤	strip	n.	两旁有商店、餐厅的街道
rickshaw	n.	人力车	physiotherapy	n.	物理疗法
valiantly	ad.	勇敢地	harrowing	a.	痛心的，悲惨的
red-rimmed	a.	眼眶红红的	brace	n.	支柱，带子
squabble	v.	争论	pullover	n.	套头衫
streak	v.	加上条纹	coax	v.	说服
tinted	a.	带色彩的	juvenile	a.	青少年的
best	v.	(口)打败			

Proper Nouns

Delhi 德里，印度一城市
Gorakhpur 戈勒克布尔，印度东北部毗邻尼泊尔的北方邦(Uttar Pradesh)的城市

News Summary

这是2012年底发生在印度德里的一宗轮奸案。星期天晚上，一对男女朋友在看完电影之后，坐上了一辆"黑巴"赶回在郊外的家。开车不久，车上的六个人，连司机在内，就开始调戏那个女孩。他们殴打那个男孩，直至他无力反抗，然后开始对女孩实施性侵，最后当他们发现那个女孩已经没有气息的时候，就把他们俩仍下车。事情发生三个星期后，记者采访了

那位男孩,他讲述了整个事件的经过。本文就是记者根据他的讲述记录和整理出来的。

Understanding Sentences

① 三个星期以来,一伙歹徒对一名23岁的学习理疗的学生实施强奸并致其死亡的事件对印度来说一直是挥之不去的恐怖。

② 潘迪先生的双眼由于过度疲劳而红肿,一只腿还用支架支撑着,他对那些在德里和其他城市上街抗议的人说,他要让他朋友的噩梦般的经历"唤醒印度"。

③ 五尺三高的约提穿着一件棕黑色的长套头羊毛衫,头发分开,脚上穿着高跟鞋。

④ 令人难以相信的痛苦的讽刺是,正是她妈给她的手机打电话,敦促他们早点回家,导致了他们两人犯了一个也是唯一的错误。

⑤ 潘迪先生不喜欢那辆中巴的样子,车窗玻璃和帘子上涂着颜色,但是她对他说别担心。

⑥ 潘迪先生空手与他们打了起来,并制服了其中的三个人,但是,这时候,歹徒们掏出了铁扦。正是这些铁扦导致了受害者身上的一些最严重的伤害。

Exercises

Ⅰ. **Understanding Ideas in the News**

1. Where were the young man and his female friend waiting for help?

   A. At the turn between the city and the suburbs.

   B. In downtown Delhi.

   C. In neon-lit hotels.

2. What did the police do after they arrived?

   A. They fetched a sheet from a hotel.

   B. They helped her into a police van.

   C. They didn't want to take the case.

3. Who called Mr. Pandey in the afternoon to suggest going out?

   A. Jyoti.　　　　　　B. His girl friend.　　　C. Dwarka.

4. Why did they get on the minibus?

   A. The minibus had tinted windows and curtains.

   B. Jyoti's mother called and urged them to be back soon.

   C. There was no rickshaw driver who would go there.

5. What did the gangsters do to the two of them finally?

   A. They raped the girl.

   B. They beat the man with iron rods.

   C. They threw them off the bus.

Ⅱ. **Language Points**

gash, inflict, harrowing, confront, valiantly 这些词用来描写这对年轻人在遭受侵犯的过程中极力反抗的情形。

gash: (砍伤) to make a deep cut, esp. on the skin   e. g. *She slipped on a rock and gashed her knee.*

inflict: (使遭受(损伤、痛苦等)) to force someone to experience something very unpleasant   e. g. *These new bullets are capable of inflicting massive injuries.*

harrowing: (痛心的, 悲惨的) extremely upsetting because connected with suffering   e. g. *For many women, the harrowing prospect of giving evidence in a rape case can be too much to bear.*

confront: (使面临, 对抗) to face, meet or deal with a difficult situation or person   e. g. *As she left the court, she was confronted by angry crowds who tried to block her way.*

valiant: (勇敢地) very brave or bravely determined, especially when things are difficult or the situation gives no cause for hope   e. g. *The company has made a valiant effort/attempt in the last two years to make itself more efficient.*

III. Questions for Further Study

This news report begins with a descriptive lead that has three paragraphs. Find out the major lead sentence in the paragraphs so that you understand what the story is about from the beginning. Why does the reporter begin the narration from the end of the event? And how does this echo with the end of the story?

2. Family sues over Hout Bay tragedy

Caryn Dolley
Cape Times
Monday, October 29, 2012

The family of Welsh tourist Peter Hyett, who died when the Miroshga capsized, plan

to take action against the vessel's owners and say a British coroner has opened an inquest into his death. ①

Yesterday, Hyett's daughter, Helen Hyett, 37, in a phone interview from her home in Bournemouth in the south of England, said: "We're planning on some sort of action because we haven't even had an apology from the owners of Miroshga. We're very upset about that."

Hyett had seen the preliminary report into the accident released last week by the SA Maritime Safety Authority (Samsa), which detailed shortcomings in maintenance and crew competency. ②

She said her family planned to take legal action against Southern Ambition Marine Safaris, the company that ran the Miroshga.

Hyett, a mother of two, was on the pleasure craft with her father, 67, and mother, Suzanne, 64, when it capsized near Duiker Island on October 13.

After arriving back home about a week ago, she identified her father's body in Britain, after also having identified it in SA.

"The UK coroner's launched an inquest into my father's death... They'll be asking for all the police reports from SA."

Hyett e-mailed Wilfred Solomons-Johannes of Cape Town's disaster risk management center about the inquest.

Solomons-Johannes confirmed yesterday he had received this email and said he would consult the British High Commission today.

Cape Times was not able to reach anyone from the high commission, but the UK's Foreign and Commonwealth website said: "A coroner in England and Wales will normally hold an inquest if a person died a violent or unnatural death overseas and the body is returned to the coroner's district."

Hyett said the inquest could take months or even years.

She and her parents had been on holiday in South Africa so Hyett could visit her birthplace, Durban.

The tragedy happened a day before they were to return home after two weeks in South Africa.

Yesterday, Hyett, who is on medication to help her sleep as she keeps having flashbacks of the Miroshga capsizing, wept as she recalled her last moments with her father. ③

Shortly after the Miroshga left Hout Bay Harbour, she noticed the vessel did not seem to be level.

"I said to my mom and dad: 'It's lifting to one side.'"

At Dulker Island, Hyett realized something was wrong with the Miroshga's engine because she heard a beep each time it was switched on.

When the back of the Miroshga started flooding, passengers were told to move to the front and life jackets were thrown to them. ④

"At that point we knew we were going to sink."

Hyett saw a small vessel approach the Miroshga and a German woman jumped overboard with her two children.

"The next second the wave threw the boat over...I coundn't see my dad. I could see my Mom," she said.

Wearing her life jacket, she was trapped in the vessel's hull with other passengers.

"Because I was struggling for air, every time a wave came in, I thought, 'This is it. I'm going to die.' I think I was in there for 30 minutes before I decided to take my life jacket off and dive under to get out.⑤"

A qualified diver, she managed to pull off her life jacket and swim under the Vessel and out.

Her clothes were dragging her down, but a man, who Hyett believed is a poacher, swam to her and helped her to safety.

About 30 minutes later, Hyett's mother, who suffered severe hypothermia, also took her life jacket off and swam out from under the Miroshga.

"We're not sure what happened to Dad. Other ladies under there said he just drifted off... He wasn't a very good swimmer." The last thing Hyett said to her father before the capsizing was: "Are you going to be okay?"

He had replied: "Yep. Fine."

Peter Hyett's funeral is expected to take place in England on Thursday. (654 words)

Words and Expressions

capsize	v.	(船)倾覆	vessel	n.	船,容器
coroner	n.	验尸官	inquest	n.	审讯
maintenance	n.	维护	competency	n.	能力
flashback	n.	急转,闪回,倒叙	poacher	n.	捕猎者(这里指下海捕捉鲍鱼的人)
hypothermia	n.	低温			

Proper Nouns

Miroshga 一艘游艇的名字

British High Commission 英国大使馆(英联邦国家之间的驻外使馆称为High Commission)

News Summary

这是开普敦当地英文报纸《开普时报》上的一篇报道。2012年10月,英国公司管理的一艘游艇在从开普敦的豪特湾开出不久之后翻船沉没,其中一名死难乘客彼得·海尔特的家属回英国以后决定对船主提出起诉。虽然起诉的事情发生在英国,但因为沉船事故发生在开普敦,所以开普敦报纸的记者还是通过长途电话对她进行采访,并把结果发表在当地报纸上。

Understanding Sentences

① 在游艇"米罗什伽"号出事时死亡的一名威尔士游客彼得·海尔特的家属准备起诉船主,并表示一名英国验尸官已对他的死亡进行调查。

② 海尔特查看了上周南非海事安全局公布的有关这一事故调查的初步报告,其中详细描述了在维修的船员能力方面的不足。

③ 昨天,一直受"米罗什伽"号翻船的困扰而不得不服用药物以帮助睡眠的海尔特女士哭着回忆了她跟父亲在一起的最后时刻。

④ 当"米罗什伽"号尾部开始进水的时候,乘客们被告知往前部移动,在那里他们得到了救生衣。

⑤ "由于我不停地在想法子呼吸,每次有大浪打过来的时候,我都想,'完了。我完了。'我想我在里面停留了约三十分钟,然后我决定把救生衣脱下来,往下潜水以离开(沉船)。"

Exercises

Ⅰ. **Understanding Ideas in the News**

1. Who would the family of Peter Hyett like to suit?

A. The crew of Miroshga.

B. The Southern Ambition Marine Safaris.

C. The SA Maritime Safety Authority.

2. According to the UK laws, under what circumstances will a coroner hold an inquest into the case?

A. If the person had an heart attack overseas.

B. If the person returned to the coroner's district.

C. If the person died in an accident outside the UK and the body is returned.

3. What had the family been doing in South Africa?

A. They were vacationing.

B. They were visiting relatives.

C. They were doing business.

4. What signs did Helen realize that there might be problems with the engine?

A. The ship did not seem to sail smoothly.

B. There was unusual sound when the engine was switched on.

C. The back of the Miroshga started flooding.

5. How did Helen finally manage to escape from the sunken ship?

A. She went to the front to get life jacket.

B. She saw a man and screamed for help.

C. She pulled off her life jacket and swam out.

Ⅱ. Language Points

capsize, vessel, overboard, coroner, inquest 这些词用来讲述这次沉船事故的发生和提出上诉的法律程序。

capsize:((船)倾覆)to (cause a boat or ship to) turn upside down accidentally while on water   e. g. *A huge wave capsized the yacht.*

vessel:(船,容器)a large boat or a ship   e. g. *a cargo/fishing/naval/patrol/sailing/supply vessel*

overboard:(自船上落下)over the side of a boat or ship and into the water   e. g. *Someone had fallen overboard.*

coroner:(验尸官)an official who examines the reasons for a person's death, especially if it was violent or unexpected

inquest:(审讯)an official process to discover the cause of someone's death   e. g. *An inquest is always held if murder is suspected.*

Ⅲ. Questions for Further Study

Study three aspects in the organization and wording of this news report, and understand the most common features in newspaper English: ①the structure of the report, into how many parts can you divide it? ②the way Helen's reminiscence of the event is reported, and ③ the transition and coherence between the single-sentence paragraphs, and what effect it may have.

3. Oscar Pistorius charged with Reeva Steenkamp murder

South Africa's Olympic and Paralympic track star Oscar Pistorius has been charged with murdering his girlfriend at his home in Pretoria.

Oscar Pistorius arrested after the killing of his girlfriend

Tiisetso Makube
Mail & Guardian
14 Feb, 2013, 13:23

Police on Thursday said they had opened a murder case after a 30-year-old woman was found shot dead at the scene in the upmarket Silver Woods gated community on the outskirts of the capital.①

Police spokesperson Katlego Mogale said a 9mm pistol had been found at the scene and a 26-year-old man was taken into custody. In South Africa police does not identify suspects until they are charged in court.

"There are witnesses and they have been interviewed this morning. We are talking to neighbours and people that heard things earlier in the evening and when the shooting took place," police Brigadier Denise Beukes told reporters outside the residential complex in Pretoria.

"At this stage he is on his way to a district surgeon for medical examination and will be appearing at the Pretoria Magistrate's Court at 2pm this afternoon."

Johannesburg's Talk Radio 702 said Pistorius was believed to have shot his girlfriend, a model, in the head and arm, although the circumstances were unclear.② The radio had said before the murder charge that he might have mistaken her for a burglar.

According to media, police are set to oppose bail for "Blade Runner"—his nickname for his racing prosthetics.

According to News24, Beukes has confirmed that there have "previously been allegations of a domestic nature at Mr. Pistorius's home".

"His gifts are thoughtful"

Reeva Steenkamp was reported to have been dating Pistorius for a year. In the social pages of last weekend's *Sunday Independent* she described him as having "impeccable" taste.

"His gifts are always thoughtful," she was quoted as saying.

Some of her last Twitter postings indicated she was looking forward to celebrating Valentine's Day on Thursday with him.

"What do you have up your sleeve for your love tomorrow???" she posted.

"We are all devastated. Her family is in shock," Steenkamp's agent, Sarita Tomlinson, said, in tears over the incident, which happened in the early hours of the morning.

"They did have a good relationship," she said. "Nobody actually knows what happened."

Pistorius, who races wearing carbon fibre prosthetic blades after he was born without a fibula in both legs, was the first double amputee to run in the Olympics and reached the 400m semifinals in London 2012.③

In last year's Paralympics he suffered his first loss over 200 metres in nine years. After the race he questioned the legitimacy of Brazilian winner Alan Oliveira's prosthetic blades, though he was quick to express his regret for the comments.

Sponsor reactions

South Africa has some of the world's highest rates of violent crime, and many home owners have weapons to defend themselves against intruders. ④

In 2004, Springbok rugby player Rudi Visagie shot dead his 19-year-old daughter after he mistakenly thought she was a robber trying to steal his car in the middle of the night.

Pistorius's lavish home is in the heart of a large estate surrounded by a 3-metre-high stone wall topped by an electric wire fence.

"It is difficult to imagine an intruder entering this community, but we live in a country where intruders can get in wherever they want to," said one of the residents, who did not want to be named. ⑤

"Oscar is a good guy, an upstanding neighbour, and if he is innocent I feel for this guy deeply," he said.

Pistorius did not answer his mobile phone on Thursday. His South African agent told Reuters he had not spoken to Pistorius but his lawyers were with him.

He is sponsored by British telecommunications firm BT, sunglasses maker Oakley, sports apparel maker Nike and French designer Thierry Mugler.

"We are shocked by this terrible, tragic news. We await the outcome of the South African police investigation," a BT spokesperson said before Pistorius was charged.

A Nike spokesperson in London said before hearing of the murder charge that the company was "saddened by the news, but we have no further comment to make at this stage". —Reuters (653 words)

Words and Expressions

custody	n.	扣押	blade	n.	刀片
burglar	n.	入屋盗窃者	brigadier	n.	旅长,准将
prosthetics	n.	弥补术	bail	n.	保释
impeccable	a.	没有缺点的,不会做坏事的	allegation	n.	断言,辩解
			devastate	v.	毁坏
fibula	n.	[解]腓骨	amputee	n.	受切断手术的人
lavish	a.	豪华的	apparel	n.	服装

Proper Nouns

Paralympics 原为脊髓病患者举行的运动会,指残疾人奥运会

"Blade Runner" "刀锋战士"(因他所用的碳纤维做的假肢形状如刀片而得名)

Springbok 南非一支有名的橄榄球队

News Summary

2013年2月的情人节前一天,一则消息震惊了整个南非社会。曾参加伦敦奥运的残疾人运动员、俗称"刀锋战士"的比思托里斯在他的住所里开枪杀死了他的女友,同样在南非社会很出名的一名模特、法律专业毕业生里娃·斯汀肯普。这是枪杀事件发生后不久的新闻,主要是说南非警察已经决定立案处理了,并简单介绍了一些背景情况,但对枪杀发生的具体情况并没有介绍,也许因为当时披露出来的信息很少吧。

Understanding Sentences

① 警察星期四说,他们已经立案侦查一起谋杀案,一名三十岁的女性在首都郊外有门卫的高档住宅区银木区的现场被发现死于枪杀。

② 约翰内斯堡的"清谈702电台"说,据信比思托里斯枪杀了他的模特女友,子弹打在头部和手上,虽然具体情况仍不清楚。

③ 比思托里斯出生时两条腿就没有腓骨,装上碳纤维做的刀片状的假肢参加比赛,是首位参加奥运的双截肢运动员,2012年在伦敦奥运会男子四百米中进入半决赛。

④ 南非的某些暴力犯罪率在世界上最高,许多人在家里备有武器,用来对付闯入者和保护自己。

⑤ "很难想象一名闯入者是怎样进入这个社区的,但我们生活在一个闯入者可以进入他们想去的任何地方的国家中,"一名不愿意透露姓名的居民说。

Exercises

Ⅰ. Understanding Ideas in the News

1. Where did the killing take place according to police?

A. Outside the residential complex in Pretoria.

B. On the outskirts of the capital.

C. In a house in Silver Woods.

2. Who was taken into custody by the police?

A. Denise Beukes.　　　　　　　　　　B. Oscar Pistorius.

C. Reeva Steenkamp

3. What is special about Oscar Pistorius?

A. He is the first double amputee to run in the Olympics.

B. His gifts are always thoughtful.

C. He was believed to have shot his girlfriend.

4. What did the radio say about the possible reason for the shooting?

A. Pretorius might have thought that it was a burglar.

B. South Africa has some of the world's highest rates of violent crime.

C. They were looking forward to celebrating Valentine's Day.

5. What was confirmed by the police Brigadier about the killing?

A. "Blade Runner" is his nickname.

B. He will be appearing at court at 2 p.m.

C. There had been quarrels at Pistorius's home.

II. Language Points

burglar, allegation, bail, custody 这些词是新闻中涉及法律方面的用语。

burglar：（入屋盗窃者）a person who illegally enters buildings and steals things

allegation：（断言，辩解）a statement which has not been proven to be true which says that someone has done something wrong or illegal   e.g. *Several of her patients have made allegations of professional misconduct about/against her.*

bail：（保释）a sum of money which a person who has been accused of a crime pays to a law court so that they can be released until their trial

custody：（扣押）the state of being kept in prison, especially while waiting to go to court for trial

III. Questions for Further Study

This news report is among the first ones to cover the shooting at Oscar's house just before Valentine's Day. It follows the format of a news report in revealing what happened first, then use a Radior's broadcast as source. Other quotes are also given to piece the information together so that it makes a complete story. Notice the tone in reporting before the suspect is confirmed. Also, in two years after the killing, the case of Oscar Pistorius has attracted attention of the media in South Africa. There have been intensive reports about the case, especially during the court trial. Find out more from the Internet and see what the final sentence is. Discuss it with your classmates.

英语报刊知识介绍

英语新闻的标题、导语和主体内容

主要的英语报刊一般有自己的记者团队，他们对重要的事件进行了解、访问等，写出自己的新闻稿。各种地方小报一般订购新闻通讯社每天提供的新闻，尤其是国际新闻。这些新闻稿到了报社编辑那里，经过层层审核、修改、设计等之后，在当天的报纸上出现时会带有标题。有些标题采用大字号，有的所占版面空间比新闻本身还大。

新闻的标题并非是记者写的。多数情况下，标题是编辑加上去的。标题最主要的就是要达意和醒目。因此，诸如省略、多用现在时、用词简短有力、各种修辞手段、成语、俗语和新创的词语等，这些都会出现。

英语新闻一般以一段简明扼要的文字开头，称为"导语"。导语段通常用一个复合句就把涉及新闻内容的几个主要方面交代清楚，如发生了什么，谁是事件主角，何时何地发生，怎样发生，以及相关的反应、讨论或评价等。这就是所谓的五个 W 和一个 H。最常见的一种导语是概括性导语，常见于对重大新闻的报道。此外，还有描述性导语、故事性导语、修辞性导语（如提出一个反问句）等。

导语之后就是新闻的主题内容，它基本上按照最重要信息放在最前面的原则安排，并且常使用引用证人的话、补充背景和插入相关链接的方法。

1. Pieces of news in a paper showing the titles and leads

Fatal Shooting Laid to Fear of A-Bomb Leak

WASHINGTON, April 1. (AP)—Fear for the safety of atomic bomb secrets was advanced tonight as the possible cause of a triple tragedy which cost the lives of an attorney associated with the project, and his wife, and left their daughter gravely wounded.

The victims were Paul P. Stoutenburgh, 45; his wife Anna, 44, and their daughter Mary, 12. The husband and wife were dead when police, summoned by relatives, broke into the house; the little girl was given scant chance to survive.

Police Inspector Robert Barrett and Lt. Jerome Flaherty said Stoutenburgh apparently shot his wife and daughter and then himself. Relatives said he had developed a "phobia" about the atomic bomb, believing its secrets were getting out.

BLAME 2 DEATHS ON WORRY OVER A-BOMB LEAK

Washington, D. C., April 1 [Special]—Worry over possible loss of atomic bomb secrets was blamed today for a triple shooting in which Paul P. Stoutenburgh, 45, and his wife were killed and their daughter, Mary, 12, wounded with a bullet in her head.

Police said Stoutenburgh, an assistant patents adviser in the atomic bomb project, had apparently shot his wife and daughter and then himself. The bodies were found in a bedroom of their home with a pistol near Stoutenburgh's hand.

Relatives said Stoutenburgh had developed a "phobia" about bomb secrets getting out and had been depressed for several months after recommendations he made to both the war and navy departments on how to protect the secrets were "ignored."

Ex-Colonel, Wife Found Shot to Death

He Reportedly Worked On A-Bomb Secrets; Child, 12, Near Death

A discharged Army officer who was said to have worked on atom bomb secrets, and his wife were found dead yesterday after a triple shooting in their home at 1521 Kalmia rd. nw.

Their 12-year-old daughter, who had lain two days in the same room with a bullet wound in her head, was near death last night.

Paul P. Stoutenburgh, a former lieutenant colonel, and his wife, Anna, both 44, were found shot to death in the second-floor bedroom of their daughter, Mary Alice, after relatives and police broke into the house.

The child, found unconscious on the floor of her room, was rushed to Walter Reed Hospital. Doctors had little hope for her survival.

A-Bomb Worker Kills Wife, Self, Wounds Daughter

WASHINGTON, April 1 (AP)—Fear for the safety of atomic bomb secrets was advanced tonight as the possible cause of a triple tragedy which cost the lives of an attorney associated with the project and his wife, and left their daughter gravely wounded.

The victims, all shot through the head in the bedroom of their home, were Paul P. Stoutenburgh, 45; his wife, Anna, 44, and their daughter, Mary, 12. The husband and wife were dead when police, summoned by relatives, broke into the house; the girl was given scant chance to survive.

Police Inspector Robert Barrett and Lt Jerome Flaherty said Stoutenburgh apparently shot his wife and daughter and then himself. A pistol lay beside his body.

See SHOOTING Page 4.

2. The front page of *The Wall Street Journal*, with news about Obama winning the second term

THE WALL STREET JOURNAL.

WEDNESDAY, NOVEMBER 5, 2008

Obama Sweeps to Historic Victory

Nation Elects Its First African-American President Amid Record Turnout; Turmoil in Economy Dominates Voters' Concerns

Obama 338 electoral votes — 51% of popular vote
McCain 140 electoral votes — 48% of popular vote

3. The headline of a front-page report on the *Daily Mail*

4. The headlines of some news reports on different newspapers

Unit 10　Environmental Protection—Saving Wild Lives

Saving wild lives has been a serious challenge facing all governments in the world today. In recent times, hundreds of species of animals have become extinct as a result of human activities, hence the issue of maintaining a balance of animal species on earth is on the agenda of jobs for many governments. Africa is the only continent that keeps game reserves where people can see wild lives roaming freely, but many of these national parks are also facing the problem of poaching. The three news reports in this chapter are all about the struggle to keep wild lives in African countries.

今天,保护野生动物已成为面对各国政府的一个严重挑战。近年来,由于人类的活动,数以百计的动物已经灭绝,因此,如何保持物种平衡已经被提到各国政府的日程上。非洲是世界上唯一的保留有野生动物公园的地方,游客在里面可以欣赏自由自在地生活的各种动物。尽管这样,许多国家公园也面对着偷猎的问题。本章收集的三篇新闻报道都与非洲国家怎样尽力保护野生动物有关。

1. Rangers in isolated Central Africa uncover grim cost of protecting wildlife

In an attack which happened about 50 miles outside the Zakouma National Park boundaries in September, five rangers were killed on the spot. One remains missing and is presumed dead. Djimet Seid, the cook, was seriously wounded.

By Jeffrey Gettleman
The New York Times
Published: December 31, 2012

ZAKOUMA NATIONAL PARK, Chad — Just before dawn, the rangers were hunched

Unit 10　Environmental Protection—Saving Wild Lives

over in prayer, facing east. They pressed their foreheads into the dry earth and softly whispered Koranic verses, their lips barely moving. A cool wind bit at their faces.

All of a sudden, Djimet Seid, the cook, said he heard "one war whoop — or maybe it was a scream".

And then: "K-k-k-k-k-k", the angry bark of a Kalashnikov assault rifle, opening up on fully automatic.

In an instant, an entire Chadian squad of rangers was cut down with alarming precision by elephant poachers who were skilled at killing more than just animals.① Crouching in the bush, the poachers fired from a triangle of different spots, concealed and deadly accurate.

"If you go look at the infantry books, it's exactly how you do a first light attack, exactly," said Rian Labuschagne, a former paratrooper and now the manager of Zakouma National Park in southern Chad. "Our guys didn't have a chance."

Out here, among the spent bullet shells and the freshly dug graves, the cost of protecting wildlife is painfully clear. As ivory poaching becomes more militarized, with rebel groups and even government armies slaughtering thousands of elephants across Africa to cash in on record-high ivory prices, a horrible mismatch is shaping up. Wildlife rangers — who tend to be older, maybe a bit slower and incredibly knowledgeable about their environment and the ways of animals, but less so about infantry tactics — are wading into the bush to confront hardened soldiers.②

The outcome, too often, is not only firefights and battles, but also coldblooded murder, with dozens of African wildlife rangers killed in recent years, many in revenge-driven ambushes.③ Ivory poachers, it seems, are becoming increasingly wily and ruthless.

This summer, in the Democratic Republic of Congo, a militia of infamous elephant poachers sneaked up to the headquarters of a wildlife reserve and killed 5 people and 14 okapis, a rare animal with a giraffelike neck and zebralike legs. One guard who narrowly escaped said the attackers sliced open the chest of a downed colleague and ate his heart. In Zimbabwe, poachers are spreading deadly poisons on elephant carcasses to kill vultures. By taking out the birds that serve as a natural early warning system that a kill has been made, the poachers make it even more dangerous for rangers because they have no idea when the poachers are around. In Mozambique, the authorities said that poachers have recently begun using land mines.

Kenya, which is considered tame compared with some of these other places, has lost six rangers this year, more than in recent memory. One of them was Florence Hadia Abae, pregnant and the mother of a small boy. In March, she was following the footprints of suspected poachers near Tsavo National Park, a fabled tourist destination, when a poacher popped out of the bush and shot her in the face.

One of her colleagues was killed in the same ambush, shot in the leg, then finished off with a short, brutish stroke of an ax.

"They had no idea what they were walking into," said Rob Dodson, a British conservationist working near Tsavo.

In the Zakouma attack, which happened about 50 miles outside the park boundaries in September, five rangers were killed on the spot; one remains missing and is presumed dead. Mr. Seid, the cook, was seriously wounded. The attack appeared to be revenge for a raid on a poachers' camp, and much of the evidence points to the Sudanese military. For years, wildlife groups have blamed the janjaweed — Sudanese horseback raiders who traditionally work in tandem with the government military — for wiping out many of Central Africa's elephant herds. ④

But specific evidence recovered from the poachers suspected of killing Zakouma's rangers strengthens the Sudanese government link, the Chadian authorities and human rights groups say. A few weeks before the attack, Zakouma rangers raided a poachers' camp nearby and discovered one uniform for Abu Tira, Sudan's notorious paramilitary service, which has been blamed for burning down villages and committing other atrocities. The rangers also found several elephant tusks and a stamped leave slip from the Sudanese Army granting four soldiers permission to go to the Chadian border. ⑤

Most incriminating, though, were the digital photos recovered from a phone showing stacks of elephant carcasses that looked similar to photos from a horrific massacre of hundreds of elephants in Cameroon this year, suggesting that the Sudanese poachers who killed the Zakouma rangers may have been involved in one of the biggest single elephant slaughters in decades.

"This is not some random group of thugs," said Jonathan Hutson, a spokesman for the Satellite Sentinel Project, a nonprofit group that helped analyze some of the evidence. "They're poaching for profit to fund mass atrocities in Sudan."

Officials at the United States Africa Command, based in Stuttgart, Germany, have also been helping analyze some of the forensics.

At first, Rabie A. Atti, a Sudanese government spokesman, reflexively dismissed the evidence.

"Pictures can be fabricated," he said.

But then he added, "If there is concrete evidence, and someone is proven to be corrupt, he can be taken to court."

There is something noble but quixotic about the 50 or so Zakouma rangers, many in their 40s, some even in their late 50s, turbans wrapped around their wrinkled, sandblasted faces, tasked with protecting a spectacularly beautiful but extremely isolated stretch of savanna in the middle of one of the poorest, least developed regions on earth. ⑥ Even the architecture of Zakouma's headquarters, with its crenulated, fortresslike walls, belies a sense of siege.

"Death can come any time," said Adoum Abdoulaye, a ranger at Zakouma. "I'm

Unit 10 Environmental Protection—Saving Wild Lives

always thinking about it. "

And people here are used to it. (947 words)

Isma'il Kushkush contributed reporting from Khartoum, Sudan.

Words and Expressions

ranger	n.	护林员	siege	n.	包围，围攻
whoop	n.	喘息声	hunch	v.	弯腰驼背，弓起背部
precision	n.	准确	assault	v.	攻击
conceal	v.	隐藏	crouch	v.	蜷缩，蹲伏
paratrooper	n.	伞兵	infantry	n.	步兵，步兵团
revenge	v.	报复	poach	v.	偷猎
okapi	n.	[动]霍加皮（产于非洲东部）	wily	a.	老谋深算的
			giraffe	n.	长颈鹿
slice	v.	切片	carcass	n.	尸体
vulture	n.	秃鹰	brutish	a.	如野兽般的，粗野的
janjaweed	n.	苏丹西部的一个民兵组织	in tandem with		一前一后
			incriminate	v.	控告……有罪
atrocity	n.	残暴，暴行	forensics	n.	辩论术
thug	n.	暴徒，凶手	quixotic	a.	堂吉诃德式的
fabricate	v.	编造，捏造	sandblasted	a.	风沙吹打的
turban	n.	穆斯林的头巾	crenulated	a.	细圆齿状的
savanna	n.	热带（或亚热带）稀树大草原			

Proper Nouns

Koran （伊斯兰教）可兰经

Kalashnikov 卡拉什尼科夫，俄罗斯人，他设计的一种机关枪以他名字命名

Zakouma 扎库马国家公园（位于中部非洲国家乍得南部）

Tsavo 肯尼亚一个国家公园

News Summary

当前，非洲还有很多地方有野生动物保护区，或叫"国家公园"。那里没有人为的开发，非洲的几种主要的大型动物，大象、河马、犀牛、长颈鹿和狮子，以及千百种物种，都任由其自然生长，保持着一种生态平衡。但是，由于利益驱动，偷猎野生动物的人也变得越来越残忍。这篇报道是美国的记者采写的，它暴露了目前在一些非洲国家中保护野生动物所面临的窘境——护林员的工作变得越来越危险。

Understanding Sentences

① 一阵子工夫，一整队乍得护林员就被消灭了，那些偷猎大象的人枪法令人可怕地准，

他们善于捕杀的不仅是动物。

② 保护野生动物的护林员——他们年纪都比较大，也许行动有点缓慢，对他们的环境和野生动物的生活方式却是非常熟悉，但对枪炮和战术却没那么精通——正在一步步朝着灌木丛走去，去面对那些凶悍的士兵。

③ 经常的结果不仅是救火和战斗，而且是冷血的谋杀，过去几年就有数十位非洲护林员被害，许多是遭遇了报复性的伏击。

④ 好多年来，保护野生动物团体一直谴责苏丹西部的一个民兵组织——那些骑着马、与政府军一前一后的偷袭者——他们消灭了许多中非的象群。

⑤ 护林员也发现一些象牙和一张盖了印的苏丹军队的请假条，批准四名士兵前往与乍得交界的边界。

⑥ 在这五十多个扎库玛的护林员身上我们可以看到崇高而又堂吉诃德式的一面，他们许多人是四十几岁，有些已经五十多了，布满皱纹的饱经风沙的脸上扎着穆斯林头巾，他们的任务是保护那一片非常壮观、美丽而又极端孤立的，位于地球上最贫穷、最不发达地区之一的深处的热带草原。

Exercises

Ⅰ. **Understanding Ideas in the News**

1. How is the attack on the squad of rangers by elephant poachers described?

    A. It is deadly accurate.

    B. It is concealed.

    C. It is professional.

2. What makes it more difficult for the rangers to deal with ivory poaching?

    A. Government armies slaughter thousands of elephants.

    B. Rangers are more knowledgeable about their environment.

    C. Ivory poachers are becoming increasingly wily and ruthless.

3. What did the elephant poachers kill in the Democratic Republic of Congo this summer?

    A. Vultures that eat carcasses.

    B. Thousands of elephants.

    C. 5 people and 14 okapis.

4. Whom did the evidence at the Zabouma attack in September point to?

    A. Government military.

    B. The janjaweed.

    C. Chadian poachers.

5. What is the dilemma that the Zakouma rangers are in?

    A. They are in a dangerous situation carrying out their duties.

    B. Even their headquarters has been attacked several times.

    C. They are no match to the forces of the poachers.

Unit 10　Environmental Protection—Saving Wild Lives

Ⅱ. Language Points

poach, atrocity, incriminate, savanna, vulture 这几个词用来描述非洲护林员所面对的危险,具有很大的地方色彩。

poach：(偷猎) to catch and kill animals without permission on someone else's land

e. g. *The farmer claimed that he shot the men because they were poaching on his land.*

atrocity：(残暴，暴行) brutal behavior　　e. g. *They're on trial for committing atrocities against the civilian population.*

incriminate：(控告……有罪) to make someone seem guilty, especially of a crime

e. g. *A secret report incriminating the company was leaked last week.*

savanna：(热带(或亚热带)稀树大草原) a large flat area of land covered with grass, usually with few trees, which is found in hot countries, especially in Africa

vulture：(秃鹰) a large bird with almost no feathers on its head or neck, that eats the flesh of dead animals

Ⅲ. Questions for Further Study

This news report also begins with descriptive lead paragraphs. They present a picture of the scene and help to create an atmosphere of danger to match the theme of the report. Then the reporter explains the situation the wild life rangers face by using the Zakouma National Park as the main location, while other locations are also mentioned. Point out all the cases mentioned in the news report and piece them together to arrive at the point the reporter wants to make.

2. Saving two-ton giraffe a tall order

Vets, residents drag the animal to safety after it got stuck in collapsed septic tank.

The two-ton male giraffe stuck in the septic tank in Marloth Park

Brendan Roane and Peter Craig-Cooper
The Star
Tuesday, July 10, 2012, 11:20

A two-ton giraffe had to be dragged out of a septic tank by ropes during a rescue by residents and vets of Marloth Park, near the Kruger National Park, after being stuck for hours. [1]

The adult male giraffe was discovered on Olifants Street early yesterday morning by a domestic worker.

The rescue was headed by Dr. Cobus Raath, director and chief vet of wildlifevets.com, based in Mbombela (Nelspruit).

The giraffe probably fell into the septic tank outside one of the park's unoccupied houses on Sunday night or early yesterday, said Raath.

He said the septic tank probably collapsed under the weight of the animal.

Marloth Park is a resort town situated along Kruger's southern border.

Residents are not permitted to erect fences around their property because the animals are allowed to roam freely in the area.

The news soon spread around Marloth Park and the rangers and honorary rangers had to control onlookers from venturing too close.

When Raath's team arrived, they found that the animal had managed to get its front legs out of the pit.

They blindfolded the giraffe and put cotton wool in its ears to reduce its stress.

The giraffe's head was pulled down to the ground and ropes were secured to the deck of the house. [2] Once the head of a giraffe is held down it cannot raise itself from the ground.

Unit 10　Environmental Protection—Saving Wild Lives

The giraffe's head had to be held in this position throughout the rescue.

Raath and other rescuers, including local residents, pulled the giraffe out of the pit on its side with ropes and straps so that they would not injure its hind legs. ③

They treated the giraffe's wounds while it lay on the ground, then turned it to face away from the pit so that it wouldn't fall back in when it was eventually freed.

There was a moment of panic while they were removing the blindfold, as the giraffe broke away and tried to lift itself up.

Ropes were still secured to its neck and Raath found himself on the underside of the giraffe's neck as it was pulled back to the ground. Luckily Raath was not injured.

When it was released, the giraffe got to its feet and stood motionless for a while, before moving back into the bush. It was photographed 10 minutes later, crossing the main road in Marloth Park.

Raath said the local rangers would monitor the giraffe for any signs of injury. (405 words)

No entry... this is a trunk road: Terror of safari Britons as bull elephant overturns their car

By Rebecca Evans
The Daily Mail
15 November, 2012

Getting up close and personal to some of nature's most fearsome beasts is the main attraction of a safari holiday.

Unfortunately for two British tourists, one elephant took his brief a little too seriously.

The newly engaged couple's car was rammed, skewered and tossed upside down by the bull elephant, which lashed out after also trying to attack the car in front. ④

Amazingly the couple, who were named locally as Chris Hare and Helen Jennings, both 40, escaped the incident at South Africa's Kruger National Park with just minor injuries.

Mr. Hare said: "When I came around the bend, the big guy was right in front of us. He walked towards us and I pulled off the road.

"The elephant appeared to walk past the car but then turned back, pushing a tusk against the passenger door and rolling the car. It was terrifying and I just thought: 'But it can't be possible that this is happening.'"

Vasti Fourie, who was travelling in a convoy through the park when she witnessed the attack on the hatchback, said: "It charged towards the side of the car, lifted it up with its tusk, dropped it on its roof and calmly walked away. ⑤

"It all happened so quickly. Once we drove around the corner, the driver of the flipped car was kneeled down in shock.

"I've never seen anything like this before in my life and I'm sure they haven't either." Mr. Hare and Miss Jennings, from Stockton-on-Tees, are understood to have been spending three days on holiday at the national park before flying on to the city of Durban.

Rangers later said they found blood on the car of the British couple and thought that the elephant might have had a tooth abscess.

It is now being tracked to see if it needs treatment. South Africa National Parks spokesman Reynold Thakhuli warned tourists to take extra care around wild animals and allow nothing to protrude from their cars.

He said: "When you see an animal approaching do not panic and try to move away as fast as you can.

"Elephants can be very dangerous when they feel threatened." (358 words)

Words and Expressions

septic tank		化粪池	roam	v.	漫游,闲逛
venture	v.	冒险	ram	v.	猛击,撞
skewer	v.	上叉,串起来	lash	v.	猛击,急速甩动
bend	n.	拐弯处	convoy	n.	护送,护卫
hatchback	n.	有仓门式后背的汽车	flip	v.	抛,翻过来
abscess	n.	脓肿,砂眼	protrude	v.	突出

Proper Nouns

Kruger National Park 克鲁格国家公园(南非的东北部与莫桑比克毗邻的地方)
Mbombela (Nelspruit) 姆本贝拉(纳尔普律斯),南非西北省地名

Unit 10　Environmental Protection—Saving Wild Lives

News Summary

与第一则新闻相比,这两则新闻属于比较轻松有趣的。第一则是关于人们怎样把一头不小心掉进陷阱里的长颈鹿拉出来的新闻,第二则是关于一头大象用它的长鼻子掀翻了一辆汽车的新闻。很多西方游客喜欢到非洲去看野生动物,是因为他们可以近距离和野生动物接触,享受这种大自然所提供的乐趣。当然那些都是比较温顺的大型动物。但是这样的接触也蕴含着某些人们没注意到的危险。

Understanding Sentences

① 在克鲁格国家公园附近的马洛斯公园,一头两吨重的长颈鹿不小心掉进一个化粪池里爬不出来,几个小时后,当地居民和兽医终于用绳子把它拉了上来。

② 长颈鹿的头被拉到地上,然后把绳索系到屋子的平台上。长颈鹿的头一旦被按倒在地上,它自己无法抬起来。

③ 拉斯和其他抢救人员,包括当地居民,通过绳子和皮带把长颈鹿侧面从粪池拉出来,这样他们不会伤到它的后腿。

④ 这对刚订婚的新人的汽车受到这头公大象的猛烈撞击,被高高举起并翻过来甩在地上。开始的时候,它企图从正面攻击汽车,之后又猛击汽车。

⑤ 在一队车队里,正穿过公园旅行的法斯提福理亲眼看到了大象攻击那辆两厢汽车的过程。她说,"它朝着汽车的侧面冲过去,用鼻子把它举起来,把汽车顶朝地摔下来,然后若无其事地走开了。"

Exercises

I . **Understanding Ideas in the News**

1. Where was the adult male giraffe found?
   A. Outside Marloth Park.
   B. In the Kruger National Park.
   C. In a septic tank of an unoccupied house.
2. What did the rescue people do to the animal to reduce its stress?
   A. They blindfolded the giraffe.
   B. They lifted its front legs out of the pit.
   C. They pulled its head down to the ground.
3. How did they manage to pull the giraffe out of the pit?
   A. They treated the giraffe's wounds.
   B. They pulled it our with ropes and straps.
   C. They lifted the giraffe up from the pit.
4. What happened to the British couple's car in Kruger National Park?
   A. An elephant lifted up the car with its tusk.
   B. An elephant went past the car.
   C. An elephant overturned the car.

5. Why was this elephant behave like that?

A. It might want to demonstrate its strength.

B. It might be scared by the car.

C. It might feel threatened.

II. Language Points

roam, ram, lash, flip, skewer 这几个动词都是单音节动词,表达各种不同的动作,在新闻中用来描述大象的动作。

roam:(漫游,闲逛) to move about or travel, especially without a clear idea of what you are going to do   e. g. *After the pubs close, gangs of youths roam the city streets.*

ram:(猛击,撞) to hit or push something with force   e. g. *Someone rammed (into) my car while it was parked outside my house.*

lash:(猛击,急速甩动) to hit with a lot of force   e. g. *The prisoners were regularly lashed with electric cable.*

flip:(抛,翻过来) If you flip something, you turn it over quickly one or more times, and if something flips, it turns over quickly.   e. g. *When one side is done, flip the pancake (over) to cook the other side.*

skewer:(上叉,串起来) to put pieces of food, especially meat, on a skewer

III. Questions for Further Study

The two pieces of news are all very typical of journalism English, with characteristics like using simple words, short sentences and one-sentence paragraphs. Analyze them to see the lead paragraphs, the structure of the news report, and the way the two incidents are presented so lively.

3. Cape's abalone is well on the way to extinction

Melanie Gosling
Cape Times

Unit 10　Environmental Protection—Saving Wild Lives

20 November, 2012

The year 2035 is when the last abalone will be taken from the southern Cape coast—an area stretching from Cape Hangklip to Cape Agulhas. And this is an optimistic projection.

The year 2035 as the Year Zero for our abalone is based on the assumption that the authorities will have reduced poaching by just over half. ① If not, the extinction will be earlier. However, attempts to stem the poaching tide have so far not delivered many discernable results.

At some parts of the coast, abalone stocks are already so low from 15 years of heavy poaching, they can be classed as the living dead—our "zombie abalone".

This is the case for the area from Cape Hangklip to Hermanus, where there are so few left that scientists regard the resource as "functionally extinct", meaning there are so few left to be able to reproduce sufficiently to increase population numbers.

Last week, fisheries scientists and official presented the stark facts to MPs in the fisheries portfolio committee. For the abalone resource to recover, poaching must be cut by 20 percent a year for the next 15 years. If not, the stocks will collapse.

When the last abalone are gone, South Africa will have lost what could have been one of its more lucrative seafood products, bringing in huge amounts of foreign exchange and creating jobs—indefinitely, if properly managed. ②

Instead, the money has lined the pockets of criminals, local and international, who are plundering the resource to extinction.

According to fisheries' statistics, about 7.8 million poached perlemoen were seized by the authorities between 2000 and 2010. Estimates are that the amount actually poached was about 50 million. The amount confiscated is estimated to be between 10 percent and 14 percent of what is poached.

Abalone is a slow-growing shellfish, putting much of its energy in its early life into creating its protective shell. While the shell may ward off marine predators, it is no match for the screwdrivers and crowbars of human predators. ③

Because it is slow-growing, it reaches sexual maturity at seven or eight years, and its minimum legal size of 11.4 centimeters for harvesting at 8 or 9 years. Scientists said smaller abalone have been poached because the bigger specimens run out.

Many of these undersized abalone are not old enough to have had a chance to breed.

And it is getting tougher for abalone to make babies. They are "broadcast spawners"; they squirt their eggs and sperms into the sea and these have to find each other floating in the currents.

In the days when abalone covered rocks in dense colonies, this was no problem. Today, poaching has meant most of these dense groups are gone, and with the remaining abalone so far apart, the eggs and sperms have much less chances of finding each other. ④

Although abalone are found from St. Helena Bay to Port St. Johns, they are sparsely distributed on the east coast. Nor do they like the colder waters of the West Coast. Historically, the most abundant abalone beds were from Cape Columbine, just south of Paternoster to Quoin Point, west of Gansbaai.

Statistics from the Department of Agriculture, Forestry and Fisheries show that in the 1960s annual landings of abalone were between 2000 and 2500 tons a year. In the late 1960s, fisheries introduced an annual quota of 1600 tons. By the 1970s this was reduced to around 750 tons.

By 2003 the level of poaching had increased so much that authorities closed the recreational sector. By 2008 poaching had got so bad the then minister, Marthinus an Schalkwyk, closed the commercial sector. Both moves were controversial, as people were angry that they were prevented from taking out abalone, while those who cocked a snook at the law hauled them in by millions.

Scientists advised that the commercial abalone industry not be reopened until there had been a 15 percent reduction in poaching every year for 15 years. ⑤ Instead, poaching increased from just under four million in 2008 to just over five million in 2010. scientists now say there needs to be a 20 percent reduction in poaching for stocks to recover.

In spite of this, Fisheries Minister Tina Joemat-Petterson reopened the commercial fishery in 2010. with a quota of 150 tons.

Because of its high price in South Asia, abalone poaching is a global problem. In California, the battle has been lost. Australia is fighting back. Oman, which put in a three-year ban with serious enforcement, has seen its stocks recover.

South Africa still has a chance to save the area from Gansbaai to Cape Agulhas. (766 words)

Words and Expressions

abalone	n.	鲍鱼	extinction	n.	消失，消灭
stem	v.	滋生，阻止	zombie	n.	僵尸
stark	a.	赤裸的	portfolio	n.	职务范围
lucrative	a.	有利的，润滑的	plunder	v.	抢劫
perlemoen	n.	（南非荷兰语）鲍鱼	confiscate	v.	没收，充公，查抄
predator	n.	掠夺者，食肉动物	crowbar	n.	撬棍
spawner	n.	产卵鱼（或虾、蟹等）	squirt	v.	喷出
sparsely	ad.	稀疏地，稀少地			

Proper Nouns

Cape Agulhas 厄加勒斯角，非洲的最南端，印度洋与大西洋的交界处
Gansbaai 杭拜斯，西开普沿海的一个小镇

Unit 10 Environmental Protection—Saving Wild Lives

News Summary

鲍鱼是一种多年生的贝壳类海洋生物,在北半球的美国西海岸、南半球的澳大利亚和南非都盛产鲍鱼。由于亚洲市场对鲍鱼的需求量很大,使南非的非法捕捞鲍鱼的活动日益增加。这就严重影响了生态平衡,会使南非政府失去一种能创造大量外汇的商品。因此,南非政府制定了一系列的法律法规来控制非法捕捞,科学家们也呼吁人们保护它。本文用很多具体数字来说明当前非法捕捞鲍鱼的严重程度,并向政府提出了一系列的保护措施。

Understanding Sentences

① 到2035年我们的鲍鱼将完全消失的预言是基于政府将能够把非法捕捞的量减少一半这一假设。

② 当最后的鲍鱼消失的时候,南非也将失去它最有利润的海产品中的一种,假如能够得到恰当的管理,它将永远地带来大量的外汇和创造工作岗位。

③ 鲍鱼是一种生长缓慢的贝壳类海产,在它生命的初期,大部分能量都花在那保护性的贝壳上。它身上的贝壳虽然能够阻止其他海生的捕猎生物,也还是敌不过人类捕猎者的螺丝刀和撬棍。

④ 今天,非法捕捞使大部分稠密的鲍鱼群已经消失了,而剩下的鲍鱼分布稀疏,它们的卵子和精子相遇的机会就少得多了。

⑤ 科学家们建议,除非在今后的15年里,每年非法捕捞的数量能够减少百分之十五,否则不能重新开放商业性的鲍鱼捕捞业。

Exercises

I. Understanding Ideas in the News

1. What does scientists predict about the population of abalone along the southern Cape coast?

   A. It will collapse in the next 15 years.

   B. It will be able to reproduce sufficiently in 15 years.

   C. It will become extinct in 2035 if poaching is not cut by over half.

2. What percentage of illegally poached abalone is confiscated in the past ten years?

   A. 7.8%.

   B. Between 10%-14%.

   C. 50%.

3. How many years does it take for a abalone to grow up to the legal size for harvesting?

   A. 8-9 years.

   B. 11.4 years.

   C. 10 years.

4. Where was abalone found abundant in the past?

   A. From Cape Columbine, south of Paternoster and west of Gansbaai.

B. From St. Helen Bay to Port St. John.

   C. Along the West Coast.

   5. How much abalone was harvested annually during the 1960s?

   A. 750 tons.

   B. Around 1600 tons.

   C. Between 2000-2500 tons.

Ⅱ. **Language Points**

extinct, zombie, plunder, predator, sparsely 这些词在新闻中用来描述人们对鲍鱼的非法捕捞行为和所引起的后果。

extinct：(消失，消灭) not now existing   e. g. *There is concern that the giant panda will soon become extinct.*

zombie：(僵尸) a dead person who is believed, in some Caribbean religions, to have been brought back to life by magic

plunder：(抢劫) to steal goods violently from a place, especially during a war   e. g. *After the president fled the country, the palace was plundered by soldiers.*

predator：(掠夺者，食肉动物) an animal that hunts, kills and eats other animals   e. g. *lions, wolves and other predators*

sparsely：(稀疏地,稀少地) small in numbers or amount, often scattered over a large area   e. g. *a sparse population/audience*

Ⅲ. **Questions for Further Study**

This news report raises the alarming prospect of the distinction of abalone in South Africa and uses statistics to prove its arguments. Analyze the structure and vocabulary of the news report to see how figures are presented and how they can make the points convincing.

英语报刊知识介绍

新闻特写、专题报道

新闻事件是每天都发生的事情,它可能就发生在我们身边,也可能在我们所在的城市,甚至在全国、世界各地。典型的新闻报道就是记者通过语言对发生的事件进行介绍,并由各种媒体发送出去。英语报刊新闻一般就指对新闻事件进行报道的文章。

新闻特写文章是叙述性的、比较长的、关于人们感兴趣的任何话题的文章,而且不一定必须跟当前所发生的事情联系起来。它经常是关于某人、某个地方、某件事的详细介绍的文章。这种新闻文章与一般的新闻区别并不大,但是通常多是叙事的语气,并且导语多是描述性或故事性的。

Unit 10　Environmental Protection—Saving Wild Lives

1. The front page of *The New York Times*, September 12, reporting on the 9.11 terrorists' attack

2. The front page of the *Los Angeles Times*, September 12, has the same feature articles about the 9.11 attack

Unit 11　Computer Technology and the Internet

Reporting on the development of technology is also one of the focuses of modern journalism. There are segments of the newspaper that cover the latest news in the field of technology. The reporters and editors provide top technology news, with investigative reporting and in-depth coverage of tech issue and events. The computer is an amazing invention of the 20th century, and computer technology is changing rapidly nowadays, hence the section on technology in the newspaper has a lot of reports and analysis on computing, the web, blogs, games, gadgets, social media, broadband connection, etc. This chapter focuses on software application and issues on the Internet only.

报道技术的发展也是当代新闻学的重点之一。报纸上有专门报道技术领域里最新消息的部分。记者和编辑们提供最新的技术方面的消息，其中有关于技术问题和事件的调查性文章，也有深度报道。计算机是20世纪的重大发明，现在的计算机技术变化很快，因此，报纸上的技术栏目部分有很多关于计算机、网络、博客、游戏、小电器、社交媒体、宽带连接等的报道和分析。本章收集的新闻主要集中在软件应用和互联网方面。

1. The web is the most conservative force on Earth

Digital technology has made us a society of mass archivers, says Charles Leadbeater. Far from rotting our brains, the web enables us to preserve all our memories.

Charles Leadbeater
The Spectator

9 July, 2008

Archiving is not regarded by most people as sexy, glamorous or even interesting. Odd then that most of us, and especially the young, hip and trendy, seem to have become avid archivists without even realising it.①

My archive, which I keep on the web, and in my computer, mobile phone and iPod, is neither particularly extensive nor interesting: several thousand digital photographs, play-lists of songs, endless dull policy reports, papers and presentations, some Internet postings, Facebook friends and connections. Teenagers, however, are archiving their lives as they happen through blog entries and photos taken on camera phones, much of which they organise collaboratively, in semi-public, on the web.② We have become a society of mass archiving.

At first sight it seems obvious that these rapidly expanding digital archives should enrich our individual and collective memory. We are more able than ever to capture, store, search, retrieve and share reminders of people and events. By tagging our digital photos with descriptions we are less at risk of forgetting who we were with, where, when and why. By sharing photos with friends on social network sites we create multiple copies and perspectives, so we should never lose anything and we should have a richer interpretation of events.③

Social networking sites will keep us in touch with friends even when our ageing minds cannot retrieve their names. That clever Sky + box will remember to record an entire series of television programmes for me even as I struggle to remember crucial things like the location of glasses, keys, credit cards and past holidays.

My parents have a large box of black and white photos in their loft, mainly of groups of smartly dressed people looking slightly uncomfortable at the seaside in the middle decades of the last century. I have no idea who most of these people were. When my parents pass away the meaning of this physical archive of family history will be lost. In future families with digital archives should not suffer this catastrophic memory loss.

From early on the computer revolution promised to create vast shared stores of memory. When Lee Felsenstein became chair of the Homebrew Computer Club in the early 1970s, he had just started a project called Collective Memory for people to share their memories using computers in public places around Berkeley. Similar projects on a much larger scale are now being run all over the world. Our expanded capacity for collective memory will make us more productive and politics more accountable.④

One of Tim Berners-Lee's motives for creating the software that spawned the web was his poor memory; he tended to lose things. One of the attractions of digital files is that it is easier to trace their history. If a software project runs into the sand, the programmer should be able to trace his way back to the fork where he took a wrong turn. Digital technology keeps older versions of the same document. That makes it easier to retrace our steps to ideas that were prematurely discarded, often one of the richest sources for innovation.

Our collective capacity for instant recall should help to make power more accountable. Hillary Clinton's mistaken memory that she arrived at Tuzla airport under sniper fire was quickly corrected. The powerful will find it more difficult to impose on us their version of the past.

The expansion of our shared memory in millions of mini-archives should be an unalloyed good, especially for an ageing society in which millions of people will be losing their memories and, as a result, their sense of themselves in the decades to come. ⑤ Yet a growing group of thoughtful skeptics — the neuroscientist Susan Greenfield, the technology critic Nicholas Carr — argue that far from supporting our minds, the web is rotting them, including our capacity for memory.

Carr argues that the web is engulfing us in a culture of distraction in which it becomes impossible to focus and think clearly. Greenfield and other neuroscientists warn that this culture of distraction is reshaping how our minds develop: destroying our capacity to organise our memory for ourselves, reducing memory to mere bits of disconnected stimulus and so, in the extreme, undermining our capacity to develop a distinct identity based on our own narrative of our lives. ⑥

Certainly cues for individual memory will be even more social in future and so in some ways less under our control. Your past will be recorded on your friends' social networking sites, warts and all. This will have downsides. I for one am very glad that YouTube and Facebook were not around when I was 17. Employers will no longer have to trust your account of your history set out in your CV; they will be able to look at your social networking profiles, blogs and other online activities. As yet the generation growing up with the web, however, seem pretty relaxed about this public display of private memories: if everyone is putting embarrassing material online, why worry?⑤

We will have to make quite different judgments about our memories and archives. For my parents' generation any memento sparked a precious memory of an important family event. Anything that could be preserved became precious just because it had survived.

Writing history is mainly an exciting act of detective work to piece together the story in scraps of material left behind by earlier generations. Historians of this period of history onwards will have the opposite problem: too much material to choose from.

We, the mass archivers, will face the same issues. Now we can keep so much, so easily, the question becomes how to distinguish the significant from the merely everyday. That is why the most contentious issue in the Wikipedia community has been the dispute over what counts as a notable entry. When everything and anything could have a

Wikipedia entry — my local cheese shop for example — why disallow something from being recorded for posterity? (967 words)

Words and Expressions

archivist	n.	案卷保管人
glamorous	a.	富有魅力的,迷人的
hip	a.	时髦的,新潮的
trendy	a.	流行的
avid	a.	渴望的
blog entry		博客内容
retrieve	v.	找回,重获
loft	n.	阁楼
spawn	v.	产生,引起
unalloyed	a.	纯粹的

skeptic	n.	怀疑论者
neuroscientist	n.	神经系统科学家
distraction	n.	分心的事物
collaboratively	ad.	合作地,协作地
catastrophic	a.	悲惨的,灾难的
prematurely	ad.	过早地
accountable	a.	应负责的,可解释的
sniper	n.	狙击兵

Proper Nouns

iPod 苹果电脑公司出品的一种随身听
Facebook 美国一个社交网站,翻译为"脸书"
YouTube 美国一个视频网站

News Summary

这是一篇关于互联网最新应用的新闻报道。计算机及互联网的出现为人们提供了另一种保存档案的方式,这种方式不仅可以帮助你保存文字、图片等资料,还提供很多工具使你保存的材料便于查阅,同时又能够与别人分享。现在,许多网站都提供了博客或个人空间等服务,每个人都可以把他的好友、通讯录、文章、照片和视频等上传到网站的服务器上,别人就可以点击浏览。当然,有些私人照片是加了密的。本文的作者把这种现象称为"大规模档案保存"。在介绍了各种保存在网络上的个人资料之后,作者指出,这种做法可能改变人们的记忆和思维方式,产生深远的影响。

Understanding Sentences

① 然而,奇怪的是,我们中的许多人,尤其是年轻人,时髦的和赶潮流的,无意间好像已经成了很热心的保管档案者。

② 但是,年轻人正通过博客文章和手机拍摄的照片把生活中发生的事情记录下来,他们还通过网络以半公开的形式集体进行整理。

③ 通过在社交网站上与朋友分享照片,我们创造了多份拷贝和多视角,因此我们永远不会失去任何东西,我们可能对事件有更丰富的解释。

④ 我们集体记忆能力的扩展将使我们更加具有生产力,将使政治更加可以追查。

⑤ 在数以百万的微型档案里我们共享扩大了的记忆应该是纯粹的好事,尤其是对于一

个在今后数十年间数以百万的人将失去他们的记忆,并因此而失去他们的自我感觉的老龄化社会来说。

⑥ 格林菲尔德及其他神经科学家警告说,这种分散注意力文化正在重新构建我们大脑的发展:摧毁我们自己组织记忆的能力,把记忆减少成仅仅是互相之间没有联系的碎片,并因此损害我们依据自己对生活的叙述而构建独特的身份的能力。

Exercises

Ⅰ. **Understanding Ideas in the News**

1. What is good about becoming a society of mass archiving?

A. It makes archiving sexy and glamorous.

B. It should enrich our individual and collective memory.

C. We will never forget who we were with, where, when and why.

2. What is the advantage of digital archives over the physical archive?

A. Its meaning won't be lost when the older generation is gone.

B. It can be captured and stored easily with digital cameras.

C. It can be made into multi-copies and shared.

3. What is one of the attractions of digital files?

A. It gives people a better memory.

B. It helps people to find their way back.

C. It is easier to trace their history.

4. In what way can our capacity for collective memory make politics more accountable?

A. Digital archives can be accessed by the public.

B. The powerful can impose on people their version of the event.

C. People can correct wrong statements by politicians.

5. What are the downsides of public display of private memories?

A. It may be in some ways out of control.

B. It may record your past on social networking sites.

C. It helps employers to read your account of your history.

Ⅱ. **Language Points**

trendy, avid, glamorous, retrieve, impose 这些词用来形容人们使用社交网站,或者表示某些动作。

trendy:(流行的) modern and influenced by the most recent fashions or ideas

avid:(渴望的) extremely eager or interested   e.g. *He took an avid interest in the project.*

glamorous:(富有魅力的,迷人的) attractive in an exciting and special way   e.g. *a glamorous woman/outfit* retrieve: (找回,重获) to find and bring back something   e. g. *We taught our dog to retrieve a ball.*

impose: (强加) to force someone to accept something, especially a belief or way of living   e. g. *I don't want them to impose their religious beliefs on my children.*

III. Questions for Further Study

The writing style of this news report is quite different from that of ordinary news reports, or journalistic English in general. First, paragraphs are longer; second, the writer uses multi-points of views, sometimes the first person, other times the third person. Most importantly, it is interpretive in nature, so find out how the writer presents his arguments, and analyze the issue in point.

2. Google pledge to downgrade piracy sites under review

Government raises prospect of fresh legislation as entertainment groups accuse Internet giant of dragging its feet.

Google search: several illegal filesharing sites are still ranked high for mp3 music downloads requests. (Photograph: Joel Saget/AFP/Getty Images)

Josh Halliday
The Guardian
Monday, 5 November, 2012

The government is to review Google's pledge to downgrade illegal filesharing websites in its search results, after entertainment groups accused the Internet giant of dragging its feet over the issue.①

The move comes a year after the search giant was warned by the then culture secretary Jeremy Hunt that new laws would compel it to demote such sites if it did not act first.

Now the department for culture, media and sport (DCMS) says it will examine the

Unit 11   Computer Technology and the Internet

technical changes promised by Google in August, when it pledged to relegate sites that persistently flout copyright laws.

A spokesman for the DCMS said the government would "consider our options" following the review, raising the prospect of fresh legislation that would force Google to downgrade pirated material in search results.

Entertainment groups, comprising the film, music and publishing industries, complained that top Google search results remain dominated by pirate sites despite repeated assurances from the Internet firm that it would push them down. ②

Government ministers see Google as central in the fight against online piracy because it is the main portal to the web for nine out of 10 Britons. The former culture secretary Jeremy Hunt privately threatened Google in September 2011 that he would introduce legislation to force it to take action against well-known pirate sites if the company did not take action voluntarily.

But even today, music fans who search Google for their favourite artist—for example "Katy Perry download" or "One Direction MP3"—will find the highest-ranked results point them to illegal filesharing sites.

Several of the most complained-about websites—most of which are listed by Google in its own transparency report—still appear prominently in search results for artists and films.

For example, the top search result for "Coldplay MP3" is for the website BeeMP3. com, which has received almost 400,000 copyright complaints from music groups according to Google's report. A search to stream the new James Bond film, Skyfall, also links to apparently infringing sites.

Google maintained that it was taking action against piracy websites and had demoted millions of sites every month.

A spokesman for Google said: "We continue to work closely with the industry to protect rights holders and their material. Sites with high numbers of removal notices are now more likely to appear lower in our results, we've made it easier to report pirated material and now take down more than seven million infringing links per month. ③"

However, entertainment groups complained that Google was still not doing enough to tackle the issue.

Geoff Taylor, chief executive of the BPI, said: "Google said it would stop putting the worst pirate sites at the top of search results. Google's transparency report shows they know clearly which are most infringing domains. Yet three months into the much-vaunted algorithm change, many of these illegal sites are still dominating search results for music downloads.

"We are talking to Google to try to establish why this is the case. With the launch of music in Google Play, now is the time to build a genuine partnership and for Google to show the world that it loves music. This means Google must stop dragging its feet and giving profile to illegal sites that it knows rip off everyone working in music."

Richard Mollet, chief executive of the publishing industry trade body the Publishers Association, said he welcomed Google's promise to demote infringing sites, but added, "We are yet to see evidence for a significant reduction in their presence in search results."

Kieron Sharp, director general of the Federation Against Copyright Theft, added, "Google claims to have taken steps to make infringing websites and the pirated content they promote less accessible, yet it seems that its search engine is still promoting these sites which are often making money from advertising or other payment mechanisms."

The way Google ranks piracy sites came to a head last year when Hunt told Google he would introduce new laws as part of the forthcoming Communications Act if the Internet firm did not take immediate action.④ Hunt, now health secretary, was replaced by Maria Miller as culture secretary, as part of David Cameron's cabinet reshuffle in September.

A spokesman for the DCMS did not rule out the prospect of fresh legislation to force Google to take urgent action on copyright.

It is understood that the government will meet with Google, Internet service providers, and rights holders before Christmas to discuss online piracy.

The DCMS is due to set out its policies on the creative industries as part of the Communications Review white paper to be published in early 2013.

Google's tough stance on its search results has been a major sticking point in its attempt to strike music licensing deals with the industry as it attempt to take on Apple's iTunes.⑤

The company says it received reports of 7.6m infringing web addresses in the past month—a sign of the significant scale of the problem.

Google has fought attempts to make it remove websites that have proved to be infringing entirely from its search results, arguing that this would amount to an attack on freedom of expression. The Internet firm has stressed that downgrading websites was not a "silver bullet" in the fight against piracy, and pointed out that there are comparatively few legal services to replace the illicit sites in search results. (890 words)

Words and Expressions

pledge	v.	保证	downgrade	v.	使降级,往后排
drag one's feet		拖延:在行动中或工作中有意延缓	demote	v.	降级
			persistent	a.	持久稳固的
relegate	v.	使贬职,使降级	pirate	v.	盗印,盗版
flout	v.	轻视,嘲笑,愚弄	portal	n.	入口

assurance	n.	保证,担保	infringe	v.	侵犯,违反
prominently	ad.	显著地	much-vaunted	a.	自夸的,吹嘘的
domain	n.	范围,领域	rip off		撕掉
algorithm	n.	[数]运算法则	stance	n.	姿态
illicit	a.	违法的			

Proper Nouns

Google　美国的一家互联网搜索服务公司,中文译为"谷歌"
iTunes　苹果公司的音乐下载播放软件

News Summary

这是英国《卫报》上刊登的一篇有关提供网络搜索服务的公司谷歌的报道。英国的大多数人通过谷歌提供的搜索引擎在互联网上寻找他们需要的信息,但搜索的结果把一些盗版网站排列在显著位置。尽管谷歌答应把它们放在后面,但是一直没有做到。因此,以娱乐集团为代表的公司提出控告,所以政府准备检查,并在必要时通过新的法律以约束谷歌的服务。

Understanding Sentences

① 在娱乐集团指控谷歌这个互联网巨头有意拖延之后,政府决定审查谷歌关于在它的搜索结果中减少非法文件共享网站的保证。

② 由电影、音乐和出版业组成的娱乐集团抱怨说,谷歌搜索结果中排在前面的仍然充满了盗版网站,尽管这家互联网公司反复保证会把它们排在后面。

③ 谷歌一名发言人说:"我们继续与行业密切合作,保护版权拥有者及他们的材料。被多次警告要撤销的网站现在更有可能在我们的搜索结果中排在后面,我们已经做到使举报盗版材料更加容易,我们现在每月降低超过七百万侵权网站的排名。"

④ 谷歌排列盗版网站的做法在去年达到顶峰,当时汉特告诉谷歌,如果他们不立即采取行动,他将在要颁布的通讯法中引进新法律,作为其中一部分。

⑤ 谷歌对其搜索结果的强硬立场在它试图和音乐行业达成版权协议的过程中一直是一个主要的难题。谷歌打算收购苹果的音乐管理软件。

Exercises

Ⅰ. **Understanding Ideas in the News**

1. What did entertainment groups accuse Google of?

   A. It is compel to demote illegal filesharing websites.

   B. It shows illegal filesharing websites in its search results.

   C. It acted slowly in downgrading illegal filesharing websites.

2. What action would the British government take against Google after the review?

   A. Forcing Google to downgrade pirated materials.

   B. Passing laws to make Google fulfill its promises.

C. Threatening Google to take action against pirating.

3. What websites do Google's search results point to even today?

A. Apparently infringing sites.

B. Music fan sites.

C. BeeMP3. com and others.

4. Who else will the government work together in the campaign to tackle online infringement?

A. Payment facilitators and online advertising bodies.

B. The DCMS and google.

C. Entertainment groups.

5. What has been a major sticking point in Google's attempt to take on Apple's iTune?

A. Attempts to remove pirated websites from its search results.

B. Google's tough stance on its search results.

C. The scale of piracy on the Internet.

II. Language Points

pirate, infringe, illicit, demote, relegate 在本新闻中用来描写谷歌在处理他们的搜索结果时对盗版网站的态度。

pirate：(盗印,盗版) to illegally copy a computer program, music, a film, etc. and sell it

infringe：(侵犯,违反) to break a rule, law, etc. e. g. *They infringed building regulations.*

illicit：(违法的) illegal or disapproved of by society e. g. *illicit drugs such as cocaine and cannabis*

demote：(降级) to lower someone or something in rank or position e. g. *The captain was demoted (to sergeant) for failing to fulfil his duties.*

relegate：(使贬职,使降级) to put someone or something into a lower or less important rank or position e. g. *She resigned when she was relegated to a desk job.*

III. Questions for Further Study

To fully comprehend this news report, you need to know Google and the search engine, as well as "filesharing websites" and "downgrade". Then analyze the structure of this news report to see where the lead paragraph is, and the key points mentioned in it. As it is a news report, its main purpose is to report on what is happening, rather than discuss the issue. The key points are also recurring throughout the reading.

3. Simultaneous translation by computer is getting closer

The Economist
Jan 5th, 2013, Seattle

IN "STAR TREK", a television series of the 1960s, no matter how far across the universe the Starship *Enterprise* travelled, any aliens it encountered would converse in fluent Californian English. It was explained that Captain Kirk and his crew wore tiny, computerised Universal Translators that could scan alien brainwaves and simultaneously convert their concepts into appropriate English words. [1]

Science fiction, of course. But the best sci-fi has a habit of presaging fact. Many believe the flip-open communicators also seen in that first "Star Trek" series inspired the design of clamshell mobile phones. And, on a more sinister note, several armies and military-equipment firms are working on high-energy laser weapons that bear a striking resemblance to phasers. [2] How long, then, before automatic simultaneous translation becomes the norm, and all those tedious language lessons at school are declared redundant?

Not, perhaps, as long as language teachers, interpreters and others who make their living from mutual incomprehension might like. A series of announcements over the past few months from sources as varied as mighty Microsoft and string-and-sealing-wax private inventors suggest that workable, if not yet perfect, simultaneous-translation devices are now close at hand.

Over the summer, Will Powell, an inventor in London, demonstrated a system that translates both sides of a conversation between English and Spanish speakers—if they are patient, and speak slowly. Each interlocutor wears a hands-free headset linked to a mobile phone, and sports special goggles that display the translated text like subtitles in a foreign film.

In November, NTT DoCoMo, the largest mobile-phone operator in Japan, introduced a service that translates phone calls between Japanese and English, Chinese or Korean. Each party speaks consecutively, with the firm's computers eavesdropping and translating his words in a matter of seconds. The result is then spoken in a man's or woman's voice, as appropriate.

Microsoft's contribution is perhaps the most beguiling. When Rick Rashid, the firm's chief research officer, spoke in English at a conference in Tianjin in October, his peroration was translated live into Mandarin, appearing first as subtitles on overhead video screens, and then as a computer-generated voice.③ Remarkably, the Chinese version of Mr. Rashid's speech shared the characteristic tones and inflections of his own voice.

Que?

Though the three systems are quite different, each faces the same problems. The first challenge is to recognise and digitise speech. In the past, speech-recognition software has parsed what is being said into its constituent sounds, known as phonemes. There are around 25 of these in Mandarin, 40 in English and over 100 in some African languages. Statistical speech models and a probabilistic technique called Gaussian mixture modelling are then used to identify each phoneme, before reconstructing the original word.④ This is the technology most commonly found in the irritating voice-mail jails of companies' telephone-answering systems. It works acceptably with a restricted vocabulary, but try anything more free-range and it mistakes at least one word in four.

The translator Mr. Rashid demonstrated employs several improvements. For a start, it aims to identify not single phonemes but sequential triplets of them, known as senones.⑤ English has more than 9,000 of these. If they can be recognised, though, working out which words they are part of is far easier than would be the case starting with phonemes alone.

Microsoft's senone identifier relies on deep neural networks, a mathematical technique inspired by the human brain. Such artificial networks are pieces of software composed of virtual neurons. Each neuron weighs the strengths of incoming signals from its neighbours and send outputs based on those to other neighbours, which then do the same thing.⑥ Such a network can be trained to match an input to an output by varying the strengths of the links between its component neurons.

One thing known for sure about real brains is that their neurons are arranged in layers. A deep neural network copies this arrangement. Microsoft's has nine layers. The bottom one learns features of the processed sound waves of speech. The next layer learns combinations of those features, and so on up the stack, with more sophisticated correlations gradually emerging. The top layer makes a guess about which senone it thinks the system has heard. By using recorded libraries of speech with each senone tagged, the correct result can be fed back into the network, in order to improve its performance.

Microsoft's researchers claim that their deep-neural-network translator makes at least a third fewer errors than traditional systems and in some cases mistakes as few as one word in eight.⑦ Google has also started using deep neural networks for speech recognition (although not yet translation) on its Android smartphones, and claims they have reduced errors by over 20%. Nuance, another provider of speech-recognition services, reports similar improvements. Deep neural networks can be computationally demanding, so most speech-recognition and translation software (including that from Microsoft, Google and Nuance) runs in the cloud, on powerful online servers accessible in turn by smartphones or home computers. (822 words)

Words and Expressions

alien	a.	外国的, 不同的	converse	v.	谈话, 交谈
simultaneously	ad.	同时地	convert	v.	转变, 转化
presage	v.	预示	clamshell	n.	蚌壳状
sinister	a.	险恶的	phaser	n.	移相器
tedious	a.	冗长乏味的	interlocutor	n.	对话者, 对谈者
goggles	n.	（复数）风镜, 护目镜	consecutively	ad.	连续地
eavesdrop	v.	偷听	beguiling	a.	欺骗的, 消遣的
peroration	n.	夸夸其谈的演讲	inflection	n.	词形变化
parse	v.	划分	constituent	n.	委托人, 要素
probabilistic	a.	或然说的	sequential	a.	连续的, 相续的
triplet	n.	三个一组, 三份	senone	n.	音团
neural	a.	神经系统的	stack	n.	堆栈
neuron	n.	[解]神经细胞, 神经元			

Proper Nouns

"Star Trek"　《星际旅行》, 美国科幻娱乐影视系列

NTT DoCoMo　日本一家3G移动电信服务公司, 译为"都科摩"。

Gaussian　高斯, 德国数学家, 他发现了高斯函数。

Android　一个开放源代码移动操作系统, 主要用于智慧型手机及平板电脑, 译为"安卓"。

News Summary

自从计算机出现以来, 利用计算机来进行翻译一直就是人们研究的一个主要课题。本篇新闻介绍了最近出现的三种翻译系统并介绍了它们各自利用的原理。文章使用了一些专业词语来解释有关计算和对人脑神经的研究。根据介绍, 最新的研究成果已经使机器翻译达到一个新的高度, 翻译的结果更加准确, 速度也更快。

Understanding Sentences

① 据说科克船长及他的水手们都戴着一种微型的、计算机控制的通用翻译器,它可以扫描异族人的大脑脑波,同时把他们的概念转化成恰当的英语词。

② 而且,更加恶意的一种说明是,好几个兵种和军用设备公司正在研制一种与移相器非常相似的高能激光武器。

③ 十月份,当公司的主要研究官员里克拉什得在天津一次会议上用英语发言时,他的演讲被现场翻译成中文,开始时好像字幕一样出现在视频投影的屏幕上,然后又传出计算机产生的声音。

④ 然后使用统计的言语模式和一种称为高斯混合函数的或然率技术来识别每一个音素,然后再重构原来的词。

⑤ 开始,它的目标不是识别单独的音素,而是三个一组的音素,叫音团。

⑥ 每个神经元估量从它周围来的信号的强度,并依据结果向其他周围的神经元发出信号,其他神经元又重复同样的动作。

⑦ 微软的研究人员声称,他们的深度神经网翻译器比传统的系统所产生的错误至少少三分之一,在某些例子上,错误少至每八个词一个。

Exercises

I. Understanding Ideas in the News

1. What is implied in the question about how long will it be that language lessons are no longer necessary?

   A. Sci-fi has a habit of presaging fact.
   B. Workable simultaneous translation devices will be available soon.
   C. Language teachers and interpreters don't like it.

2. What does each interlocutor using Will Powell's system wear?

   A. Eye-glasses.
   B. A mobile phone and sports glasses.
   C. A headset and goggles.

3. What is significant about NTT DoCoMo's translation service?

   A. It uses a firm's computer.
   B. It is very fast.
   C. It translates between four languages.

4. What improvement did the translator Mr. Rashid demonstrated make?

   A. It identifies sequential triplets of phonemes.
   B. It uses a probabilistic technique.
   C. It is computer-generated voice.

5. What is the limitation of speech-recognition software in the past?

   A. It may be irritating in voice-mail jails.

B. It cannot recognize and digitize speech.

C. It works only with a restricted vocabulary.

II. Language Points

converse, convert, simultaneous, constituent, sequential 这几个词用来介绍有关机器翻译的最基本的知识。

converse:（谈话，交谈）to talk between two or more people in which thoughts, feelings and ideas are expressed, questions are asked and answered, or news and information are exchanged e. g. *She's so shy that conversing with her can be quite difficult.*

convert:（转变，转化）to (cause something or someone to) change in form, character or opinion e. g. *Could we convert the small bedroom into a second bathroom?*

simultaneous:（同时的）happening or being done at exactly the same time e. g. *There were several simultaneous explosions in different cities.*

constituent:（委托人，要素）one of the parts that a substance or combination is made of e. g. *What are the basic constituents of the mixture?*

sequential:（连续的，相续的）following a particular order e. g. *The publishers claim that the book constitutes the first sequential exposition of events and thus of the history of the revolution.*

III. Questions for Further Study

This technology report comes from the British weekly *The Economist*. News reports for a magazine may be quite different from that for a newspaper, and technology news may not be the same as hard news. Study this article carefully and sum up some of the difference in magazine articles, such as the longer paragraph and more advanced vocabulary.

英语报刊知识介绍

新闻分析、深度报道

新闻分析或深度报道的文章对有关新闻进行深入全面的报道,通常提供比较多的信息,并把整个新闻事件的过程重现出来。新闻分析还把对新闻事件的报道和记者的分析结合起来,帮助读者理解有关新闻事件的含义和影响。

深度报道这一概念最早出现于西方新闻学论著。美国新闻学者认为,深度报道是解释性报道的深化和发展。解释性报道提供事实,展现背景和意义,深度报道则通过挖掘新闻的具体材料和背景,揭示其意义。

1. A news-in-depth from *The Atlantic* entitled "If America Left Iraq"

HYPOTHETICALS
If America Left Iraq
The case for cutting and running

BY NIR ROSEN

At some point—whether sooner or later—U.S. troops will leave Iraq. I have spent much of the occupation reporting from Baghdad, Kirkuk, Mosul, Fallujah, and elsewhere in the country, and I can tell you that a growing majority of Iraqis would like it to be sooner. As the occupation wears on, more and more Iraqis chafe at its failure to provide stability or even electricity, and they have grown to hate the explosions, gunfire, and constant war, and also the daily annoyances: having to wait hours in traffic because the Americans have closed off half the city; having to sit in that traffic behind a U.S. military vehicle pointing its weapons at them; having to endure constant searches and arrests. Before the January 30 elections this year the Association of Muslim Scholars—Iraq's most important Sunni Arab body, and one closely tied to the indigenous majority of the insurgency—called for a commitment to a timely U.S. withdrawal as a condition for its participation in the vote. (In exchange the association promised to rein in the resistance.) It's not just Sunnis who have demanded a withdrawal: the Shiite cleric Muqtada al-Sadr, who is immensely popular among the young and the poor, has made a similar demand. So has the mainstream leader of the Shiites' Supreme Council for the Islamic Revolution in Iraq, Abdel Aziz al-Hakim, who made his first call for U.S. withdrawal as early as April 23, 2003.

If the people the U.S. military is ostensibly protecting want it to go, why do the soldiers stay? The most common answer is that it would be irresponsible for the United States to depart before some measure of peace has been assured. The American presence, this argument goes, is the only thing keeping Iraq from an all-out civil war that could take millions of lives and would profoundly destabilize the region. But is that really the case? Let's consider the key questions surrounding the prospect of an imminent American withdrawal.

Would the withdrawal of U.S. troops ignite a civil war between Sunnis and Shiites?

No. That civil war is already under way—in large part *because* of the American presence. The longer the United States stays, the more it fuels Sunni hostility toward Shiite "collaborators." Were America not in Iraq, Sunni leaders could negotiate and participate without fear that they themselves would be branded traitors and collaborators by their constituents. Sunni leaders have said this in official public statements; leaders of the resistance have told me the same thing in private. The Iraqi government, which is currently dominated by Shiites, would lose its quisling stigma. Iraq's security forces, also primarily Shiite, would no longer be working on behalf of foreign infidels against fellow Iraqis, but would be able to function independently and recruit Sunnis to a truly national force. The mere announcement of an intended U.S. withdrawal would allow Sunnis to come to the table and participate in defining the new Iraq.

But if American troops aren't in Baghdad, what's to stop the Sunnis from launching an assault and seizing control of the city?

Sunni forces could not mount such an assault. The preponderance of power now lies with the majority Shiites and the Kurds, and the Sunnis know this. Sunni fighters wield only small arms and explosives, not Saddam's tanks and helicopters, and are very weak compared with the cohesive, better armed, and numerically superior Shiite and Kurdish militias. Most important, Iraqi nationalism—not intramural rivalry—is the chief motivator for both Shiites and Sunnis. Most insurgency groups view themselves as waging a *muqawama*—a resistance—rather than a *jihad*. This is evident in their names and in their propaganda. For instance, the units commanded by the Association of Muslim Scholars are named after the 1920 revolt against the British. Others have names such as Iraqi Islamic Army and Flame of Iraq. They display the Iraqi flag rather than a flag of *jihad*. Insurgent attacks are meant primarily to punish those who have collaborated with the Americans and to deter future collaboration.

Wouldn't a U.S. withdrawal embolden the insurgency?

No. If the occupation were to end, so, too, would the insurgency. After

2. A news analysis on the front page of *Los Angeles Times*

GAZA'S DILEMMA: WAR OR BLOCKADE

For some, end to Israeli embargo is greater goal

By Alexandra Zavis
and Batsheva Sobelman

GAZA CITY — Fatima Helles desperately wants Israel's war with Hamas to end.

Her family of 19 was driven from its home in the northern Gaza Strip by fierce Israeli shelling. All of them moved in with her husband's family, but the fighting followed them there. They are now living under a tree at Gaza City's main hospital, Shifa.

But when asked whether she supports efforts to negotiate a cease-fire, the grandmother hesitates.

"I don't want to die. I don't want my people to die," she said. But she doesn't want life to go back to the way it was either.

"We can't breathe," she said. "Most of my kids can't find work. We live on handouts."

It is a common sentiment on the Gazan side of this war. Despite more than two weeks of intense shelling that has claimed nearly 700 Palestinian lives and sent more than 100,000 people fleeing from their homes, many insist that they want their leaders to keep fighting until they achieve Hamas militants' stated demand: an end to the years-old embargo on Gaza.

Israel and Egypt impose tight restrictions on movement in and out of the narrow coastal strip, which has been controlled by the Islamic militant group since 2007. They say the blockade is necessary to limit Hamas' access to materiel, including the rockets it has been firing by the hundreds at Israel.

But Palestinians say it has choked economic development in Gaza, separated families, prevented young people from getting an education and kept residents isolated from the world.

"I think the fact that people, even in the midst of this terrible physical destruction, are still talking about the economy is testament to how devastating the closure has been for people living in Gaza," said Sari Bashi, co-founder of Gisha, an Israel-based legal center that advocates for greater freedom of movement for Palestinians.

As Secretary of State John F. Kerry and United Nations Secretary-General Ban Ki-moon shuttled among regional leaders Wednesday trying to enlist support for a cease-fire in the 16-day-old conflict, Hamas militants
[See Gaza, A6]

CAROLYN COLE *Los Angeles Times*

IN GAZA CITY, Palestinians line up for water at a shelter. The 16-day-old conflict between Hamas and Israel has claimed nearly 700 Palestinian lives and displaced more than 100,000 people.

In explaining the need for secrecy, federal agents wrote that the Sheriff's Department had interfered with previous FBI investigations. The agents described instances in which sheriff's officials allegedly retaliated against an informant, denied agents access to a key source in jail and prevented a federal task force from gaining access to "jail communications."

As further justification for secrecy, FBI agents wrote that a nephew of Baca's who worked in the jails was suspected of being "one of the most egregious inmate beaters." The nephew has never been charged, and through his attorney, he denied any misconduct.

The FBI records also cited "a long history of criminal allegations" against Baca himself and two of his undersheriffs, including claims that Baca issued concealed weapons permits to reward campaign contributors and that sheriff's employees pressured tow truck companies for political donations. None of the allegations led to criminal charges, and some appear to have been based on little more than news reports or unconfirmed tips from informants.

Nevertheless, FBI agents wrote that the allegations and past instances of obstruction led "to the inescapable conclusion that this investigation could only be worked independent of the Los Angeles [County] Sheriff's Department."

The confidential documents vividly illustrate the depth of the bureau's distrust of Baca and his inner circle. The records indicate that FBI agents searched their files on Baca to make the case that he and his con-
[See Baca, A12]

Unit 12　Science and Technology

As science and technology is becoming more and more important in the world today, the news paper carries news reports on the recent development of scientific research and latest products of technology. Most of the news reports in this genre are not academic, professional articles, but popular readings that explains some profound theory or any significant discovery in common language that can be understood by the reader. There might be sub-divisions into the topics grouped under this heading, such as earth science, engineering or medicine, and this chapter contains three articles on smoking, the climate and ecosystem.

　　由于科学技术在今天的世界上已经变得越来越重要,报纸也刊登有关科学研究的最新成果和技术应用的最新产品。此类新闻报道的大部分不是学术性和专业性的文章,而是用简单语言说明某种深奥的理论或重大发明的文章,一般读者都能看得懂的。科学技术这一总题目还可以分成不同的类别,如地球科学、工程或医学等。本章收集的三篇报道是关于吸烟的副作用和气候、生态系统等的。

1. Grandma's curse

Some of the effects of smoking may be passed from grandmother to grandchild.

Unit 12 Science and Technology

Think of your grandchildren!

The Economist
Nov. 3rd, 2012

ONE of biology's hottest topics is epigenetics. The term itself covers a multitude of sins. Strictly speaking, it refers to the regulation of gene expression by the chemical modification of DNA, or of the histone proteins in which DNA is usually wrapped. ① This modification is either the addition of methyl groups (a carbon atom and three hydrogens) to the DNA or of acetyl groups (two carbons, three hydrogens and an oxygen) to the histones. Methylation switches genes off. Acetylation switches them on. Since, in a multicellular organism, different cells need different genes to be active, such regulation is vital.

What has got a lot of people excited, though, is the idea that epigenetic switches might be transmitted down the generations. Some see this as contrary to Darwinism, since it would permit characteristics acquired during an organism's lifetime to be passed on to its offspring, as suggested by a rival theory of evolution put forward by Jean-Baptiste Lamarck. ② This is an exaggeration. The DNA sequence itself is not being permanently altered. Even those epigenetic changes that are inherited seem to be subsequently reversible. But the idea that acquired characteristics can be inherited at all is still an important and novel one, and a worrying example of the phenomenon has been published this week in *BioMed Central Medicine*. ③

The study in question, by Virender Rehan of the Los Angeles Biomedical Research Institute, and his colleagues, was of the intergenerational effects of nicotine. It was done in rats, but a rat's physiology is sufficiently similar to a human's to suspect the same thing may be true in *Homo sapiens*. In a nutshell, Dr. Rehan showed that if pregnant rats are exposed to nicotine, not only will their offspring develop the asthma induced by this drug, so will the offspring of those offspring. ④

Dr. Rehan and his team injected their rats with nicotine when they were six days pregnant. (Rat pregnancies last 22 days.) They then allowed them to give birth and raised the pups to the age of three weeks, before some were examined. The rest were allowed to mature and breed, and their own offspring were similarly examined. There was, however, no further administration of nicotine.

The pups of the treated mothers had asthmatic lungs. The organs' airways were constricted, and molecular analysis showed abnormally high levels of fibronectin and collagen—which would stiffen the lung tissue—and also high levels of receptor molecules for nicotine. ⑤ That was expected, since the developing embryos were exposed to the nicotine when their mothers were treated. However, when the team did similar tests on the grand-offspring of the treated mothers, they got similar results. Those grand-offspring had not been exposed to nicotine.

The cause of the grand-offsprings' asthma, Dr. Rehan believes, is epigenetic modification. Nicotine is not only affecting lung cells, but also affecting sex cells in ways that cause the lungs which ultimately develop from those cells to express their genes in the same abnormal ways.

Exactly what those epigenetic changes are is hard to track down. The team have started looking, but could find no clear pattern except that one form of nicotine-induced acetylation, that of H3 histones (histones come in five varieties), could be blocked by a molecule called RGZ. This molecule is also known to protect lungs against the asthma-causing effects of nicotine. That suggests it is the acetylation of H3 histones rather than the methylation of DNA itself that is creating the effect.

Which crucial genes these histones surround remains obscure. Nor have the team yet found out whether the epigenetic effect they have discovered reaches further than grand-offspring. If it does, though, it suggests that epigenetics really might act like the biblical curse: that the sins of the fathers (or, in this case, the mothers) will be visited on the sons, even unto the third and fourth generations. (639 words)

Words and Expressions

epigenetics	n.	表征遗传学	gene	n.	[遗传]基因
histone	n.	[生化]组织蛋白	protein	n.	蛋白质
wrap	v.	包，覆盖	methylation	n.	甲基化作用
acetylation	n.	[化]加乙酰基于	multicellular	a.	多细胞的
transmit	v.	遗传，传播	reversible	a.	可逆的
nicotine	n.	烟碱	asthma	n.	[医]哮喘
pup	n.	小狗，幼畜	constrict	v.	压缩
fibronectin	n.	纤维蛋白（一种高分子量糖蛋白）	collagen	n.	胶原质
			receptor	n.	受体
stiffen	v.	变黏，变硬	modification	n.	更改，修改
embryo	n.	胚胎，胎儿			

Proper Nouns

DNA　脱氧核糖核酸，可组成遗传指令的一种生物大分子
Darwinism　达尔文主义（达尔文是英国生物学家，提出进化论）
Jean-Baptiste Lamarck　让·巴蒂斯特·拉马克，法国科学家，1809年阐述了他的进化论
Homo sapiens　智人，意为"有智慧的人"

News Summary

吸烟危害健康，这是大家都知道的事实。在发达国家里，公共场合吸烟也受到限制。这篇新闻主要是报道洛杉矶生物医学研究所进行的一项关于烟碱（俗称"尼古丁"）在遗传上

的作用的研究。这项研究初步发现,烟碱的作用可以遗传到第三代,但对其中这一胚胎学上的变化具体是如何发生的还不清楚。也就是说,吸烟可以危害到第三代。为了帮助读者,文章的开头用了两段话介绍有关基因变异的知识。

Understanding Sentences

① 严格地说,它(表征遗传学)指脱氧核糖核酸的化学改变对基因表露的调节作用,或对通常包裹着脱氧核糖核酸的组蛋白的调节作用。

② 有些人认为这是跟达尔文主义相反的,因为它会允许一个有机体在它的生命中获得的特点被遗传给后代,这正如让·巴蒂斯特·拉马克所提出的另一种进化论所主张的一样。

③ 但是获得的特点毕竟能够被继承,这一说法仍是一个重要和新颖的理论,而这一现象的一个令人担心的例子在本周的《生物医学中心医学》上发表了。

④ 里汉医生在一个坚果壳里展示了如果怀孕的老鼠接触到烟碱,不仅它们的后代会获得由这种药物诱发的哮喘病,它们后代的后代也会得病。

⑤ 这个器官的呼吸通道被收窄了,分子分析表示它的纤维蛋白和胶原质的含量异常高——这些会使肺部的组织变得坚硬——同时也有很高含量的接纳烟碱的分子。

Exercises

Ⅰ. **Understanding Ideas in the News**

1. What is epigenetics?
A. The effect of DNA on gene expression.
B. The modification of histone proteins.
C. The addition of methyl groups.
2. What is exciting in epigenetics studies?
A. New development on Darwinism.
B. The DNA sequence itself is permanently altered.
C. Acquired characteristics can be inherited.
3. What did Dr. Rehan and his team show in their research?
A. Pregnant rats exposed to nicotine may not have offspring.
B. The effect of nicotine may be shown in the third generation.
C. Nicotine is injected into their rats when they are pregnant.
4. How did Dr. Rehan explain the findings of the experiment?
A. Nicotine also affects sex cells.
B. The lungs are ultimately developed from those cells.
C. The gene can be expressed even in the third generation.
5. What does Dr. Rehan believe is the cause of the grand-offsprings' asthma?
A. A molecule called RGZ.   B. The H3 histones.
C. Epigenetic modification.

Ⅱ. **Language Points**

epigenetics, histone, asthma, transmit, inherit 这几个是比较专业化的词语。

epigenetics: (表征遗传学) the study of cellular and physiological traits that are inheritable by daughter cells and not caused by changes in the DNA sequence

histone: (组织蛋白) highly alkaline protein found in eukaryotic cell nuclei that package and order the DNA into structural units called nucleosomes

asthma: (哮喘) a medical condition which makes breathing difficult by causing the air passages to become narrow or blocked

transmit: (遗传,传播) to pass something from one person or place to another   e. g. *a sexually transmitted disease*

inherit: (继承, 遗传而得) to be born with the same physical or mental characteristics as one of your parents or grandparents   e. g. *Rosie inherited her red hair from her mother.*

III. Questions for Further Study

This news report is more interpretive in nature than narrative, but as a news report, it has all the characteristics of reporting an event—the findings of some scientific research. Analyze how the main idea of the news is expressed in the lead paragraph. Also notice how interpretation is given in the reporting so as to make this professional issue easy to understand by the layman.

2. It's snowing, and it really feels like the start of a mini ice age

Something is up with our winter weather. Could it be the Sun is having a slow patch?

By Boris Johnson
The Daily Telegraph
9:54PM GMT, 20 Jan, 2013

Unit 12　Science and Technology

"The Sun is god!" cried JMW Turner as he died, and plenty of other people have thought there was much in his analysis. The Aztecs agreed, and so did the pharaohs of Egypt. We are an arrogant lot these days, and we tend to underestimate the importance of our governor and creator. ①

We forget that we were once just a clod of cooled-down solar dust; we forget that without the Sun there would have been no photosynthesis, no hydrocarbons — and that it was the great celestial orb that effectively called life into being on Earth. ② In so far as we are able to heat our homes or turn on our computers or drive to work it is thanks to the unlocking of energy from the Sun.

As a species, we human beings have become so blind with conceit and self-love that we genuinely believe that the fate of the planet is in our hands — when the reality is that everything, or almost everything, depends on the behaviour and caprice of the gigantic thermonuclear fireball around which we revolve. ③

I say all this because I am sitting here staring through the window at the flowerpot and the bashed-up barbecue, and I am starting to think this series of winters is not a coincidence. The snow on the flowerpot, since I have been staring, has got about an inch thicker. The barbecue is all but invisible. By my calculations, this is now the fifth year in a row that we have had an unusual amount of snow; and by unusual I mean snow of a kind that I don't remember from my childhood: snow that comes one day, and then sticks around for a couple of days, followed by more. ④

I remember snow that used to come and settle for just long enough for a single decent snowball fight before turning to slush; I don't remember winters like this. Two days ago I was cycling through Trafalgar Square and saw icicles on the traffic lights; and though I am sure plenty of readers will say I am just unobservant, I don't think I have seen that before. I am all for theories about climate change, and would not for a moment dispute the wisdom or good intentions of the vast majority of scientists.

But I am also an empiricist; and I observe that something appears to be up with our winter weather, and to call it "warming" is obviously to strain the language. I see from the BBC website that there are scientists who say that "global warming" is indeed the cause of the cold and snowy winters we seem to be having. A team of Americans and Chinese experts have postulated that the melting of the Arctic ice means that the whole North Atlantic is being chilled as the floes start to break off — like a Martini refrigerated by ice cubes.

I do not have the expertise to comment on the Martini theory; I merely observe that there are at least some other reputable scientists who say that it is complete tosh, or at least that there is no evidence to support it. ⑤ We are expecting the snow and cold to go on for several days, and though London transport has coped very well so far, with few delays or cancellations, I can't help brooding on my own amateur meteorological observations. I wish I knew more about what is going on, and why. It is time to consult once again the learned astrophysicist, Piers Corbyn.

Now Piers has a very good record of forecasting the weather. He has been bang on about these cold winters. Like JMW Turner and the Aztecs he thinks we should be paying more attention to the Sun. According to Piers, global temperature depends not on concentrations of CO2 but on the mood of our celestial orb. Sometime too bright the eye of heaven shines, said Shakespeare, and often is his gold complexion dimmed. That is more or less right. There are times in astronomical history when the Sun has been churning out more stuff — protons and electrons and what have you — than at other times. When the Sun has plenty of sunspots, he bathes the Earth in abundant rays.

When the solar acne diminishes, it seems that the Earth gets colder. No one contests that when the planet palpably cooled from 1645 to 1715 — the Maunder minimum, which saw the freezing of the Thames — there was a diminution of solar activity. The same point is made about the so-called Dalton minimum, from 1790 to 1830. And it is the view of Piers Corbyn that we are now seeing exactly the same phenomenon today.

Lower solar activity means—broadly speaking—that there is less agitation of the warm currents of air from the tropical to the temperate zones, so that a place like Britain can expect to be colder and damper in summer, and colder and snowier in winter.⑥ "There is every indication that we are at the beginning of a mini ice age," he says. "The general decline in solar activity is lower than Nasa's lowest prediction of five years ago. That could be very bad news for our climate. We are in for a prolonged cold period. Indeed, we could have 30 years of general cooling."

Now I am not for a second saying that I am convinced Piers is right; and to all those scientists and environmentalists who will go wild with indignation on the publication of this article, I say, relax. I certainly support reducing CO2 by retrofitting homes and offices—not least since that reduces fuel bills. I want cleaner vehicles.

I am speaking only as a layman who observes that there is plenty of snow in our winters these days, and who wonders whether it might be time for government to start taking seriously the possibility — however remote — that Corbyn is right. If he is, that will have big implications for agriculture, tourism, transport, aviation policy and the economy as a whole. Of course it still seems a bit nuts to talk of the encroachment of a mini ice age.

But it doesn't seem as nuts as it did five years ago. I look at the snowy waste outside, and I have an open mind. (1044 words)

Words and Expressions

| pharaoh | n. | 法老王 | clod | n. | 土块 |

celestial	a.	天体的		orb	n.	球,块
species	n.	物种		conceit	a.	自大,骄傲
meteorological	a.	气象学的		astrophysicist	n.	天体物理学家
caprice	n.	无常,任性		thermonuclear	a.	热核的
bashed-up	a.	深埋起来的		slush	n.	融雪
icicle	n.	冰柱		empiricist	n.	经验主义者
strain	v.	紧张,拉紧		postulate	v.	假定
floe	n.	冰块		tosh	n.	废话,胡说
bang	v.	发巨响		complexion	n.	面色,肤色
churn	v.	搅拌,搅动		solar acne		太阳黑点
palpably	ad.	可触知的		diminution	n.	减少,减低
agitation	n.	激动,兴奋		indignation	n.	愤慨
retrofit	v.	重新安装				

Proper Nouns

JMW Turner　约瑟夫·玛罗德·威廉·特纳,十九世纪英国浪漫派风景画家
the Aztecs　阿扎克人,指墨西哥中部的一个民族
Dalton minimum　以英国天文学家约翰·道尔顿命名的一个太阳活动不活跃的时期
the Maunder minimum　墨得尔最少论,指十七至十八世纪太阳黑子活动减少的时期

News Summary

这是英国《每日电讯报》上的一篇专栏文章,作者谈论了2012年英国遭遇到一个寒冷的冬天。作者先描写了他所观察到的一些现象,以说明今年冬天的雪下得大,而且好几天都不融化。然后引用天体物理学家比埃斯的观点,试图说明造成这种格外寒冷的天气的原因是由于太阳黑子减少和太阳活动的放慢,而不是更多地由于大气中二氧化碳含量的增加。文章还引用了一些文学大师的语言,风格幽默。

Understanding Sentences

① 这些年来,我们越来越自高自大,忽视了上天和造物主的重要性。

② 我们忘记了我们曾经只是冷却下来的太阳系尘埃构成的一块土,我们忘记了没有太阳就没有光合作用和碳水化物,我们忘记了正是这个巨大的天体使地球上有了生命。

③ 作为一种物种,我们人类已经因为自大和自爱而变得如此盲目,以至于我们真诚地相信这个星球的命运掌握在我们手中——事实是,一切,或几乎一切,依赖于我们绕着它旋转的那个巨大火球的行为和喜怒。

④ 按我的计算,今年是连续第五年有这么大的降雪,我指的是从我孩提时代以来不曾记得的如此大的雪:今天下的雪,留在地面上好几天,接着又下起雪来了。

⑤ 我并不懂专业知识,无法评论这种关于马提尼的说法,我只是想说,至少还有一些有名望的科学家说这是完全的胡说八道,或至少并没有证据可以支持这一说法。

⑥ 广泛地说,比较低的太阳系活动意味从热带地区向温带地区流动的暖气流活动较

少,因此像伦敦这个地方夏天可能比较冷和潮湿,冬天可能更冷,下更多雪。

Exercises

Ⅰ. **Understanding Ideas in the News**

1. What did the cold weather prompt the writer to think of?
   A. The importance of environmental protection.
   B. The importance of the Sun to people on Earth.
   C. The poems written by Shakespeare.

2. What special scenes did the writer observe as proof of an extraordinary cold winter?
   A. The flowerpot and barbecue.
   B. The snow in the garden and icicles on the traffic lights.
   C. The slush along the street.

3. How does the "global warming" theory explain for the cold and snowy winters?
   A. The melting of the Artic ice chills it.
   B. It is to "strain" the language.
   C. The floes start to break off.

4. According to Piers Corbyn, what does global temperature depend on?
   A. The concentrations of CO_2.
   B. The moving the Earth round the Sun.
   C. The behavior of the Sun.

5. What point does the writer want to make about the cold weather and the different theories?
   A. He doesn't want to counter the CO_2 theory.
   B. He only observes that there is plenty of snow this winter.
   C. He thinks it might be time to reconsider the theory of a mini ice age.

Ⅱ. **Language Points**

slush, floe, diminution, agitation, complexion 这些词在新闻中用来描述作者对气候变化的观察。

slush:(融雪) snow that is lying on the ground and has started to melt

floe:(冰块) a large area of ice floating in the sea

diminution:(减少,减低) the act or process of diminishing; a lessening or reduction
e. g. *Regular exercise can result in a general diminution in stress levels.*

agitation:(激动,兴奋) the act of agitating or the state of being agitated e. g. *The anti-war agitation is beginning to worry the government.*

complexion:(面色,肤色) the natural appearance of the skin on a person's face, especially its colour or quality e. g. *a dark/fair complexion*

Ⅲ. **Questions for Further Study**

There is a variety of newspaper articles called comment, which usually follows the coverage of a certain event in the newspaper. Comments are usually written by the editors of a newspaper, or by some senior reports, and in the name of a columnist. It may also begin with a descriptive lead, and with explanation about the ideas in question. Read this comment and find out on what topic the writer comments on, and how he makes the language vivid.

3. Climate change alters ecosystems from Walden Pond to "The Shack"

Using historical data collected by famous naturalists and authors Henry David Thoreau and Aldo Leopold, scientists have linked early flower blooms to warm springs. This is the first time researchers have analyzed patterns in these two sets of data together.

Walden Pond has seen warmer temperatures and earlier spring flowerings since Henry David Thoreau first stayed there in 1852.

By Tia Ghose
Christian Science Monitor
January 16, 2013

The warmest springs on record caused flowers to bloom at their earliest dates in decades at two historic sites, according to new research.

The findings, published online today (Jan. 16) in the journal *PLOS ONE*, show just how much climate change has altered ecosystems throughout the temperate areas of the United States. ① The study used 161-year-old data on flowering times from Henry David Thoreau's notebooks, as well as nearly 80-year-old data from the famous naturalist Aldo Leopold.

Scientists had previously described the Thoreau records but they hadn't combined the two naturalists' findings until now.

"Record warm temperatures (in 2010 and 2012) have resulted in record early flowering times," said study researcher Elizabeth Ellwood of Boston University.

Famous naturalists

Henry David Thoreau was one of the most iconic figures of the 19th century. The famous naturalist and poet wrote the book *Walden* about his years living at idyllic Walden Pond in Concord, Mass. Starting in 1852 and at different points throughout his life, he also created the first "spreadsheets of flowering dates" for many well-known flowers, including the wild columbine, the pink-lady slipper orchid and the marsh marigold, Ellwood said. ②

Similarly, the naturalist Leopold took detailed records of first flowering times at a site called "The Shack" in wilderness near the Wisconsin River, starting in 1935.

"It's the iconic equivalent to Walden Pond for Wisconsinites," Ellwood told LiveScience.

While scholars knew of these flowering observations, many were scattered in different libraries and archives, and no one had systematically analyzed their patterns, she said.

Hotter springs, earlier blooms

To do so, Ellwood and her colleagues gathered all of Thoreau's flowering records from several archives. They then compared flowering dates with spring temperatures for 32 different flowering plants.

They found that as temperatures warmed over the last 161 years, the date of first blooms of the season crept forward, too — about 10 days earlier than when Thoreau first visited the site. ③ During the record-breaking years of 2010 and 2012, flowering happened a full 20 to 21 days earlier. The average spring temperature at Walden Pond has increased about 6 degrees Fahrenheit (3.4 degrees Celsius) since Thoreau's time.

Similarly, at The Shack, as average spring temperatures rose about 3 degrees Fahrenheit (1.7 degrees Celsius) over the last eight decades, first flowering came a week early for the 23 species they studied. During the hottest years in the United States (2010 and 2012), flowering came 24 days earlier than in Leopold's time.

Still adapting

The research may have tracked just two sites, but has broad implications, said Elizabeth Wolkovich, a climate change ecologist at the University of British Columbia who was not involved in the study.

"One is deep within the country and one is on the coast," Wolkovich said.

That means the findings probably apply to temperate climates throughout a large swath of the United States, she told LiveScience.

Though Thoreau and Leopold's works have highlighted how much climate change alters ecosystems, in some ways, the findings are good news.

At some point, the climate will get too hot for plants to survive without evolving, but the fact that the plant flowering time is still changing in step with the temperature means they haven't hit that point yet, said David Inouye, a University of Maryland biologist who was not involved in the study. ④ (558 words)

Words and Expressions

ecosystem	n.	生态系统		iconic	a.	具有肖像特点的
idyllic	a.	田园短诗的		columbine	n.	耧斗菜
orchid	n.	兰，兰花		marsh	n.	湿地，沼泽，沼泽地
marigold	n.	[植]万寿菊，金盏草		shack	n.	小室
creep	v.	爬，蹑手蹑脚		temperate	a.	（气候）温和的
swath	n.	（某种特定类型的）大区域				

Proper Nouns

PLOS ONE 科学网（美国加州公共科学图书馆出版的一种开放型、同行匿名评审的网络期刊）

Walden Pond 沃尔登湖，美国麻省康科德市的一个湖

Henry David Thoreau 亨利·戴维·梭罗，十九世纪美国作家

Aldo Leopold 奥尔多·利奥波德，二十世纪美国生态学家

News Summary

这篇新闻是关于科学家对气候变化及气温升高使植物开花的时间提前的研究的。科学家们不仅研究了当前越来越温暖的气候对植物的影响，而且还通过以前的档案资料，研究了十九世纪美国两个不同地方的野花在春天开花的时间与温度的关系，得出结论说，一百六十一年来，随着春天温度上升提早到来，开花的日期也比以前提早了约十天。

Understanding Sentences

① 今天（1 月 16 日）在网络期刊《科学网》上发表的研究结果说明了气候变化怎样改变了美国整个温带地区的生态系统。

② 埃尔伍德说，从 1852 年开始至他一生中的不同时间点，他也为许多有名的花，如耧斗菜、粉红兰花和万寿菊等野生花创建了一份"开花时间报表"。

③ 他们发现，由于在过去的 161 年中温度上升，这些花初次开花的日期也悄悄提前了，比梭罗首次访问这个地点提早了大约 10 天。

④ 没有参与这个研究的、来自马里兰大学的生物学家大卫·印欧页说，到了（温度的）某个点，气候将变得过热，使得植物如果不进化的话就无法生存。但是，植物的开花时间仍然跟随温度变化的步伐这一事实意味着，还没达到那个（温度的）点。

Exercises

Ⅰ. Understanding Ideas in the News

1. What is the study on flowering times in two sites in the US based on?

A. Data published online today in the journal *PLOS ONE*.

B. Records of temperature in the two locations.

C. Data recorded by Henry David Thoreau and Aldo Leopold.

2. In addition to writing *Walden*, what else did Thoreau do?

A. Keeping records of flowering times of some wild flowers.

B. Growing flowers like wild columbine and marsh marigold.

C. Researching on the relation between temperature and flowering times.

3. Where did Aldo Leopold live and observe the flowering times?

A. Walden Pond.   B. Concord, Mass.   C. The Shack.

4. How many days was the flowing date advanced at Walden in 2010 and 2012?

A. 24 days.   B. 20—21 days.   C. About 10 days.

5. What does the findings in this research apply to?

A. A large area of temperate climates in the US.

B. On the coastal areas.

C. In tropical areas

II. Language Points

ecosystem, temperate, creep, swath, idyllic 这些词文章中用来描述对气象的研究。

ecosystem：(生态系统) all the living things in an area and the way they affect each other and the environment   e.g. *Pollution can have disastrous effects on the delicately balanced ecosystem.*

temperate：((气候)温和的) (of weather conditions) neither very hot nor very cold   e.g. *a temperate climate*

creep：(爬,蹑手蹑脚) to move slowly, quietly and carefully, usually in order to avoid being noticed   e.g. *She turned off the light and crept through the door.*

swath：((某种特定类型的)大区域) a long strip or large area especially of land   e.g. *Huge swathes of rain forest are being cleared for farming and mining.*

idyllic：(田园短诗的) of a place or experience that is extremely pleasant, beautiful or peaceful   e.g. *an idyllic childhood/summer*

III. Questions for Further Study

This news report is not as long and difficult as the previous ones, because it is written for the newspaper. It is in essence still a science report, but as the topic is less complicated, it is relatively easier to report. Find more readings similar to this from websites, and analyze them in the way as this reading.

英语报刊知识介绍

社论、专栏文章、读者来信以及博客和微博

社论一般是报社的编辑部人员写的文章,主要针对当前报道的重大事件发表评论。英语报刊的社论并不一定代表报社的态度,更不声称代表官方的态度。专栏文章通常是针对时事的评论。每种报纸都有一些专栏作家,他们定期向报社发送他们的文章。由于每个作家的风格不同,所针对的话题也不同,所以他们的文章可以满足不同读者群的阅读兴趣,这样能为报纸争取读者群。读者来信是报纸保持与读者的联系,从而确保其发行量的一种方式。这是一种传统的方式,它通过把读者的反馈全部或摘录刊登的方式,反映读者的意见和建议,听取来自一般读者的声音。

随着互联网的广泛应用和电子报刊的出现,博客、微博等形式也开始出现,这改变了传统报纸的"读者来信"专栏的功能,以及传播消息的手段。

1. A stack of British newspapers

2. A clip of newspapers writings put together

Unit 13 World Economy

The world economy, or global economy, generally refers to the economy, which is based on economies of all the world's countries' national economies. Also global economy can be seen as the economy of global society and national economies—as economies of local societies, making the global one. Today, economic activities in countries in the world are more and more related, so interest in getting news about the world economy is growing. In addition to some newspapers that specialized in reporting on this special field, such as *Wall Street Journal* and the *Financial Times*, all newspapers devoted pages and sections to the topic of world economy every day. There are three reports in this chapter: about the expectation of the US economy, the IMF, and mobile network.

世界经济,也称全球经济,一般指以全球各国的国家经济为基础的经济。同时,全球经济也可以看作是全球社会和国内经济的总体——作为由各地域的经济组成的全球整体。今天,世界上各国的经济活动越来越联系紧密了,因而对获取世界经济新闻的需求也不断增长。除了专门报道经济方面的报纸,如《华尔街日报》和《财经时报》之外,几乎所有报纸每天都有报道世界经济的版面或专栏。本章收集了三篇经济新闻,分别是关于美国经济发展的预期、关于国际货币基金组织和关于欧盟和韩国联合研发移动网络的。

1. The economy is holding up surprisingly well in a year of austerity

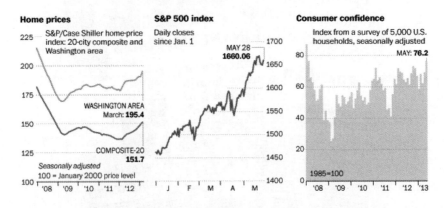

(Sources: S & P/Case Shiller, Bloomberg News, Conference Board. The Washington Post. Published on May 28, 2013, 9:13 p.m.)

By Neil Irwin and Ylan Q. Mui
The Washington Post

May 28, 2013

A U. S. economy that was supposed to be barely hanging on is starting to look surprisingly robust.

Housing prices rose faster over the past year than they have in the past seven, according to data out Tuesday. Consumer confidence hit its highest level in five years. The stock market rallied another 0.6 percent as measured by the Standard & Poor's 500, leaving it just short of an all-time high reached last week. ① And the national retail price of gasoline fell for six days straight through Monday and is down 16 cents a gallon since late February.

The market keeps on rising.

It adds up to this reality: In a year when tax increases and spending cuts by the federal government were expected to bleed life out of the economy, the strengthening housing and financial markets are proving to be more powerful than acts of Congress. ②

Americans with higher incomes are wealthier thanks to the stock market's 16 percent rise so far in 2013. Middle-income earners, whose assets are disproportionately tied up in their homes, are becoming wealthier thanks to higher housing prices — up 10.2 percent in 20 major cities in the year that ended in March, according to the S&P/Case-Shiller home price index released Tuesday.

And lower-and middle-income consumers have benefited from falling gasoline prices. Those are likely key factors behind overall economic data that has suggested growth that, while hardly gangbusters, is a bit better than the past few years. ③ Gross domestic product rose at a 2.5 percent rate in the first quarter, a bit better than the average over the past several years, and the nation added an average of 196,000 jobs a month in the first four months of 2013, up from 180,000 in the second half of 2012.

Meanwhile, the direct evidence is scarce that government's tighter control over spending is damaging growth. A 2 percentage point increase in payroll taxes that took effect Jan. 1, reducing the take-home pay of all American workers, would be expected to put a big damper on consumer spending. ④But personal consumption expenditures rose at a 1.2 percent annual rate in the first quarter, a not-too-shabby result.

Lynn Franco, director of economic indicators at the Conference Board, said that budget wars in Congress and the payroll tax increase dampened consumers' mood over the winter, but that Americans seemed to weather Washington's troubles. "They were shocked," she said. "They've absorbed it. They've processed it."

The Conference Board's consumer confidence index rose to 76.2 in May, the highest since February 2008 and up from 68.1 in April. Similarly, while there are ample reports of impact from the automatic spending cuts known as the sequester — such as government contractors being furloughed or unemployment insurance being reduced — the effects are not really noticeable so far in the broad economy. ⑤ For example, March and April employment data show steady job creation and no major change in the trend for government employment, or in categories that include large concentrations of federal contractors such as professional and business services.

So was the impact of Washington's austerity oversold? Not necessarily. Growth is holding up well in 2013, but would be even stronger if the federal purse strings were not being tightened, according to economic models used by both private forecasters and independent agencies like the Congressional Budget Office.

"All else being equal, growth in 2013 should be better than 2012, because the headwinds holding it back are diminishing," said Michelle Girard, chief economist of RBS. "The impact of the fiscal drag isn't things getting worse, it's the absence of things getting much better."

It is also evident that economists' intuition about how people will respond to changes in policy doesn't always hold up in the real data.⑥ For example, a worker whose after-tax paycheck dropped by 2 percent Jan. 1 may not have immediately cut back on spending by that amount, judging by retail sales data. Perhaps workers are phasing in the adjustment over months, or keeping up their spending levels but reducing their rate of saving instead.

The same could be said of a federal employee seeing reduced paychecks due to furloughs. In addition, the full economic brunt of sequestration probably hasn't hit yet. It went into effect March 1, but many government agencies and their contractors may have delayed their response in hopes that Congress would reduce or eliminate certain cuts. Now economists see it as more likely to have its full impact later in the year.

And there are more caveats to the spate of good news. For example, the pleasant surprises from housing, the stock market and gasoline prices are driving consumer confidence, but that will not necessarily translate into actual consumer spending. "Over the longer run, households still need to save more, and that's going to be a restraint on growth," said Gus Faucher, a senior economist at PNC Bank.

For the economy to continue growing even as the sequestration and tax increases have their full effects, higher housing prices will need to translate into more home construction, higher stock prices will need to translate into companies making new investments, and consumers' higher level of confidence will need to translate into spending more money.

Until those things happen, there will not be the kind of full-throated economic boom that, four years since the great recession ended, America is still desperately waiting for.
(890 words)

Words and Expressions

robust	a. 健康和有力的	sequestration	n. 自动减支

bleed	v.	榨取,勒索		rally	v.	重整旗鼓,集结
proportionate	a.	成比例的		asset	n.	资产
payroll	n.	工资单		gangbuster	a.	具有很大影响的
dampen	v.	消除,抑制		damper	n.	起抑制作用的因素
furlough	n.	休假,暂时解雇		sequester	n.	自动减支计划
purse strings		钱袋口上的绳子,金钱		austerity	n.	严峻,严厉,朴素
phase in		逐步采用		intuition	n.	直觉,直觉的知识
caveat	v.	[律]中止诉讼手续的申请,警告,告诫		brunt	n.	冲击,冲势
				spate	n.	大量

Proper Nouns

Standard & Poor's 500 标准普尔500指数(又译为"史坦普指数",美国股市记录500家上市公司的一个股票指数)

Case-Shiller 标准普尔属下的一种房价指数

RBS 苏格兰皇家银行,the Royal Bank of Scotland

PNC Bank 匹兹堡国家公司银行

News Summary

2008年以来,美国的经济连续几年出现衰退,政府增加税收缩减开支,股市下跌,房价下降,消费者信心指数也下降。因此,曾经有经济学家对美国2013年的经济也持悲观态度。但是这篇发表于2013年上半年《华盛顿邮报》上的新闻却注意到了美国经济复苏的一些迹象。文章列举了这些方面,基本上都有实际的数据,并引用了权威部门的统计结果,因此读起来可信度高。

Understanding Sentences

① 股票按照标准普尔500来估算收复了另一个百分之零点六,结果是差点达到上周的最高。

② 所有这些加起来的现实是:在这一年中,尽管联邦政府想通过增加税收和减少支出来紧缩经济,但强劲的住房和金融市场证明比国会通过的法令更强大。

③ 那些可能就是整体经济数据背后的主要因素,这表明虽然增长几乎没有造成什么影响,但已经比过去几年要好一点了。

④ 从一月一日开始生效的工资税增加了两个百分点,减少了所有美国工人实际拿到的工资,预料将在很大程度上影响消费者的花费。

⑤ 同样的,尽管有很多关于自动减少支出计划所造成影响的报告,比如政府承办商被解雇,或失业保险减少等,其在大范围经济内的效果目前看来还确实不明显。

⑥ 也有证据表明,经济学家关于人们将会对政策的改变做出什么样反应的直觉,并不总是和实际数据一致。

Exercises

I. Understanding Ideas in the News

1. What is the most important indicator of the American economy recovering?
   A. The federal government enforced tax increases and spending cuts.
   B. The housing prices rose slowly compared to the past seven years.
   C. The stock market reached almost the all-time high last week.

2. What is the factor that makes middle-income earners wealthier?
   A. Stock Market's 16% rise.   B. Higher housing prices.
   C. Tax increase policies.

3. What happened to consumer spending despite the payroll taxes increase?
   A. Consumption expenditures rose at an annual rate of 1.2%.
   B. Gross domestic product rose at a 2.5 percent rate.
   C. An average of 196,000 jobs a month is created.

4. What are the effects in the broad economy of automatic spending cuts?
   A. Consumer confidence index rose.
   B. Not really noticeable.
   C. It dampened consumers' mood.

5. Why is it that economists' intuition about how people will respond to changes in policy is not always supported by statistics?
   A. The tax increase of 2% is insignificant.
   B. Federal employees want to have more vacations.
   C. People are phasing in the adjustment over months.

II. Language Points

austerity, sequester, gangbuster, damper, intuition 这几个词用于介绍美国经济。

austerity: （严峻，严厉，朴素）(from austere: without comfort; plain and without decoration; severe) e.g. *The wartime austerity* (= lack of luxuries and comfort) *of my early years prepared me for later hardships.*

sequester: （自动减支计划）a package of automatic spending cuts that's part of the Budget Control Act

gangbuster: （具有很大影响的）with great impact, vigor, or zeal

damper: （起抑制作用的因素）(put a damper/dampener on sth.) to stop an occasion from being enjoyable e.g. *Both the kids were ill while we were in Boston, so that rather put a damper on things.*

intuition: （直觉）an ability to understand or know something immediately without needing to think about it, learn it or discover it by using reason

III. Questions for Further Study

This news report is divided into three parts: first, the lead paragraph at the beginning states that the American economy starts to look surprisingly dynamic; then statistics are quoted to support it from three fields, and finally some warnings to these optimistic signs. In writing economy news, one important feature is the use of statistics and data by established financial institutes. There are also some standard terms and institutes in the field of economy that one needs to be familiar with.

2. IMF calls on UK to do more to boost economy

Associate Press
May 22, 2013

LONDON (AP) — The International Monetary Fund has issued a tough assessment of U. K. economic policy, urging the coalition government and Bank of England to do more to boost demand in the economy.

The IMF's report of its latest consultation with British authorities released Tuesday called for more stimulus, either through further rounds of quantitative easing or by a further cut in the all-time low base lending rate of 0.5 percent.

Since coming to power in 2010, the U. K.'s coalition government has introduced an extensive austerity program of state spending cuts and reforms aimed at bringing down the country's deficit. However, as the IMF report states, that while the U. K. has "made substantial progress toward achieving a more sustainable budgetary position", the country has fallen back into recession and "the hand-off from public to private demand-led growth has not fully materialized." ①

The Bank of England, meanwhile, has been working to keep inflation — which halts income growth and squeezes household spending — down to a target 2 per cent. Latest figures released Tuesday show that consumer price inflation fell from 3.5 percent in March to 3 percent in April, a bigger drop than expected.

The BoE has also paused in its program of quantitative easing — buying high-quality assets to free up the flow of money in the economy — after spending 325 billion pounds ($ 513 billion) to support the economy.

The IMF said that by cutting rates and introducing another round of QE "inflation could take longer than expected to return to target, with convergence being further delayed by additional monetary easing.② Nonetheless, the cost of such a delay is likely to be low relative to the benefits of a more rapid closing of the output gap."

Britain's Treasury chief, George Osborne, welcomed the IMF report as an endorsement of the government's policies.

"The IMF couldn't be clearer today. Britain has to deal with its debts and the government's fiscal policy is the appropriate one and an essential part of our road to recovery," Osborne said.

The opposition Labour Party, however, has called for more emphasis on promoting growth.

"In Britain, cutting spending and raising taxes too far and too fast has backfired, with the resulting slow growth and high unemployment," said Ed Balls, Labour's economic spokesman in Parliament.

Blerina Uruci at Barclays Capital Research said there appeared to be little prospect of a change of course by the government, "even if the economic recovery were to go further off track."

"In this respect, at least, the IMF's message is likely to fall on deaf ears," Uruci said.

The drop in April's consumer price inflation does give the government and BoE added leeway to respond to the IMF's call for more action to boost demand.③ "The signs are that the Bank of England is keeping the door fully open to more QE given the major uncertainties over both the growth and inflation outlooks," said Howard Archer, European economist at HIS Global Insight.

The IMF also warned that the difficulties facing the economy of 17 country eurozone — which is the U.K.'s biggest export market — is the biggest threat to the U.K. economy.

"An escalation of stress in the euro area could set off an adverse and self-reinforcing cycle of lower confidence and exports, higher bank funding costs, tighter credit, and falling asset values, resulting in a substantial contractionary shock," the IMF said.④

While the government will be encouraged by the inflation data, the April budget surplus of 16.5 billion pounds was below the market consensus of 20 billion pounds. The transfer of Royal Mail pension fund assets pushed the account into surplus for the month.

The government's tax take was down 0.9 percent compared to a year earlier. Excluding the pension fund effect, "the deficit of 11.5 billion pounds looks pretty nasty," said Vicky Redwood, chief U.K. economist at Capital Economics. (636 words)

Unit 13　World Economy

Words and Expressions

assessment	n.	估价，被估定的金额	boost	v.	推进
stimulus	n.	刺激物，促进因素	deficit	n.	赤字，亏损额
sustainable	a.	足可支撑的，养得起的	recession	n.	衰退，不景气
halt	n.	停止，暂停，中断	convergence	n.	集中，一体化
backfire	n.	逆火	leeway	n.	可允许的误差，退路
eurozone	n.	欧元区	escalation	n.	扩大，增加
adverse	a.	不利的，相反的	consensus	n.	一致同意

Proper Nouns

the International Monetary Fund, IMF　国际货币基金组织

QE　量化宽松政策（Quantitative Easing Monetary Policy），指一国货币当局通过大量印钞等方式向市场注入超额资金

Barclays　巴克莱银行，英国第二大银行，具有超过300年历史

HIS Global Insight　HIS全球观察，是世界第一的经济和金融信息顾问公司

Royal Mail　英国皇家邮政

News Summary

这篇新闻是关于英国经济的报道。自2010年工党下台、新的联合政府成立以来，英国采取一系列措施削减开支、增加税收，以应付庞大的财政赤字，但是这些措施也导致了经济衰退。因此，国际货币基金组织通过对英国政府这些政策的评估和实际的经济数据，要求英国政府采取新一轮的量化宽松政策，降低利率，以刺激经济发展。文章同样用恰当的、针对性很强的数据来分析说明问题。

Understanding Sentences

① 但是，正如国际货币基金组织报告所说，虽然英国已经"朝着形成一个更加可持续的预算位置取得了实在的进步"，但该国已经跌回到了经济衰退中，而且"从公共领域转移到私人领域的需求性增长并没有完全实现"。

② 国际货币基金组织说，通过降低利率和开启新一轮的货币宽松政策，"随着一体化被额外的宽松货币政策所推迟，通货膨胀可能比预期需要更长时间回归目标"。

③ 四月份消费者价格通胀的下跌确实给了政府和英国银行多余的空间，来回应国际货币基金组织采取更多行动刺激需求的要求。

④ 国际货币基金组织说，"欧元区压力的升级可能导致不断自我强化的恶性循环，影响投资者的信心和出口量，造成更高的银行融资成本，更紧缩的信用，以及资产价值下跌，结果是巨大的紧缩性震动。"

Exercises

I. Understanding Ideas in the News

1. Which is one of the measures the IMF wants the UK government to do to boost demand?

   A. A new round of quantitative easing.

   B. Assessment of the economy.

   C. More stimulus to the economy.

2. What is the result of the austerity program introduced by the coalition since 2010?

   A. The country's deficit has been brought down.

   B. Inflation has been reduced to 2 percent.

   C. The country has fallen back into recession.

3. What did George Osborne think about IMF's assessment of UK's economy policy?

   A. He agreed with IMF that another round of quantitative easing is needed.

   B. He thought that IMF supported the government's policies.

   C. He disagreed with IMF's call for more stimulus to the economy.

4. What is Labour Party's attitude toward the British economy?

   A. More emphasis should be placed on promoting growth.

   B. They should turn a deaf ear to IMF's message.

   C. The government should cut spending and raise taxes.

5. According to statistics, what is the budget surplus in April?

   A. 20 billion pounds.   B. 16.5 billion pounds.

   C. 11.5 billion pounds

II. Language Points

boost, stimulus, deficit, recession, convergence 这些是新闻中用来谈论经济的词汇。

boost: (推进) to improve or increase something   e.g. *The theatre managed to boost its audiences by cutting ticket prices.*

stimulus: (刺激物,促进因素) something that causes growth or activity   e.g. *Foreign investment has been a stimulus to the industry.*

deficit: (赤字,亏损额) the total amount by which money spent is more than money received   e.g. *The country is running a balance-of-payments/budget/trade deficit of $250 million.*

recession: (衰退,不景气) a period when the economy of a country is not successful and conditions for business are bad   e.g. *The country is sliding into the depths of (a) recession.*

convergence: (集中,一体化) the act of converging and especially moving toward

Unit 13 World Economy

union or uniformity e. g. *a convergence of interests/opinions/ideas*

III. Questions for Further Study

This is from the website of the Associate Press, and is typical of wire news. News agencies provide wire news to subscribers, which in turn may edit and add headlines to them and publish in local newspapers. Analyze this news report to see how the main idea is presented and supporting evidence or data is given, followed by less-important information about the topic.

3. EU, South Korea to ally on faster mobile access

In South Korea, more than one mobile device is in use for each person. (*Agence France-Presse/Getty Images*)

By Frances Robinson in Brusssels and
Min-Jeong Lee in Seoul
The Wall Street Journal
Monday, June 16, 2014

In the race to get the world's fastest mobile Internet, South Korea and the European Union on Monday will unveil a major new pact to join forces on so-called 5G networks, according to a draft of the agreement seen by *The Wall Street Journal*. [①]

The deal sets up a joint group to develop systems, set standards and get radio frequencies ready to accommodate the new technology. The aim is to have a global consensus and vision on 5G by the end of 2015.

The agreement could be crucial for the EU, which is lagging behind in the global telecommunications race after late and patchy implementation of the current 4G standard. [②] While users can download a one-hour high-definition film in six minutes on 4G mobile Internet, 5G would slash the time to six seconds, according to EU data.

European businesses have long warned that Europe's growth will suffer if the bloc continues to trail its rivals on mobile technology. The 5G race is already on: Huawei South Koreans Technologies Co. of China is investing heavily—$600 million through 2018—in the next-generation network. The U. S. doesn't have a nationally backed program, but universities are researching various aspects of the next-generation standard.

The EU is eager to regain its position as a global leader in mobile standards. The European GSM led the world when people first started using portable phones.

While Europe rested on its laurels, South Korea pushed ahead to set out fresh revenue streams, with the first comers to the technology expected to hold a leading share in the industry. ③

South Koreans are perhaps the world's most dedicated smartphone users. The country's mobile-penetration rate of more than 100% means that more than one mobile device is in use for each person.

Forging ahead together would benefit both Europe's mobile-equipment manufacturers—such as Ericsson, Nokia Siemens Networks Oyj and Alcatel-Lucent SA—and, among others, South Korea's Samsung Electronics Co., the world's largest maker of smartphones.

Samsung is expected to play an active role in realizing South Korea's goal of seizing a firm foothold on patent rights on related telecom technologies.

Last year, the company claimed a breakthrough in the development of 5G technology, saying that it found a way to transmit large volumes of data using a much higher frequency band than conventional ones, which would eventually allow users to send massive data files at much faster speeds through their mobile devices, "practically without limitation." ④ In January, the South Korean government announced its road map for 5G wireless-communication technology, with a goal of being the first to bring the technology to commercial markets, in December 2030.

This would be achieved through joint private-sector efforts involving the country's mobile carriers—SK Telecom Co., KT Corp. and LG Uplus Corp—and manufacturers such as Samsung and LG Electronics Inc. The government forecast the country would invest a combined 1.6 trillion won ($1.57 billion) over the next seven years in attempting to bring the technology live.

Under the plan, the government is aiming for total revenue of 331 trillion won from sales of mobile devices and network equipment that support 5G communications technology, during the 2020-26 period. ⑤

From the EU side, in December 2013 the European Commission said that it would allot 700 million ($948 million) and industry partners more than 3 billion to conduct exploratory research into 5G without delay. The Commission intends to select the first set of projects to fund at the end of this year, with 125 million to allocate.

The partnership will be led by two groups: Europe's 5G PPP, which is based in Belgium and includes European technology and telecom companies such as Telefonica SA and Nokia Oyj; and its South Korean equivalent, the 5G Forum.

Work on 5G should start "the sooner the better—it is extremely important that we take the lead again," said EU digital commissioner Neelie Kroes. "In the '90s we were in the driver seat, talking about GSM, so it would nice to be back in that position." (671 words)

Words and Expressions

unveil	v.	揭开，揭幕	pact	n.	合同，公约，协定
patchy	a.	补丁的，不调和的	slash	v.	（大幅度）削减
trail	v.	拉，拖	laurel	n.	桂冠，殊荣
smartphone	n.	智能手机	forge ahead		向前迈进
trillion	n.	万亿	revenue	n.	国家的收入，税收
allocate	v.	分派，分配	allot	v.	（按份额）分配，分派

Proper Nouns

5G　第五代移动通信技术的简称
GSM　全球移动通信系统
Alcatel-Lucent SA　阿尔卡特-朗讯（一家美国与法国合作的电讯设备和服务公司）

News Summary

这篇新闻是关于韩国将和欧盟联合研制第五代移动通信技术的消息。新闻的重大意义在于两个方面：第一，第五代移动通信技术在2014年开始便成为一个热门词，因为它的速度快，据说几秒钟就可以下载一部一个多小时长的DVD片子。第二，新的技术可以带来巨额的收入，包括服务和各种硬件的销售。文章接着分析了欧盟和韩国方面各种的背景和计划，以及各自的主要移动通信设备制造商和提供服务的公司。

Understanding Sentences

① 根据《华尔街日报》所接触到的一份协议草稿，在一场争夺世界上最快的移动网的比赛中，韩国和欧盟在星期一将宣布一项合作研究第五代移动通信技术的新协议。

② 该协议对于欧盟来说是很关键的，欧盟执行当前的第四代标准比较晚，而且是零碎的，因此在全球电子通信赛跑中落在后面。

③ 当欧洲躺在它的桂冠上休息的时候，韩国不断向前推进，创造新的收入来源，这个技术上的新来者预计在该行业中占有主要市场份额。

④ 去年，该公司宣布在第五代移动通信技术研发上取得突破，声称其找到了一个利用超高频率的波段传输大量数据的方法。这一技术最终将使用户可以通过移动终端以更快的速度传输大数据文件，"基本上不受任何限制"。

⑤ 根据这一计划，政府将在2020至2026年期间，从销售支持第五代移动通信技术的移

动装置和网络设备那里获得总数为三百三十一万亿的收入。

Exercises

Ⅰ. **Understanding Ideas in the News**

1. What is the aim of the cooperation between South Korea and the EU?

    A. To develop a new kind of mobile phone.

    B. To set international standards on 5G by the end of 2015.

    C. To help the EU catch up in global telecommunications race.

2. In what field had Europe been leading the world?

    A. The GSM.　　　　　B. 5G.　　　　　C. Smartphone.

3. Who would be benefited by the cooperation between South Korea and the EU?

    A. Smartphone makers.　B. Erocsspm.　　　C. Both sides.

4. What is South Korea's goal in this telecommunications race?

    A. To control the telecom industry firmly.

    B. To acquire most of the patent rights on 5G technology.

    C. To be the first to make breakthrough in 5G technology.

5. What will the European Commission do at the end of this year?

    A. To spend 700 million on research.

    B. To cooperate with the Korean company Samsung.

    C. To pick some projects to support.

Ⅱ. **Language Points**

pact, slash, patchy, trail, allot 在介绍韩国与欧盟合作研究第五代移动通信技术时，本文用了这些简短有力的词．

pact：（合同，公约，协定）a formal agreement between two people or groups of people　e. g. *The United States and Canada have signed a free-trade pact.*

slash：（（大幅度）削减）to greatly reduce something, such as money or jobs　e. g. *Prices have been slashed by 50%.*

patchy：（补丁的，不调和的）only existing or happening in some parts　e. g. *Southeast England will start with some patchy rain/patchy cloud at first.*

trail：（拉，拖）to (allow something to) move slowly along the ground or through the air or water, after someone or something

allot：（分配，分派）to give (especially a share of something available) for a particular purpose　e. g. *They allotted everyone a separate desk.*

Ⅲ. **Questions for Further Study**

This piece of economy news is published in *The Wall Street Journal*, a professional daily newspaper dedicated to reporting world-wide events in the field of economy. The news is written in the typical style of journalist English, with the structure clearly divided into three sections. The use of short, one-syllable words is also one important feature of

Unit 13　World Economy

this news. Analyze the reading in details according to the instructions given above.

英语报刊知识介绍

经济(商业)新闻、体育新闻

所谓新闻报道,就是对最近发生的事件的求实性报道,它的特点是用事实说话。当然,事实的形式不一定百分之百是摆在人们面前的东西,它可能是亲身经历者或目击者的讲述,或是权威机构发布的数据、信息等。新闻可以按照几个不同的层面来划分基本的类型,以便于我们学习。按照新闻事实发生的地域和范围来分,可以有本地新闻、国内新闻、国际新闻等。按照新闻的性质来分,可以有政治新闻、经济(商业)新闻、科教新闻、军事新闻、社会新闻、娱乐新闻、体育新闻,还有其他的实用或休闲类的文章,如汽车、园林、房地产、分类广告等。

经济(商业)新闻主要是关于经济贸易方面的、涉及国内国际的、内容包括了从股票市场到汽车销售、从投资设厂到电子产品新产品上市等的报道。体育新闻主要是报道各种竞技体育比赛及相关消息。

1. A front page of *The Times*

2. A front page of *The Guardian*

Unit 14　Business News

Business news is news about business activities in a country and the whole world. It is also call "business journalism", which tracks, records, analyzes and interprets the economic changes that take place in a society. It could include anything from personal finance, to business at the local market and shopping malls, to the performance of well-known and not-so-well-known companies. Most newspapers and magazines carry a business segment. This chapter puts together three business news reports, one is about Chinese company in Africa, one about the e-business in Australia, and one about the EU levying on Chinese solar panels.

商业新闻指有关一个国家或全球的商业活动的新闻。它也称"商业新闻学",主要是追踪、记录和分析在某个国家发生的经济变化。它可以包括个人理财、当地市场或购物中心的营业状况,以及有名或不那么有名的公司的运作情况等的报道。大多数报纸都有专版刊登商业新闻。本章收入了三篇商业新闻,一篇是关于中国公司在非洲发展的,一篇是关于澳大利亚的电子商务发展情况的,还有一篇是关于欧盟对中国的光伏产品征收高关税的。

1. Chinese trade with Africa keeps growing; fears of neocolonialism are overdone

The Economist
Mar. 23rd, 2013, Nairobi

A GROUP of five tourists from Beijing passes low over Mount Kenya and into the Rift Valley in their private plane before landing on a dusty airstrip surrounded by the yellow trunks and mist-like branches of fever trees.① They walk across a grassy opening where zebras and giraffes roam, snapping pictures while keeping an eye out for charging buffaloes. When they sit down at a table, they seem hungry but at ease. "Last year I went to the South Pole with some friends," says one of two housewives, showing off iPhone pictures of a gaggle of penguins on permafrost.

Chinese are coming to Africa in ever greater numbers and finding it a comfortable place to visit, work in and trade. An estimated 1m are now resident in Africa, up from a few thousand a decade ago, and more keep arriving. Chinese are the fourth-most-numerous visitors to South Africa. Among them will be China's new president, Xi Jinping, who is also going to Tanzania and the Democratic Republic of Congo on his first foreign outing as leader.

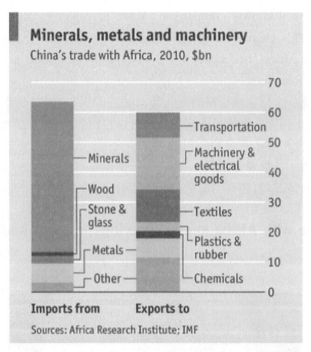

The origin of China's fascination with Africa is easy to see. Between the Sahara and the Kalahari deserts lie many of the raw materials desired by its industries.② China recently overtook America as the world's largest net importer of oil. Almost 80% of Chinese imports from Africa are mineral products. China is Africa's top business partner, with trade exceeding $166 billion. But it is not all minerals. Exports to Africa are a mixed bag (see chart). Machinery makes up 29%.

The size of China's direct investment in Africa is harder to measure than trade. Last summer China's commerce minister, Chen Deming, said the number "exceeded $14.7 billion, up 60% from 2009"③. Around the same time the Chinese ambassador to South Africa, Tian Xuejun, said: "China's investment in Africa of various kinds exceeds $40 billion." Apparently, the first figure is for African investments reported to the government. The second includes estimates of Chinese funds flowing in from tax shelters around the world.

Sino-African links have broadened in the past few years. The relationship is now almost as diverse as Africa itself. But Mr. Xi will search in vain for the e-mail address of a single African leader who can speak for the rest, rather as Henry Kissinger legendarily struggled to find a single phone number for Europe.

Until recently China concentrated on a few big resource-rich countries, including Algeria, Nigeria, South Africa, Sudan and Zambia. But places like Ethiopia and Congo, where minerals are scarce or hard to extract, are now getting more attention, not least as more Chinese businesses branch out into non-resource sectors. ④ State-owned companies compete with private firms—both tempted by margins often far higher than at home. Young Chinese private-equity funds are also coming to Africa.

China's image in Africa, once marred by suspicion, is changing. Businessmen facing Chinese competition, especially in farming, retail and petty trading, still complain. In Malawi, Tanzania, Uganda and Zambia, new rules restrict the industries or areas in which Chinese can operate. Yet a growing number of Africans say the Chinese create jobs, transfer skills and spend money in local economies. ⑤ In small countries, where the Asian behemoth was most feared, the change is especially noticeable. Michael Sata, president of Zambia and a long-standing China critic when in opposition until 2011, changed his tune once in office. Last year he demoted his labour minister, who had lambasted Chinese and Indian business interests. He also sent his vice-president to Beijing to discuss links between his Patriotic Front and the Chinese Communist Party.

Other popular fears triggered by China's growing presence have also proved hollow. It has not stoked armed conflict. On the contrary, China has occasionally played peacemaker, although motivated by self-interest. Sudan and South Sudan are both big Chinese trade partners. When they hovered on the brink of war last year, China intervened diplomatically along with other powers.

Only in Africa's largest economies has China become less popular. There it is increasingly seen as a competitor. Jacob Zuma, South Africa's president, who long cultivated Chinese contacts, was last year forced by domestic critics to change posture. In Nigeria the central-bank governor recently excoriated the Chinese for exuding "a whiff of colonialism". Other Africans guffawed—in the past it was often the Nigerians and the South Africans who muscled into their markets. (730 words)

Words and Expressions

fever tree		金鸡纳树	snap	v.	拍快照
gaggle	n.	鹅群,一群	permafrost	n.	永久冻结带
diverse	a.	不同的,变化多的	tempt	v.	引诱,吸引
margin	n.	利润,差数	mar	v.	毁坏,损害
behemoth	n.	河马,巨兽	lambaste	v.	痛打,严责
hover	v.	盘旋	excoriate	v.	批判

| exude | v. | 渗出,发散 | whiff | n. | 一阵气味 |
| stoke | v. | 给(炉子)添加燃料,引起 | guffaw | v. | 哄笑,狂笑 |

Proper Nouns

the Kalahari deserts   卡拉哈里沙漠(非洲南部一大平原沙漠)
the Sahara deserts   撒哈拉沙漠

News Summary

这是英国《经济学家》杂志上的一篇文章,风格与前两单元所选的出自该杂志的文章差不多,只是话题不同。文章也以一个描写性的导语段开头,旨在突出现在中国人的富有。文章接着介绍中国与非洲的贸易及投资的增长,着重指中国从非洲进口原材料。作者也没忘记从西方的立场观点来看待中国与非洲的日益紧密的关系。

Understanding Sentences

① 一队五个来自北京的游客乘坐私人飞机在肯尼亚山上空低飞,进入断裂谷,最后在一条被金鸡纳树黄色的树干和雾一般的树枝包围的、布满尘埃的跑道上降落。

② 在撒哈拉沙漠和卡拉哈里沙漠之间蕴藏着其工业所需要的许多种原材料。

③ 中国在非洲的直接投资规模比贸易更难估计。去年夏天,中国商务部部长陈德铭说,这个数字"超过147亿,比2009年上升百分之六十"。

④ 但是,像埃塞俄比亚和刚果这样的地方虽然矿物比较少,又难以提炼,但现在由于越来越多的贸易进入非资源性的领域,也不比其他地方少受人注意。

⑤ 但是,越来越多的非洲人说,中国人在当地经济中创造了工作岗位,传授了技术和投入了资金。

Exercises

I. Understanding Ideas in the News

1. What is the number of Chinese living in Africa now?

   A. About one million.   B. Several thousand.

   C. Tens of thousands

2. Why are the two figures of China's investment in Africa different?

   A. The second figure excludes other funds.

   B. The figures are reported by different people.

   C. The first figure is reported to the government.

3. Why do Chinese state-owned companies compete with private firms in Africa?

   A. The profit is higher than at home.

   B. The difference is greater than at home.

   C. There are more resources than at home.

4. In what fields do businessmen complain facing Chinese competition?

A. Oil and minerals.

B. Farming, retail and petty trading.

C. Machinery.

5. In what African country is China seen as a competitor?

A. Nigeria.   B. South Africa.   C. Malawi.

II. Language Points

tempt, mar, excoriate, exude, whiff 这些词既有常用的,也有不常用的,但在文中都用得很恰当。

tempt:(引诱,吸引) to make someone want to have or do something, especially something that is unnecessary or wrong   e.g. *The offer of a free car stereo tempted her into buying a new car.*

mar:(毁坏,损害) to spoil something, making it less perfect or less enjoyable e.g. *Sadly, the text is marred by careless errors.*

excoriate:(批判) to state the opinion that a play, a book, a political action, etc. is very bad   e.g. *His latest novel received excoriating reviews.*

exude:(渗出,发散) to produce a smell or liquid substance from inside   e.g. *Some trees exude from their bark a sap that repels insect parasites.*

whiff:(一阵气味) a brief smell, carried on a current of air   e.g. *He leaned towards me and I caught/got a whiff of garlic.*

III. Questions for Further Study

This news report not only presents some facts about China's increasing presence in Africa, but also the writer's feeling about it, both positive and negative. Analyze the language of the article to see how the writer expressed his attitude, either openly, or in a more subtle way as can be read between the lines.

2. "We're happy" — Frenzy drives traffic to retailers

When the Click Frenzy site was down, shoppers just went straight to the participating retailers.

Glenda Kwek *Business Reporter*
Sydney Morning Herald
November 21, 2012 — 4:47p. m.

Some retailers say their online sales jumped as a result of the Click Frenzy promotion, despite consumer complaints following the website's crash on Tuesday.

Retailers such as Woolworths and Windsor Smith said consumers bypassed the Click Frenzy website when it went down and shopped at their online stores instead.①

"We did phenomenal figures and we were very happy with it," said Jane Mance of Windsor Smith, a wholesale footwear retailer. "We got what we would normally get in a month in one night as far as unique visitors to our website, and I have to attribute that to Click Frenzy."

Ms Mance said unique visitors to the site reached six-digit figures on Tuesday night.

Benedict Brook, a spokesman for Woolworths, which manages two brands taking part in the promotion — Dan Murphy's and Masters Home Improvements — said their websites saw a spike in visitors, especially when the Click Frenzy website became unavailable.

"We had around 200 per cent more customers than usual," Mr. Brook said.

"**Prepared for the additional load**"

Both retailers said they were prepared for the additional load, with Windsor Smith conducting repeated tests to its servers — managed by a Melbourne digital company — to ensure their site could handle up to 500,000 unique visitors at any given time.②

However, Melbourne IT, which monitored the availability and response times for 153 websites that participated in Click Frenzy, said between 6 p. m. and midnight on Tuesday night "about two-thirds of the participating sites had issues, which is not good".

Woolworths and Westfield, another participating retailer, said they would always be keen to be involved in any promotion that would boost the image of their brands and clients to consumers.

Ms Mance said she was surprised to find that even items not on sale being snapped up.

"Even the day before, we were getting incredible sales on our full-price items. Last night, our full-price items sold neck-to-neck with our [sale items]."

Up to $30,000 to advertise on Click Frenzy site

Click Frenzy's owners would have made a tidy sum too, with the company charging retailers up to $30,000 for advertising space on the website.

On the low end, an "initial brand set-up and first listing" would cost a retailer $1500 plus GST, a Click Frenzy advertising booklet states.③ At the premium end,

$30,000 plus GST would get a retailer featured deals on the homepage or site-wide advertising excluding the homepage.

Senior industry analyst Naren Sivasailam of IBISWorld said despite the technical problems, the Click Frenzy event was an opportunity for Australian retailers to acknowledge that going online represented the present and future of the industry.

"It's a testament to the fact that online retail is well and truly in the mainstream consciousness," he said, adding that Australian retailers should have shored up their online presence five years ago.

"I think it's an acknowledgement that this is where it's going and [Australian retailers] do have to get with the program, and participating in sales like this... if the retailers have experienced a spike in sales, is a taste of things to come. Multi-channelling retailing to some extent is the future."

"We were not prepared for the scale"

Click Frenzy said in a statement released on Wednesday that the number of consumers visiting its website was "multiple times greater than the maximum capacity we had"④. The company said it was prepared for one-million unique visitors within 24 hours.

Click Frenzy also stated that it had received "very positive responses" from retailers such as Booktopia and Chemist Warehouse.

"Phenomenal sales for Booktopia so far. Site never missed a beat. In the past hour we were doing 11 sales a minute with customers doing large orders," Tony Nash of Booktopia reportedly told Click Frenzy.

Julia Salter of EzyDVD said in a statement that its site saw "a 550 per cent increase in sales and already trends suggest we'll do the same sales number in the next 12 hours".

"Seventy-five per cent of all visitors are new to the site which bodes well for future sales especially around the key holiday period. We couldn't be happier."

Continued growth of online retail

Craig White of Elan, which operates EzyDVD, said he believed the increased traffic and sales were set to continue.

"It will only get bigger and bigger and I believe the early mistakes customers experienced will be long forgotten given the scale of success we are seeing," he said. ⑤ "Having to compete against iconic global retailers such Amazon teaches you a lot. We were prepared for Click Frenzy but not for the scale of sales response."

Mr. Brook could not say if Woolworths would participate in Click Frenzy again next year, but added the retail giant would not be seeking compensation from the company following the website crash.

"Many, many customers came through to our websites and are coming through Click Frenzy. We saw a lot of customers and we are pleased with the result," he said.

Mr. Sivasailam said online sales in Australia would continue to show double-digit growth, at the very least, for the next 12 months. (851 words)

Words and Expressions

click	n.	咔嗒声	frenzy	n.	狂暴
crash	v.	（系统）崩溃	bypass	v.	绕过
phenomenal	a.	显著的，能知觉的	spike	n.	猛增
premium	n.	高级，优质	shore up		支持
bode	v.	预示			

Proper Nouns

Woolworths　沃尔沃斯，英国最大的日用品连锁超市
Windsor Smith　澳大利亚一家高档鞋店
Westfield　西田集团（澳大利亚一家跨国商场管理集团）
GST　澳大利亚的消费税
Booktopia　澳大利亚一家最大的网上书店

News Summary

这篇新闻是关于澳大利亚的一个网上商店，由于一下子增加了很多的访问量导致其瘫痪了。这个网站在圣诞节前做促销，联合其他的各零售商做减价销售活动，结果一下子就吸引了很多顾客。文章是典型的新闻报道，每个自然段就是一个句子，由于涉及的话题简单，所以很容易看懂。

Understanding Sentences

① 沃尔沃斯和温莎史密斯等零售商说，当"疯狂点击"网站瘫痪了的时候，有些顾客直接跳过它到他们的网店上购物。

② 两家零售商都说他们对额外增加的点击有所准备，温莎史密斯已经对其由墨尔本一家数字公司管理的服务器进行过反复测试，确保他们的网站在任何时间都可以应付五十万以上的访问。

③ 在"疯狂点击"的一本宣传册里说，在低端，一个"品牌最初的产品首次上目录"，零售商应付的广告费是 1500 澳元外加消费税。

④ 在星期三公布的一份声明中，"疯狂点击"说访问他们网站的顾客人数是"我们所能应付的最大能力的好多倍以上"。

⑤ 他说，"业务将越来越大，我相信，考虑到我们看到的成功的规模，顾客在早些时候所碰到的错误将很快地被遗忘。"

Exercises

Ⅰ. Understanding Ideas in the News

1. What did Windsor Smith gain from the promotion by Click Frenzy?

A. Their sales reached six-digit figures on Tuesday night.

B. They received many unique visitors.

C. They had the business for the whole month in one night.

2. What do participating retailers think about the promotion by Click Frenzy?

A. It helps them to sell full-price items, too.

B. It is good to boost the image of their brands and clients.

C. It causes their servers to go down on Tuesday night.

3. What did the Click Frenzy event make the retailers realize?

A. Online shopping will become popular.

B. There are technical issues involved.

C. It is an opportunity for retailers to expand.

4. How was business of Booktopia as it participated in Click Frenzy?

A. They had 11 sales in a minute.

B. They missed some beats.

C. They had a 550 percent increase in sales.

5. What did the participating retailers not prepare for?

A. The website crash.　　　　　　　　　B. The competition.

C. The scale of sales response.

II. Language Points

click, crash, bode, bypass, spike　这些都是常用于新闻报道中的词。

click：(咔嗒声) a light short sound, or to make something do this　e. g. *The key turned with a click.*

crash：((系统)崩溃) If a computer or system crashes, it suddenly stops operating.
e. g. *My laptop's crashed again.*

bode：(预示) to be a sign of something that will happen in the future, usually something particularly good or bad　e. g. *These recently published figures bode ill/do not bode well for the company's future.*

bypass：(绕过) to avoid something by going around it　e. g. *We were in a hurry so we decided to bypass Canterbury because we knew there'd be a lot of traffic.*

spike：(猛增) a sudden large increase in sth.　e. g. *A spike is expected this year.*

III. Questions for Further Study

This is a very typical news report, with short paragraphs and simple, one-syllabus words. The main idea is clearly expressed in the beginning paragraph, and some sub-headlines are given to help the reader catch the main idea in each section. Analyze the structure of this news report, with emphasis on the division of sections and the use of sub-headlines.

3. EU duties on Chinese solar panels losing member state support

Chinese workers examine solar panels at a plant in Huaibei in China's Anhui province. (Photograph: AP)

By Robin Emmott and Ethan Bilby
Yahoo News
Mon, May 27, 2013

BRUSSELS (Reuters)—A majority of EU governments oppose a plan to impose hefty duties on solar panel imports from China, a survey of member states showed on Monday, undermining efforts by Brussels to pressure Beijing over its trade practices.①

The European Commission, the EU's executive, accuses Chinese firms of selling solar panels at below cost in Europe—a practice known as "dumping"—and plans to impose duties, making it far harder for China to gain market share.

The duties, averaging 47 percent, will come into force from June 6 for a trial period and could be withdrawn if both sides reach a negotiated settlement.②

It is the largest trade case the Commission has undertaken, with about 21 billion euros of China-made solar panels sold in the EU.

The duties are being proposed by the EU's trade commissioner, Belgian lawyer Karel De Gucht, who met with Chinese Vice-Minister of Commerce Zhong Shan for an informal meeting in Brussels on Monday.

The Chinese side described the meetings as "constructive" and said the pair discussed solar duties as well as an EU threat to open an investigation into mobile telecom equipment makers Huawei and ZTE.

But Zhong said that either EU move would lead to a definitive Chinese response.

"Such practices of trade protectionism are not acceptable to China," a spokeswoman for the Chinese mission to the European Union said in a statement, and would "seriously sour the climate on bilateral trade and economic engagement". ③

"The Chinese government would not sit on the sidelines, but would rather take necessary steps to defend its national interest, if the EU went ahead," the statement said.

The fear of Chinese reprisal and potential loss of business has led Germany, Britain and the Netherlands to be among at least 14 member states to oppose the sanctions, diplomats told Reuters. ④

The Commission said China was pressuring some EU countries to oppose the duties.

"Commissioner De Gucht... made it very clear to the Vice-Minister that he was aware of the pressure being exerted by China on a number of EU member states, which explains why they are positioning themselves as they are in their advisory positions towards the European Commission," the Commission said in a statement.

The EU's 27 countries had until last Friday to submit a formal, written response to De Gucht's plans. While the trade commissioner would still have the right to impose the duties, doing so in the face of member states' opposition would be hard.

The Commission statement said De Gucht told China's vice-minister he wanted "to examine the possibility of a negotiated settlement in partnership with the United States should this become necessary."

Provisional duties will more than likely still go ahead on June 6, once they are published in the European Union's official journal, officials say, but the pressure to roll them back before they become permanent in December will be intense. ⑤

The split underlines the depth of division in the EU over how to deal with China, a critical market for many EU exporters and the region's second biggest trading partner over all.

Reuters spoke to 21 of the EU's 27 countries and confirmed that 15 opposed the duties, while six supported them. The other six either declined to say or were unreachable.

France and Italy are leading a group of countries that say De Gucht is right to go ahead with sanctions, arguing that China's rapid rise in solar panel output to more than the world's entire demand could not have happened without illegal state support. ⑥

Chinese companies have captured more than 80 percent of the European market from almost zero a few years ago.

De Gucht met China's deputy commerce minister for informal talks in Brussels on Monday, a day after Chinese Premier Li Keqiang and German Chancellor Angela Merkel, meeting in Berlin, called for an end to the dispute, as well as another conflict over Chinese telecoms companies accused of dumping in Europe.

Germany initially supported De Gucht's plans for duties, and it was a German company, Solar World, that first raised the complaint against the Chinese.

But rather than punitive measures, Merkel now appears to favor a negotiated solution, wary of the potential impact on German exporters if China were to take retaliatory steps.

"There is no need for more sanction measures," German Economy Minister Philipp Roesler told a news conference on Monday after talks with Li. (739 words)

Words and Expressions

hefty	a.	重的，高昂的	undermine	v.	破坏
dumping	n.	倾销	definitive	a.	最后的，确定的
bilateral	a.	有两面的，双边的	reprisal	n.	报复
sanction	n.	制裁	provisional	a.	临时的
punitive	a.	惩罚性的	wary	a.	机警的
retaliatory	a.	报复的			

Proper Nouns

Huawei 华为公司（中国一家民营电讯设备公司）
ZTE 中兴公司（中国一家国营电讯设备公司）
Angela Merkel 安克拉·默克尔（现任德国总理）

News Summary

2013年，中国与欧盟之间发生了一次有关中国光伏板在欧洲倾销的贸易摩擦。这篇新闻就是有关这一事件的许多报道之一。欧盟同时还要对我们的华为和中兴的通讯产品进行调查。但是，由于欧盟各国具体情况不同，他们对此的态度也不尽相同，如新闻最后提到的德国总理默克多的态度就比较灵活。

Understanding Sentences

① 星期一，一份对成员国的调查显示，大多数欧盟政府反对一项向从中国进口的光伏板征收高额关税的计划，影响了布鲁塞尔对北京的贸易做法施加压力所作出的努力。

② 这项平均为百分之四十七的关税将在六月六日开始的一段试验期内生效，如果双方能达成一致意见，也可能会撤销。

③ 中国驻欧盟代表团一位女发言人在一份声明中表示，"这种贸易保护主义的做法是中国无法接受的，它将严重影响双边贸易和经济合作的关系。"

④ 外交人士告诉路透社，由于担心中国方面的报复和贸易上可能的损失，使德国、英国和荷兰加入反对制裁的至少十四个成员国之中。

⑤ 官员说，一旦它们在欧盟的官方记录上发表，临时关税将很有可能还是从六月六日开始实行，但是，在这些关税在十二月成为永久的之前，希望撤销的压力还是很强的。

⑥ 以法国和意大利为首的若干国家表示，德古切决定实行制裁是正确的，他们认为，没有政府的非法支持，中国光伏板产量迅速上升至超过全球需求的事实不太可能发生。

Exercises

Ⅰ. Understanding Ideas in the News

1. What did the European Commission accuse Chinese firms of?
   A. Selling solar panel products at high prices.
   B. Dumping solar panel products in Europe.
   C. Occupying a large market share for solar panels
2. What did the Chinese side say about EU's decision to impose high duties on solar panel imports from China?
   A. China wouldn't give a definitive response.
   B. It is constructive.
   C. It is unacceptable to China.
3. Why did Germany and Britain side themselves with other countries that opposed the duties?
   A. They didn't agree with other countries.
   B. They received pressure from China.
   C. They were concerned about loss of business.
4. Why would it be hard for the trade commission to impose the duties on China's solar panels?
   A. The majority of EU member states are opposed to it.
   B. China is exerting pressure on a number of EU member states.
   C. The EU countries have to submit a formal, written response.
5. What did France and Italy argue for impose the duties on China's solar panels?
   A. Chinese companies are supported by the state.
   B. Chinese solar panel output increases too fast.
   C. The global demand for solar panels is met already.

Ⅱ. Language Points

hefty, punitive, wary, retaliatory, reprisal 文章中用这些词谈论中国和欧盟之间的贸易纠纷。

hefty：(重的,高昂的) large in amount, size, force, etc   e.g. a hefty bill/fine

punitive：(惩罚性的) intended as a punishment   e.g. *The UN has imposed punitive sanctions on the invading country.*

wary：(机警的) not completely trusting or certain about something or someone   e.g. *I'm a bit wary of/about giving people my address when I don't know them very well.*

retaliatory：(报复性的) from retaliate: to hurt someone or do something harmful to them because they have done or said something harmful to you   e.g. *If someone insults you, don't retaliate as it only makes the situation worse.*

reprisal：(报复) activity against another person, especially as a punishment by military forces or a political group   e.g. *economic/military reprisals*

III. Questions for Further Study

This news report tells the reader that many EU member states oppose a plan to impose high duties to import of solar panel from China, then explains why. There are two outstanding features of journalistic English to be noticed: (1) the quoting of authorities to support the statement; (2) putting more additional information at the end. Analyze this article carefully to see how these are achieved.

英语报刊知识介绍

新闻英语的词汇特点

由于新闻报道的主题范围很广，各种新闻所使用的文体不同，因此，作为一个整体的英语新闻的词汇量也很大，尽管我们说掌握了一定数量的新闻词汇，就可以阅读很多的英语新闻了。新闻英语所用的词汇，有一个基本的总体特点，就是词语生动，但固定句子的套式和常用句型却大致相同。词语生动指记者大多喜欢使用常用的又能准确表达意思的词语，同时尽量避免重复，当表达同一个意思时，多用同义词，以免给人一种枯燥单调的感觉。此外，为了避免重复和节省篇幅，使用指代词、缩略词等也比较多，因为话题的关系而使用区域英语的词汇也比较多。如本书中介绍穆斯林开斋节的新闻就用了一些阿拉伯语词，报道发生在南非的新闻又用了一些南非英语常用的词，或来自南非荷兰语的一些词汇。最后，英语标题所用的词又有它们的特色，有些人甚至总结出了好几百个英语新闻标题的常用词。

1. Newspaper clips of various headlines, noticing the use of words in the headlines

2. An example of the use of newspaper English in "Police tipped to vending theft ring"

Police tipped to vending theft ring by suspect using quarters for bail

By JOHN SULLIVAN
Journal-Bulletin Staff Writer

PORTSMOUTH — When a man arrested early Sunday for allegedly stealing from vending machines tried to pay his bail with a knapsack full of quarters, police suspected there was more to the case.

Later, Vierra said, Rosa asked for a bright-red backpack in the pickup's cab.

When police checked the pack, they discovered about $400 in change and keys used to open vending machines. As a result, they arrested Rosa's passenger, Jason N. Perez, 20, ▓▓▓▓▓▓▓▓▓▓▓▓. Both were charged with larceny, receiving stolen goods and possession of burglar's tools.

Unit 15　The London 2012 Olympics

The 2012 Summer Olympic was held in London, the UK, from 25 July to 12 August, 2012. London is the city to have hosted the Olympic games three times, in 1908, 1949 and 2012 respectively. The opening ceremony received widespread acclaim throughout the world, and was widely covered by the media. In this chapter, we collect three news reports about the games. The first one is a report from the American newspaper *USA Today*, from which we can see how the Americans commented on the opening. The second is a report from a British newspaper *Daily Mail*, from which we can see the British people's enthusiasm about the games. And the last one is a report on Usain Bolt's winning the 100-meter dash.

2012年的夏季奥运会于7月25日至8月12日在英国伦敦举行。伦敦是曾经分别于1908、1949和2012年三次承办奥运会的城市。本次奥运会的开幕式也别具一格，在世界上得到好评和各地媒体的大量报道。我们在本章收集了关于本次奥运的三篇报道。第一篇是来自美国的报纸《今日美国》的新闻,从中可看到以美国为首的外国媒体对开幕式的评价。第二篇是英国的报纸《每日电讯报》对开幕式的报道,它反映了英国人对主办本届奥运的热情。第三篇是对世界著名短跑运动员尤赛因·波尔特赢得一百米短跑的报道。

1. London Olympics opening ceremony quirky, fun, loud, British

By Mike Lopresti,
USA TODAY
7/28/2012, 7:07 a.m.

The Queen in her screen acting debut as a James Bond girl, certainly an opening ceremony first. *Rowan Atkinson* running with the lads from *Chariots of Fire*. *Harry Potter and William Shakespeare* and *Paul McCartney*. Bicycles made up to be doves, *Muhammad* Ali holding the Olympic flag.

And in the end, the flame lit not by a famous face but seven young people, igniting more than 200 copper petals — one for each country — that converged into a burning flower of Olympic best wishes and hopes. ①

It wasn't Beijing. Not as exotic, not as magical. And not as expensive. This opening ceremony was quirky and fun and loud and British.

There were not the wow moments of Beijing, just many very cool ones among the $3\frac{1}{2}$ hours. There was more humor than we usually see from an opening ceremony, with puns and pop culture among the pomp and circumstance. ②

During the athletes' parade, Fiji marched in to the music of the Bee Gees. And was that really dozens of Mary Poppins floating in from the sky?

It was a show that did not take itself too seriously. The guess is that played well on television back in the colonies.

Queen Elizabeth and Daniel Craig sharing a scene was not to be missed. "It's believed this is the first time Her Majesty has acted on film," the program noted.

Atkinson banging out the *Chariots of Fire* theme with one finger on a piano and then somehow showing up on the beach running with the track team was priceless.

The infield turning from a quiet countryside with sheepdogs and horses and ducks into an industrialized city with belching smokestacks was gold medal set design. ③

The torch lighting was a deft twist in the road, an artistic wonder that put the attention on the moment itself, rather than whoever was doing it. Probably not everyone's cup of English tea.

The dropping of 7 billion pieces of paper from a helicopter onto the assembled teams — representing every person on the planet — was inspired. Except to the clean-up crew. That's going to take a lot of brooms.

The collage of pictures of lost family members — spectators were invited to provide them — was moving, but one wonders about the thoughts of the Israeli delegation, which repeatedly has been shunned by the IOC in its request for a moment of silence at the opening ceremony for the victims of the 1972 Munich massacre. ④

And there was the same show-stopper every other city gets. The parade of athletes never goes out of style, though if more countries keep coming, it will take longer than the marathon. The organizers tried to move things along by playing music at 120 beats per minute to promote quicker walking by the athletes, but Greece started the march at 10:21 p.m. local time and the home team from Great Britain did not enter the stadium to end it until 11:54 p.m., to the music of David Bowie. ⑤

It's one of the nights of their lives. Who wants to hurry?

The flag bearers for the countries might have been the 205 proudest people in the world Friday night, and their diversity was a snapshot of the tapestry of the Games.

There were wealthy professional tennis players: Maria Sharapova for Russia and Novak Djokovic for Serbia. But also the archer from Bhutan, Sherab Zam's biography claiming she practices every day from 8 a.m. to 6 p.m.

There was Jamaica's Usain Bolt, who runs for world records and fame. And shooting's Bahya Mansour Al Hamad — the first female Olympian ever from Qatar — who says she hopes to encourage other women.

Only two men's basketball players were picked: Spain's Pau Gasol and China's Yi Jianlian.

But 11 taekwondo athletes were chosen.

North Korea track athlete Song-Chol Pak led his delegation, and it was comforting to see they had handed him the correct flag.

The USA chose a fencer from Notre Dame, Mariel Zagunis. The Americans came in snazzy blue and white outfits. China, the nation that produced them, should be proud.

And for a poignant history lesson, the Israel team marched in behind sailing's Shahar Zubari, 40 years after Munich. His uncle Gad Zubari was a wrestler in 1972, and the only Israeli to escape from the terrorists.

Ceremony director Danny Boyle's *Slumdog Millionaire* won eight Oscars, so he didn't need this to pay the bills. It must be a little nerve-wracking to have your work judged by an audience of 4 billion. ⑥He said he took on the Olympics partly because his father was such a big fan of the Games.

His father died 18 months ago. Friday would have been his birthday.

He'd have had reason to be proud. Good show, indeed. (786 words)

Words and Expressions

debut	n.	初次登场	dove	n.	鸽子
exotic	a.	异国情调的	quirky	a.	诡诈的，离奇的
pomp	n.	壮丽，盛况	belch	v.	冒烟，喷出
deft	a.	灵巧的	collage	n.	抽象拼贴画
shun	v.	避开，避免	tapestry	n.	织锦，挂毯
taekwondo	n.	跆拳道	fencer	n.	击剑者
snazzy	a.	时髦的	nerve-wracking	a.	伤脑筋的
archer	n.	射手，弓术家			

Proper Nouns

James Bond　詹姆士·邦德（英国一部系列侦探电影主角）
Chariots of Fire　《烈火战车》
Harry Potter　《哈利·波特》，英国幻想小说

Unit 15　The London 2012 Olympics

News Summary

　　由于每四年一度的奥运会开幕式往往成为世界关注的中心,所以各主办国都想尽办法创造能代表其文化的开幕式。美国报纸对于英国人主办的2012年奥运会开幕式的评价,就这么四个词:神奇、趣味、喧嚣和英国式的。这篇刊发于《今日美国》的报道,文字精练,评论中肯,但没有花很多笔墨在细节上,尤其是表演的细节。相反,它比较详细地报道了各国运动员代表团出场的最主要特点。

Understanding Sentences

　　① 最后,火炬不是由熟悉的面孔点燃,而是由七名青年一起点燃了两百多个铜制的花瓣——每一个代表一个国家——这些火苗串在一起,点燃了代表奥林匹克最好祝愿和希望的火炬。

　　② 开幕式上我们看到的幽默比任何其他仪式上的都要多,在这豪华壮观的场景中出现了许多妙语和流行文化元素。

　　③ 场上的景象从遍地牛羊、马匹和鸭子的农村变成了烟囱冒烟的一座工业城市,这正是金牌的背景设计。

　　④ 由家人提供的那些死去的家庭成员的照片组合非常感人,这使人们想起以色列代表团的反应。国际奥委会一直避开以色列提出的在开幕式上为1972年慕尼黑事件中的死难者默哀的要求。

　　⑤ 大会组织方通过播放快速节奏的音乐来使运动员入场的步伐加快,可是在当地时间10时21分希腊代表团才开始入场,而主办方英国代表团直到11时45分才跟着大卫·波伊的音乐迈进体育场。

　　⑥ 你的作品要由四十亿观众来评定,这肯定有点伤脑筋。

Exercises

Ⅰ. Understanding Ideas in the News

　　1. How was the Olympic torch lit at the end?
　　　A. By seven young people.　　　　　B. By Mohammad Ali.
　　　C. By Rowan Atkinson.

　　2. How does the reporter compare the London 2012 Olympic open to that of the Beijing 2008 Olympic?
　　　A. It was less expensive.　　　　　B. It was quick.
　　　C. It was as magical.

　　3. What did the opening ceremony begin with?
　　　A. Videos taken earlier of the Queen parachuting.
　　　B. The scene of James Bond and his girl.
　　　C. Pictures of celebrities together.

　　4. What was noticed about the parade of athletes?
　　　A. Each team shows the unique culture of the nation.

B. There were more countries coming.

C. There was a flag bearer to each team.

5. Which of the following athlete came from the smallest country in the world?

A. The archer.　　　　B. Sherab Zam.　　　　C. Yi Jianlian.

II. Language Points

quirk, exotic, deft, snazzy, nerve-wracking　这些是用于描述伦敦 2012 年奥运会开幕式的一些词。

quirky：(诡诈的，离奇的) unusual in an attractive and interesting way　e. g. *He was tall and had a quirky, off-beat sense of humour.*

exotic：(异国情调的) unusual and often exciting because of coming (or seeming to come) from a distant, especially tropical country　e. g. *exotic flowers/food/designs*

deft：(灵巧的) skilful, clever or quick　e. g. *Her movements were deft and quick.*

snazzy：(时髦的) modern and stylish in a way that attracts attention　e. g. *Paula's wearing a very snazzy pair of shoes*!

nerve-wracking：(伤脑筋的) describing something that is difficult to do and causes a lot of worry for the person involved in it　e. g. *My wedding was the most nerve-racking thing I've ever experienced.*

III. Questions for Further Study

This news report from *USA Today* has all the characteristics of news published in that newspaper—briefness and conciseness. And the order of narration is a little special—after a summary of the ceremony, it recaps the scenes from the beginning, until the end of the athlete parade. Notice how the reporter select the scenes to be reported.

2. Licence to thrill! London welcomes the world with spectacular three-hour Olympic Opening Ceremony celebrating Great Britain

By Jonathan McEvoy
Daily Mail
23:55 GMT, 27 July, 2012

Unit 15 The London 2012 Olympics

Good evening, Mr. Bond. Welcome, world. The Olympic Games arrived in London on Friday night with peals of bells, tableaux of drama and paroxysms of cheers that split the black velvet sky. ①

And with those four words of introduction from The Queen to Daniel Craig's 007 in a scene recorded in Buckingham Palace, corgis in attendance.

The artistry could do nothing but lift the spirits and set the tone for 16 days of magical competition across 26 sports. Yet for all the creative flair to be marvelled at, the vision of Britain sent out from here across the world at times bordered on left-wing propaganda. ②

Danny Boyle, the opening ceremony's ringmaster, has a creative mind of manic genius. He also has a history of gritty films and grim themes. For all his Oscars and Baftas, the *Slumdog Millionaire* director was a risky appointment for this seminal event.

NHS beds dominated the infield for so long that it seemed more a political message than a tribute to our hardworking nurses. The Jarrow marchers were given a prominent role. Churchill featured only fleetingly. Still, Boyle's £27million creation dazzled, winning him thousands of new Twitter followers by the second.

But the stars of this show — the one that stretches out before us over the most lavish sporting fortnight this island has ever staged — are the athletes. So who better to start the ceremony than our Tour de France hero, Bradley Wiggins, wearing the yellow jersey, ringing the bell before popping back to get ready for Mark Cavendish's road race challenge on Saturday morning? ③ By 9.05pm he had exited the stage and was tucked up in bed for his next endeavour.

Once the Jarrow marchers and the rolling kaleidoscopic scenery had delivered their brilliant tapestry, it was the athletes' turn to parade in. All 204 nations, predominantly in alphabetical order, though with Britain as hosts last into the stadium.

We now think of what Sir Chris Hoy, the proud flag bearer and the 240 who marched behind him can achieve. The first desire is to believe in the Olympic oath that was uttered by Britain's Taekwondo star Sarah Stevenson, who lost both her parents as she prepared for the Games.

On behalf of the 10,500 fellow London Olympians, she pledged to compete "for the glory of sport and the honour of our teams" by abiding by the rules and spirits of the movement we celebrated here.

She will, no doubt, compete free of stimulants but not everyone will be honouring her commitment. Nine drugs tests were failed in the build-up to Friday night's extravaganza. More will have cheated their way to London.

But it is the fun of competition, the joy of sharing in the best day of someone's life, of watching the super-human effort of the Bolt and Phelps and the rest, of history being made, that beckons us. ④

The success of the Games will be determined to an extent on how many British medals are won — 19 golds from Beijing is the yardstick. ⑤ But there is more than that parochial concern to concern us.

As a nation we are heirs to a rich tradition that forbids such short-sightedness. Greece, as the home of the ancient Olympics, has the greatest right to laud its sporting heritage in this quadrennial setting. Yet London has hosted the modern Games three times, a singular distinction and one that was touched upon by no less than the president of the International Olympic Committee, Jacques Rogge.

It is as relevant to Hoy and his team-mates who marched in their flashy Elvis-style white jackets as it was on the playing fields of Victorian Britain.

The Olympic torch's journey summed up so much that we can celebrate as a nation. It travelled its final stages to the Olympic Stadium along the Thames from Hampton Court Palace to the Tower of London aboard the Diamond Jubilee barge Gloriana.

The flame began on Mount Olympus, when it was lit by vestal virgins with a mirror and the sun's rays, was transported around Greece and flown over on BA Flight 2012 to start its 70-day, 8,000-mile trek across Britain. Sure there have been too many celebrity stooges brought in to run a leg of it.

David Beckham was seen with the torch on Friday night, a poster boy excluded from competition. The best argument for his inclusion in the football squad has always been that he was desperate to be an Olympian in every facet of the experience. That was hardly true of everyone his sport.

And, lo and behold, who should have missed out on the ceremony but the team captain Ryan Giggs and his fellow Welshman Craig Bellamy. Injury necessities or wilful absences?

London 2012 is massively different from the other Games the country hosted, in 1908 and 1948. They are bigger; Britain's place in the world post-imperial.

"One hundred years ago we were everything," said Boyle pre-show. "I hope there is an innate modesty in what we do. You have to learn your place in the world."

In fact, the best of British always was modest but with bold ambitions. It is still so as the Games of the XXX Olympiad, presented with brilliance and bias as midnight closed in over east London, begin. (875 words)

Words and Expressions

peal	n.	隆隆声，响亮的钟声	tableau	n.	静态画面、场面
paroxysm	n.	一阵发作	velvet	n.	天鹅绒，柔软，光滑
corgis	n.	威尔士矮脚狗	artistry	n.	艺术性，艺术才华
flair	n.	才能，本领	ringmaster	n.	表演指导者
manic genius		躁狂者	gritty	a.	坚忍不拔的
seminal	a.	种子的	lavish	a.	过分丰富的，浪费的
fleetingly	a.	飞快地，疾驰地	kaleidoscopic	a.	万花筒的，五花八门的
jersey	n.	运动衫	extravaganza	n.	内容狂妄的作品
stimulant	n.	兴奋剂	laud	v.	赞美，称赞，颂歌
parochial	a.	教区的，地方范围的	stooge	a.	配角，丑角，帮手
quadrennial	a.	每四年一次的	vestal	n.	处女，修女
barge	n.	驳船，游艇			

Proper Nouns

Baftas　英国电影学院奖
the NHS　英国国民健康保险制度
Elvis-style　猫王式的外套（猫王是美国一流行歌星的绰号）
Jarrow March　1936 年英国的一次游行

News Summary

这篇新闻同样是报道伦敦2012年奥运会开幕式，但由于记者所代表的国家不同，他们所报道的重点和报道方式也不同。新闻以两自然段的描述性导语段开头，然后很简单地总结了表演的经过。在报道运动员进场时只集中提到英国运动员，而且还总结了英国的体育精神。最后文章以介绍奥运圣火点燃的经过和简单的议论结束。

Understanding Sentences

① 星期五晚上，奥林匹克运动会在伦敦开幕，钟声清脆响亮，戏剧场面壮观，阵阵欢呼声冲破了漆黑的夜空。

② 然而，在赞美那些创造性的天才之作的同时，从这里向世界发出的英国的形象有时接近左翼的宣传。

③ 所以，有谁比我们的环法自行车比赛选手布勒·利魏金斯更合适来开始这场典礼呢？他穿着黄色运动衣，摇着车铃，但是星期六早上就要准备好参加在马克·卡文迪斯路段的比赛了。

④ 但是，正是比赛所带来的乐趣，正是与人分享一生中最好的几天的乐趣，正是欣赏像波尔特和菲尔斯这样的超人的表演的乐趣，正是创造历史的乐趣，召唤着我们到来。

⑤ 在一定程度上,这次运动会的成功取决于英国队能获得多少枚金牌,北京奥运会上我们获得了19枚金牌可以作为参照基准。

Exercises

Ⅰ. **Understanding Ideas in the News**

1. What did the Queen say in the recorded scene shown before the ceremony started?

   A. Good evening, Mr. Bond.

   B. The Olympic Games begin.

   C. Hello, welcome to London.

2. Who was the director of the performance at the opening?

   A. Danny Boyle.

   B. Daniel Craig.

   C. Bradley Wiggins

3. What message was sent by the NHS beds that dominated the infields for so long?

   A. Political.

   B. A tribute to the nurses.

   C. Economic.

4. How were the athletes expected to behave during the two weeks of competition?

   A. They are supposed to abide by the rules and spirits of the Games.

   B. They are supposed to compete fiercely and defend the national honor.

   C. They are supposed to win as many gold medals as they can.

5. How did the Olympic torch travel to the stadium for the final stage?

   A. By boat along the Thames.

   B. On BA Flight 2012.

   C. Carried by David Beckham.

Ⅱ. **Language Points**

tableaux, paroxysm, artistry, flair, tapestry 这些词用来表述开幕式上精彩的表演。

tableaux:（静态画面、场面）an arrangement of people who do not move or speak, especially on a stage, who represent a view of life, an event, etc

paroxysm:（一阵发作）a sudden and powerful expression of strong feeling, especially one that you cannot control e.g. *In a sudden paroxysm of jealousy he threw her clothes out of the window.*

artistry:（艺术性,艺术才华）great skill in creating or performing something, such as in writing, music, sport, etc e.g. *You have to admire the artistry of her novels.*

flair:（才能,本领）natural ability to do something well e.g. *He has a flair for languages.*

tapestry:（织锦,挂毯）a piece of cloth whose pattern or picture is created by sewing or weaving different coloured threads onto a special type of strong cloth

III. Questions for Further Study

This news report focuses more on the performance at the opening ceremony and the British players, as well as the artists who participated in the design and performing. Compare it to the first reading to see some differences in the following aspects: (1) the organization and presentation of ideas; (2) the view and focuses of the reporters.

3. Don't Deny the Joy of Usain Bolt

By JASON GAY
Wall Street Journal
August 11, 2012, 5:20 a.m. ET

You loved him. Come on. If you offer an objection, I'm not buying it for a moment. It's a pose. It's what you think you're supposed to say, but you don't really feel it. If we cut you open and investigate, those bright red insides of yours will reveal the truth. And the truth is you have adored every second of him. How could you not?

The 100. The 200. The finger point. The shhhhhhhh. The bow and arrow.

The push-ups. (The push-ups were truly the best)

Over-the-top? Yes. Funny? Totally. Obnoxious? Borderline.

But unforgettable, all of it.

The Jamaican sprinter Usain Bolt is not to be missed at these 2012 Summer Olympics in London. He has won gold medals in the 100 and 200 meters, breaking his own Olympic record in the first event, and getting pretty close in the second; he would have broken his 200 mark Thursday night had he not stopped to order a macchiato and take a phone call with 30 meters to go. ①

In a Games rich with thrilling moments, Bolt towers above all. He has embraced the world's attention, as if it charges him and propels his stride. A week ago, there had been speculation that Bolt was about to lose his title as the World's Fastest Human, but seven days have made that conjecture sound ridiculous. Everyone who came to London was running for second place. Deep second place. You got a silver medal, and, for the rest of your life, you get to be in a lot of Usain Bolt posters.

He's fast. It's official, again.

Still, the most satisfying part of Bolt—even more than his brilliant runs—is how much he demolishes the myth that the world wants humble athletes. This is the belief that superstars are supposed to always carry themselves as paragons of modesty, never calling the spotlight to themselves, never crossing some bright, imaginary line that exists dividing the attention-deserving from the attention-seeking. ②

This is also known as the Boring Line.

The Boring Line is a big deal in sports. It's a frothy topic on talk radio after every silly scoring celebration or overly demonstrative occasion on a field or a court. Violations of the Boring Line are good for manufactured outrage and highlight shows, and they make social media go crazy. ③

But the Boring Line is tedious. I have been hearing about how excessive celebrations are ruining sports as long as I have been watching sports. So have you. It made little sense then and makes less sense now. It's not ruining anything. You like this stuff or you don't; a fancy end-zone dance is definitely not everyone's favorite thing, and I'm sure it's pushed some fans away from the game. But these are the kind of people who hate pizza and scream at dogs.

What's great about Bolt is that he crashes over this line and nobody cares. He's just too good. The finger pointing, the shhhhh, the push-ups, the bow and arrow, the underappreciated somersault he did after the 100 last Sunday—he does all the things you're allegedly not supposed to do. ④

Doesn't matter. Earth loves Bolt.

It helps that Bolt loves Earth, too, and does everything with a wink.

He possesses a light, showman's touch, and even when post-win celebrations are choreographed, they're clever. His signature bow and arrow thunder has a touch of whimsy—an exaggerated sense of the moment, not to mention a nod to his last name. ⑤ It's so clear Bolt feeds off the theater of it all, the joy he provokes, converting the cauldron of flashbulbs inside Olympic Stadium into energy.

But he also moves to his own, amusing inner clock. I have reached the point—and I believe I am not alone—at which I almost enjoy watching Bolt run a heat as much as a final (I said almost). Finals provide history, but heats offer the entertaining sight of Bolt regulating his Bolt-ness. Watching him back off in his 200 meters semifinal was hilarious. People have run more spiritedly down the aisle on "The Price is Right". Bolt draws back, like a sommelier realizing he's accidentally poured an expensive bottle the customer didn't order. Hold on, he seems to be saying. You'll get the good stuff later.

There will be some who argue that winning exonerates everything, and that Bolt's personality wouldn't be so intoxicating if he was finishing second. To this, I'd say: you're right.

But this is another truth that Usain Bolt, who runs a final time Saturday as part of Jamaica's 4×100 relay, exposes. For all our belief in humility, for all the veneration of the modest and supposedly modest, there is no visual in sports quite as satisfying as the called shot—the athlete who says he or she will go out and do it, and then does it. ⑥ There's no use denying the thrill of a boast delivered. It is as fun as it gets. Bolt acts like it's the greatest thing we've ever seen, because it kind of is the greatest thing we've ever seen.

Let's not pretend. He's Usain Bolt, and you approve his message. (856 words)

Words and Expressions

adore	v.	崇拜	obnoxious	a.	不愉快的，讨厌的
sprinter	n.	赛跑选手	macchiato	n.	滴注式咖啡壶
conjecture	v.	推测，臆想	demolish	v.	毁坏，破坏
paragon	n.	模范	somersault	n.	筋斗
allegedly	ad.	据说，据传	wink	n.	眨眼
choreograph	n.	舞蹈设计	whimsy	n.	怪念头，奇想
flashbulb	n.	闪光灯泡	hilarious	a.	欢闹的
sommelier	n.	〈法语〉斟酒服务员	exonerate	v.	免除责备，证明无罪
humility	n.	谦卑	veneration	n.	尊敬，崇拜

Proper Nouns

Usain Bolt   尤赛恩·博尔特（牙买加短跑运动员）
the Boring Line   无聊线（指运动员在获得胜利时做出的各种过分夸张的动作）

News Summary

这篇新闻评论是关于奥运会上的明星运动员牙买加短跑选手尤赛恩·博尔特的。比赛之前，有传言说博尔特的"世界上跑得最快的人"的称号将不保，但是七天来的比赛打破了这一谣传。博尔特在短跑的几项比赛中还是第一。而且，他每次取得好成绩之后总是做出一些动作，夸耀他的成绩，显得十分兴高采烈的样子。作者表示，这是运动员自信的表现，是一种兴奋的表达，完全无可非议。

Understanding Sentences

① 他已经赢得了100米和200米比赛的金牌，在第一项中破了他自己的奥运记录，在第二项中非常接近；星期四晚上他原本可以破他200米的记录，要是他在最后30米时不停下来要一杯咖啡和打了一个电话的话。

② 这是人们通常的看法，他们认为超级明星应该总是谦虚谨慎的模范，从不吸引公众

注意，从不哗众取宠，超越不该跨过的红线。

③ 违反了这一无聊线就会使人们愤怒和关注，这使社交媒体兴奋不已。

④ 上星期天在一百米比赛之后，他手指指向前方，他发出嘘嘘声，他做俯卧撑，他做出射箭状，他翻筋斗，他做出你肯定不会做的动作。

⑤ 他那射箭状的标志性动作带有怪念头的成分，是那个时刻做出的夸张的表现，也是对他自己的姓的认同。（英语的 bolt 具有"像弓箭那么快"的意思）

⑥ 我们崇尚谦虚，我们尊敬谦虚，在体育中，没有什么比这种大胆的表达更令人满意的了——运动员说他或她将尽全力去做，然后真正做到了。

Exercises

Ⅰ. **Understanding Ideas in the News**

1. Why didn't Usain Bolt break his own record for the 200 meter event?

   A. He slowed down with 30 meters to go.

   B. He stopped to order coffer.

   C. He had broken his 100m record.

2. What myth did Bolt demolish with his gestures after the race?

   A. Superstars are supposed to be modest.

   B. He was about to lose his title as the World's Fastest Human.

   C. He crossed the line that exist dividing people.

3. What is a hot topic after every celebration or obvious occasion?

   A. The Boring Line.   B. Usain Bolt.

   C. World's Fastest Human.

4. What do some athletes do after they win the match, or score a goal?

   A. They show some very exaggerative gestures.

   B. They dance to the music.

   C. They eat pizza and scream at dogs.

5. What does Bolt's signature bow and arrow thunder show about himself?

   A. He possesses a light, showman's touch.

   B. He is overjoyed with winning.

   C. He wants to provoke joy among the audience.

Ⅱ. **Language Points**

wink, whimsy, conjecture, demolish, exonerate　这些词用来谈论博尔特赛跑后常做出的招牌动作。

wink：(眨眼) closing one eye briefly as a way of greeting someone, or of showing that you are not serious about something you have said

whimsy：(怪念头，奇想) something that is intended to be strange and amusing but in fact has little real meaning or value　e. g. *Personally I've always considered mime to be a lot of whimsy.*

conjecture: (推测,臆想) an opinion or idea that is not based on definite knowledge and is formed by guessing   e.g. *This conjecture is not supported by real evidence.*

demolish: (毁坏,破坏) to totally destroy a building, especially in order to use the land for something else   e.g. *A number of houses were demolished so that the supermarket could be built.*

exonerate: (免除责备,证明无罪) to show or state that someone or something is not guilty of something   e.g. *The report exonerated the crew from all responsibility for the collision.*

III. Questions for Further Study

This is a news comment that appears on *The Wall Street Journal*. It makes comments on the exaggerative gestures Usain Bolt acts out after he completes the race and won the first. In this article there are some expressions that are very funny but hard to get at. Analyze the article by pointing out those expressions and interpreting them in your own language.

英语报刊知识介绍

新闻照片

新闻照片是传统新闻报道的一个重要组成部分,通讯社一般都提供新闻照片服务,报刊上的头条新闻至少都配有一张现场发回来的照片,这使读者对新闻的内容有比较直观的了解。各种新闻杂志上的照片也很多。而在报刊的网站上可以看到更多的照片。

一些通讯社每年还评选本年度最佳的照片。

1. Bystanders standing around the body of a suspected Ebola victim lying in a street in the town of Koidu, Kono district in Eastern Sierra Leone (Reuters / Thursday, December 18, 2014)

2. A woman kissing a Ukrainian serviceman through the gate as he stands on the territory of a military unit located in the village of Lyubimovka near a local airfield, southwest of Simferopol, Crimea's capital (Reuters/Monday, March 03, 2014)

Unit 16 Culture News

As different peoples in the world have their own different cultures, we are interested in knowing about the culture, folk tradition and customs of other peoples. The newspaper is one source for us to get information on culture. News reports about cultures may be stories about the history, tradition, custom, literature, arts and lifestyle, etc. There are segments on many newspapers that are devoted to topics like these; some may be very interesting for us to read. This chapter has three news reports: one is about the Muslim festival of Eid Al-Adha, the other two are about novels that don't have an ending in English literature.

由于世界上不同的民族有自己的不同文化,我们对此很感兴趣,很想了解其他民族的文化、民间传统和习俗。报纸是我们获取有关文化信息的一个资源。关于文化的新闻报道可以是有关一个民族的历史、传统、习俗、文学、艺术和生活方式的报道。许多报纸都有专门用来报道这些话题的专栏,有些对我们来说也许很有意思。本章包含了三篇文化新闻,一篇是关于穆斯林开斋节的,另两篇是关于文学阅读的,它们都讨论英语文学中一些没有结尾的小说。

1. Eid Al-Adha, the story and traditions

Eid Al-Adha, also called the Feast of Sacrifice or the Greater Bairam, is one of two important religious holidays celebrated by Muslims worldwide.

Man sharpens knives in preparation for the ritual slaughter of animals for Eid. (Photo by Hassan Ibrahim)

By Rana Muhammad Taha, Nouran El-Behairy and Hend Kortam
Daily News (Egypt)

October 25, 2012

The day of Eid starts with Eid prayer. Al-Adha has a special prayer; it takes place sometime after *Fajr* when the sun loses its reddishness. It's a congregational prayer that consists of two *rak' ah* (praying units) followed by a sermon, which is usually given by the Imam.

The ruling of Eid prayer is disputed among scholars, some maintain the prayer is compulsory and thus those who do not pray without reasonable excuse are sinners; while others hold it is recommended but not obligatory. ①

After the prayer comes the ritual of sacrificing the animal which is usually a sheep, goat, cow, ram or camel. The sacrifice has certain criteria, regarding the age, the health condition and the ownership of the animal. The sacrifice can be made anytime from after the prayer on the first day of Eid until the sunset of the fourth day.

For a few days before and after the Adha Eid, the streets of Cairo are filled with blood from the slaughtering of the cattle. It is impossible to avoid the sight of blood, inches high in some places. In some neighbourhoods, if you're on the street after a cattle beast was slaughtered you will see the butchers, at their most lucrative time of the year, covered in blood and with an array of different sized knives in their pockets. ②

Slaughtering cattle in Islam follows certain rules regardless of whether it is Eid or any normal day. The difference is that in Eid, the act itself is a religious symbol. Doctor Mohamed Mokhtar Al-Mahdy, a member of the committee of the senior Al-Azhar scholars and head of the Legitimate Committee for the Supporters of the Sunnis, explained the rules that must be followed when slaughtering the cattle and the extent to which they are followed in Egypt.

"The rightful slaughter in Islam, and Christianity and Judaism is unified. It is cutting the veins but not directly beneath the chin, you leave a vertebra or two and then slaughter the animal and wait for the blood to drain," he said. ③

"The cattle is slaughtered in the direction of the Qibla and the person who slaughters it has to say 'Allahu Akbar'," Al-Mahdy added. He said that the words "God is Great" have a huge significance when slaughtering. "It means that I have not assaulted this animal, but I am slaughtering it in the name of God," Al-Mahdy explained.

Al-Mahdy said that these words mean that God has created both the slaughterer and the animal and that he is more powerful than both of them.

Al-Mahdy spoke about the need to be merciful towards the cattle when slaughtering it. "The animal should not see the knife before it is slaughtered and should not be slaughtered in front of a slaughtered animal," Al-Mahdy said. ④ Often, animals will be slaughtered in the same place. Once they witness the slaughtering of another animal, they are in shock. "This way the animal is tortured," he said.

Al-Mahdy described the current way in which the animals are slaughtered, in which they may witness other animals being slaughtered as wrong and cited a *Hadith* (saying) of Prophet Mohamed proving that it is wrong to subject the animals to this. He added that before slaughtering the animals, the blade of the knife that is going to be used to slaughter the cattle must be sharpened. ⑤

The meat is then divided into three shares, the family retains one third to eat, another goes to relatives, neighbours and friends and the third is distributed among the poor. It was also recommended by scholars to carry out the sacrifice right after the prayer to be able to have its meat for breakfast.

Like any Egyptian celebration, the Adha Eid is famous (or rather notorious) for its special meals. Unlike the Fitr Eid where you have sweet, sugary Kahk for breakfast, the Adha is all about the meat. Yes, ladies and gentlemen, Egyptians have meat for breakfast, be it stir-fried liver or meat cubes; and it might well be coupled with some delicious *Fatta* (rice with toasted bread chips and tomato sauce).

The meat intake doesn't quite die out by lunch/dinner time but there is some slight variation. If one hasn't already taken their generous share of Fatta and meat cubes, it is mandatory that they do so during lunch. ⑥ Otherwise, lots of other Egyptian dishes are waiting in line, ranging from the classic *Ro'a'* (crispy pie-like dough layered with minced meat) and the ever popular lamb cutlets.

Putting the food department behind us, other priorities also fall into place; namely family reunions. If the entire family doesn't get together to share this mouthwatering banquet, then they're sure to meet up some time after lunch. It is at that time when grown-ups get to catch up and little kids get to show-off their new Eid clothes and spend their entire Eid allowances, *Eideyas*, on homemade fireworks.

The exchange of greetings and visits was recommended by prophet Mohamed; some scholars even mentioned that he encouraged Muslims going to the Eid prayer to take a different route as they returned home, to get the chance to meet and greet more people.

These activities aim to bring Muslims closer together and to encourage helping the poor by seeing that no one is left without meat during Eid. (888 words)

Words and Expressions

prayer	n.	祈祷		congregational	a.	(教堂)会众的
Imam	n.	[伊斯兰]阿訇,教长		compulsory	a.	被强制的,义务的
obligatory	a.	义不容辞的		sacrifice	n.	牺牲,祭品
vertebra	n.	脊椎骨,椎骨		mandatory	a.	命令的,强制的
mince	v.	切碎		cutlet	n.	肉片

Proper Nouns

Eid 开斋节

Eid Al-Adha 宰牲节

the Sunnis （穆斯林教的）逊尼派
Judaism 犹太教
Qibla 朝拜
Eid Al-Fitr 开斋节

News Summary

穆斯林的开斋节是一个主要节日，那天几乎所有的家庭都屠杀一头牲畜来祭祀，或是牛，或是羊。伊斯兰教对于屠杀动物有一套规矩，整个过程表现出这是天意，人只是奉神的意旨办事。这篇新闻介绍在埃及人们是这样过开斋节的。

Understanding Sentences

① 学者们对开斋节祈祷的规定有争论。有些人认为，这些祈祷是强制性的，因此，那些没有合理的理由而不祈祷的人就是罪人，其他人则认为它是推荐性的，因而不是非做不可的。

② 在某些社区，如果你在一头动物被屠杀以后走到街上，你会看到那些屠夫，衣服上沾满血迹，口袋里带着各种大小不一的刀子，那是他们一年中收获最大的时刻。

③ 这样做是切断血管，而不是直接在下巴的部位上割一刀，刀子停留在一两个脊椎骨上，然后把动物杀死，等着血管里的血慢慢流干净。

④ "那头动物在被杀掉之前不应该看到刀子，也不应该在一头已经被杀死的动物面前被屠宰，"阿里·马哈地说。

⑤ 他补充说，在屠杀这头动物之前，准备用来杀死它的刀子锋面必须磨砺。

⑥ 假如一个人还没有享用那很大一份的米饭和肉粒，那么他必须在午餐的时候吃，这是强制性的。

Exercises

Ⅰ. Understanding Ideas in the News

1. When does the Eid prayer begin?
   A. In the morning.
   B. In the evening.
   C. When the sun is setting down.
2. What is the rightful slaughter of an animal in Islam?
   A. The animal should be killed in front of a dead one.
   B. The knife much cut through the vertebra.
   C. It is cutting the veins and letting the blood drip.
3. Why must the blade of the knife be sharpened before slaughtering the animal?
   A. They want to be able to kill the animal quickly.
   B. They want to be merciful towards the cattle.
   C. They want to cut the bones of the animal.
4. What is different between the Fitr Eid and the Adha Eid?

A. The Adha Eid is all about eating the meat.
B. The meat is divided into three shares.
C. The Fitr Eid has stir-fried liver for breakfast.
5. What is the Egyptian food Fatta made up of?
A. Stir-fried liver and meat cubes.
B. Rice, toasted bread and tomato sauce.
C. Crispy pie-like dough with minced meat.

II. Language Points

congregational, obligatory, mandatory, prayer, sacrifice 这些词用在介绍伊斯兰教的开斋节。

congregational: ((教堂)会众的) from congregation: a group of people gathered together in a religious building for worship and prayer   e.g. *The vicar asked the congregation to kneel.*

obligatory: (义不容辞的) describing something you must do because of a rule or law, etc.   e.g. *The medical examination before you start work is obligatory.*

mandatory: (命令的,强制的) describing something which must be done, or which is demanded by law   e.g. *The minister is calling for mandatory prison sentences for people who assault police officers.*

prayer: (祈祷) the act or ceremony in which someone prays   e.g. *I found her kneeling in prayer at the back of the church.*

sacrifice: (牺牲,祭品) (a) religious offering to God or a god, esp. of an animal by killing it ceremonially.

III. Questions for Further Study

This news report was carried on an English newspaper published in Egypt. It introduces the Muslim custom of observing the Eid Al-Adha, a festival that centres on the slaughtering of cattle for meat. It devotes the main part to explaining the rules that must be followed in slaughtering the animal. It also tells us how the Egyptians share the meat and the joy of festival among people. Pay attention to the Arabic words and their meanings.

2. Coming to bad ends: stories that refuse closure

Narratives that finish without resolving their plots—such as *Brighton Rock* and *An Inspector Calls*—are unending torture for readers.

Make it stop... Richard Attenborough in the 1947 film of *Brighton Rock*. (Photograph: Ronald Grant Archive)

Russell Williams

The Guardian

20 November, 2012

Fully resolved tragedy, leaving stage and page a sluice with blood or tears, induces a washed-clean calm in the reader, even as it plays havoc with her mascara.① Muslin-clad romances crushed in embraces on the last page, or chocolate-box mysteries tied off with a flourish of resolving ribbon, leave me sighing and replete. Even endings presaging inevitable sequels, wherein a vital protagonist or quest object has yet to be freed or found (YA trilogies, I'm looking at you) can increase my sense of wellbeing; if I enjoyed the book's world and its writing, another to look forward to is no bad thing. But there is a tiny subset of unresolved and evil endings that leave their protagonists poised, helpless, on the brink of cataclysm, with the reader forever conscious, forever appalled and forever powerless to intervene.② I call these Sword of Damocles endings, and avoid them like the black catarrh.

The first of these beastly, brain-seizing denouements I encountered was a theatrical one—JB Priestley's *An Inspector Calls*, which I studied at school. It wasn't the relentlessly succeeding revelations about the Birling family's collaborative doing-to-death of Eva Smith, sacked, shamed and driven to suicide by bourgeois callousness and hypocrisy, that gave my 12-year-old head the dramatic equivalent of an earworm.③ It wasn't even the "fire and blood and anguish" the Inspector calls down on them in recompense, although I remember confusedly expecting literal flames, and possibly the appearance of the *Demon King*, on the class trip to the actual show. It's the fact that the play ends with a phone call about a young girl's suicide, and the family's realisation that while the Inspector might not have been what he seemed, they haven't been let off after all—their shame and sorrow have simply been postponed.④ Both the arse-covering elders and the repentant kids are held in that moment forever, without the possibility of ever facing their tragedy or finding redemption beyond it. Like Eva Smith, they're not given any second chance; only a brief bubble of illusory hope, which bursts as the curtain falls.

Similarly, Graham Greene's *Brighton Rock* plucked the lowest string in my brain when I read it in my teens, and has left it humming since. The precise, savage planes of the novel, sharp as a stabbing bird's beak, are clear to the reader from its justly famous opening ("Hale knew, before he had been in Brighton three hours, that they meant to murder him"). Pinkie the baby-faced killer and his simple-complex vileness, alternately treading down and encouraging naive Rose's spaniel love, makes for repeated wincing on the reader's part; so does his cheerful nemesis, Ida, and her somehow hideous implacability, peeping out like withered children from the jolly robe of the Spirit of Christmas Present. But its ending, which leaves the widowed, pregnant Rose walking "rapidly" towards "the worst horror of all", the disc on which Pinkie has recorded a hissed message of hatred instead of the love-words she thinks will give her courage, makes me want to beat on the glass panel between reader and book until it breaks, seize her by the shoulders and distract her while someone else breaks the record over his knee and sets fire to the pieces. ⑤

As for Mo Hayder's *Hanging Hill*, it has bounced around my unquiet cerebellum since I read it earlier this year, and is still popping up every now and then to play merry hell with my peace of mind. Its protagonists, estranged sisters Sally and Zoë, navigate the book's moral maze clumsily and with frequent, increasingly cataclysmic false steps. ⑥ The worse they do, the worse is done to them, and the greater the reader's agony on their behalf. Hayder's masterful evocation of how calmly murderous a parent can become in defence of a child—the moment when Sally sets fear aside, birthing "a thing that was skinless and sharp-toothed, with the long face of a dragon"—is closely followed by the cruel revelation that her saved child has blithely been sent off into a wilderness of unmapped lanes with a nondescript, gently-spoken killer, her mother missing the frantic phone messages that bring the news too late. Part of my mind is still driving through those lanes with a shotgun, and I think it always will be.

Is anyone else living vicariously under a suspended literary sword, desperate for the resolution they're never going to get without some Annie Wilkes-style author-kidnap? And can you steer me away from any other brain-melting not-quite-coups de grace? (750 words)

Words and Expressions

sluice	n.	水闸;(水闸控制的)水	muslin	n.	一种薄细的棉布,[总称]女性
mascara	n.	染眉毛油			
crush	v.	压碎,碾碎	replete	a.	充满的
sequel	n.	续集,结局	protagonist	n.	(戏剧、故事、小说中的)主角
poise	v.	保持平衡,保持均衡			
appal	v.	使胆寒,使惊骇	cataclysm	n.	灾难,大洪水,地震
denouement	n.	结局	catarrh	n.	(医学)卡他,黏膜炎
revelation	n.	显示,揭露	relentlessly	ad.	无情的

callous	a.	无情的，冷淡的	sack	v.	解雇
recompense	v.	报偿	hypocrisy	n.	伪善
arse	n.	屁股，〈英〉饭桶，笨蛋	repentant	a.	后悔的，悔改的
pluck	v.	勇气	redemption	n.	赎回，偿还
tread	v.	踏，行走，踩碎	vileness	n.	讨厌，卑劣
wince	v.	退缩	spaniel	n.	西班牙长耳狗
implacability	n.	不缓和，不安静	distract	v.	转移
cerebellum	n.	小脑	estrange	v.	疏远
nondescript	a.	难以区别的	maze	n.	曲径，迷宫
coups de grace		最后一击	evocation	n.	唤出，唤起
vicariously	ad.	产生同感的	blithely	ad.	愉快地，快乐地
havoc	n.	大破坏，浩劫	nemesis	n.	报应，复仇女神

Proper Nouns

Sword of Damocles　　达摩克利斯之剑，指悬在头上的迫切而永久的危险
JB Priestley　　约翰·普里斯特利，英国小说家
An Inspector Calls　《探长来访》
Demon King　《最后大魔王》，日本作家的小说
Graham Greene　　格雷厄姆·格林，英国小说家
Brighton Rock　《布莱登棒棒糖》
Mo Hayder　　莫海德，英国犯罪小说家，生于1962年
Hanging Hill　《悬山》

News Summary

这篇新闻是英国《卫报》的副刊上的一篇文章，讲的是关于一些文学作品的结尾故意留下伏笔和余地让读者思考，可是像本文作者这样的人，对于这类结尾苦思不得其解，反而被它折磨得吃睡不安宁。作者接着谈了三位不同时期的英国作家所写的三本小说，第一本就是著名的普利斯特利写的《探长来访》。

Understanding Sentences

① 结局完整的悲剧，不管是在舞台上还是在书里到处是血和泪，在读者心中引起的是一种清洗干净了的平静，即使它描写了红颜祸水。

② 但是，有一小类没有解决问题且又邪恶的结局，让故事的主角处于一种无法平衡、无助或面临大灾难的边缘，而让读者一直在猜想中，一直在恐惧中，一直处于无力干预的状态。

③ 在我那十二岁的脑袋里像一条爬虫般挥之不去的，不是那一个接一个无情的关于伯令一家可能参与了导致伊娃·史密斯死去的阴谋的暴露；也不是被解雇、又被羞辱了的伊娃，在资产阶级的厚颜无耻和虚伪的迫使下，一步步地走向了自杀。

④ 这出戏的结局是电话响起，电话那头传来一个声音说有个女孩自杀了，这时一家人才知道，虽然探长也许心里想的跟他看起来的样子不同，他们并没有被他放过——他们的耻

辱和悲哀只不过被推迟了。

⑤ 但是,它的结尾让成了寡妇又怀孕的露西"疾速地"朝着"所有最恐怖的地方走去",那张苹基在上面录了嘶哑声音的怨恨话语而不是她觉得会给她带来勇气的爱情话语的光盘,使我很想敲打在读者和书之间的那层玻璃,直到它破裂,一把抓住她的肩膀把她拉开,让其他人把光盘用膝盖打碎,点火烧掉。

⑥ 故事的主角是已经被疏远了的两姐妹萨丽和左伊,他们在书中道德的迷宫中笨拙地摸索着,越来越经常地迈出灾难性的步子。

Exercises

Ⅰ. Understanding Ideas in the News

1. According to the writer, what kind of ending to novels makes him feel comfortable?

   A. Endings with blood and tears and death on the scene.

   B. Endings that foretell the destiny of the protagonist in the following part.

   C. Endings of sudden reversal to the plots before it.

2. What is left to the mind of the audience by *An Inspector Calls* when the curtain falls?

   A. The relentlessly succeeding revelations about the Birling family.

   B. A brief bubble of illusory hope for the Birling family.

   C. The "fire and blood and anguish" the Inspector calls down on them.

3. Who killed Eva Smith in *An Inspector Calls*?

   A. The Birling family.

   B. An Inspector.

   C. Bourgeois callousness and hypocrisy.

4. Why is the ending of *Brighton Rock* so unbearable to the writer?

   A. It does not give an answer to the fate of Rose.

   B. It shows Rose's affection for Pinkie.

   C. It does not reveal what Pinkie had recorded.

5. What makes the writer's mind still driving through those lanes with a shotgun?

   A. He wants to kill the nondescript, gently-spoken killer.

   B. He wants to listen to the missed phone messages.

   C. He wants to find out where the abnormal baby has been sent.

Ⅱ. Language Points

denouement, revelation, evocation, poise, replete 这些词是作者用来描写那些没有结局的小说的。

denouement:(结局) the end of a story, in which everything is explained, or the end result of a situation

revelation:(显示,揭露) when something is made known that was secret, or a fact that is made known   e.g. *a moment of revelation*

evocation: (唤出, 唤起) from evoke: to make someone remember something or feel an emotion   e.g. *That smell always evokes memories of my old school.*

poise: (保持平衡, 保持均衡) balance; be balanced   e.g. *A bird poised on the branch.*

replete: (充满的) full, especially with food   e.g. *After two helpings of dessert, Sergio was at last replete.*

III. Questions for Further Study

Reading the literature section in a newspaper can be very challenging, yet helpful to the student of English. This news report is a good piece of exercise, though a little difficult. The writer raises the issue of unending stories that make the reader feel bad, then discuss the endings of three novels. To fully understand the reading, try to analyze the meanings of some key sentences and the literary terms.

3. The Box and the Keyhole

(Illustration by Roman Muradov.)

Posted by Brad Leithauser

The New Yorker

November 21, 2012

Recently, I drove into a patch of rainy fog and everything in my head turned clear. A memory came back—gently, vividly—of another rainy drive. This was more than a dozen years ago. Four of us were driving back home to Massachusetts from a family friend's wedding in Philadelphia. We figured on six or seven good hours in the car, and we'd brought along a number of books on tape. We were listening to Daphne du Maurier's *My Cousin Rachel*. As it happens, that story, too, opens with a wedding.

The wedding *we'd* attended had been an auspicious occasion—but not so the wedding in the book. While wintering in Italy for his health, the narrator's guardian and cousin, an English country gentleman named Ambrose Ashley, had fallen in love with an impoverished contessa, his distant cousin Rachel, and precipitately married her. ① The joys of married life were destined to be short lived, though, and Ambrose soon sank into a feverish decline and died—but not before scribbling to his cousin back in England a couple of urgent, unsettling, and possibly febrile letters hinting that lovely Rachel just might not be the angel he'd first taken her for.

Both in the book and along the New Jersey Turnpike, it began to rain. One big, whistling truck after another threw a blinding wash across our windshield. The narrator, young Philip, raced off to Italy to investigate his cousin's death and, notwithstanding his grave suspicions, himself fell madly in love with Rachel. ② Indeed, he was so besotted that he soon began making plans to transfer his inheritance to her...

Clearly, no good could come of such a plan, and yet the precise shape of the oncoming disaster remained in question. Rachel herself remained in question. Without doubt, she was unwise and credulous in her personal relations—her friend the lawyer Rainaldi was a *creep*. Or was she in fact a canny soul, and were she and Rainaldi colluding as swindlers and trysting as secret and shameless lovers? ③ In any case, it was a bad idea to put her in charge of any sizable fortune, for she was wildly—uncontrollably—extravagant. Or was she something far worse? Was she the sort of woman capable of killing in order to replenish her purse?

Questions piled up faster than answers, and when, through Philip's negligence, Rachel plunged to her death off a tottery bridgeway, nobody in our car could say whether she was merely bad news, or truly *bad*. ④ We were as confused as poor undone Philip, for beautiful Rachel took her secrets to the grave.

"But what was Rachel really like?"

This came from fifteen-year-old Emily, sitting in the back seat but leaning so far forward she seemed almost perched on my shoulder—just where, in Saturday-morning cartoons, the imp Conscience hovers and whispers reproaches into a person's ear. I replied that perhaps Rachel wasn't *really* like anything—that sometimes writers deliberately leave their characters ambiguous. ⑤ Emily listened patiently as I droned on (I teach undergraduates for a living) and then she said:

"O.K., but what do you *think* Rachel was really like?"

And I explained that sometimes one of the greatest pleasures in reading is to watch a writer straddle a fence. That my favorite American fiction writer, Henry James, was a master of this, and in his novella "The Turn of the—"

"O. K. , but what do *you* think Rachel was really like?"

Clearly, we each suspected that the other wasn't being quite logical. From Emily's point of view, Rachel had either done away with cousin Ambrose or she hadn't. *We might not know the truth about her, but Rachel had to be one thing or the other:* innocent widow or scheming murderess.

If at that moment I'd been more articulate, I might have explained to Emily that some of the modern writers I loved best—James and Proust and Nabokov and Cheever—occasionally took enormous satisfaction in the final unreality of their characters; these were creative artists ever yearning to announce that their creations were mere puppets and that the one living soul inside their homemade theatre was the writer, the puppet master. And if Emily had been more articulate, she might have spoken of the godlike power of authorial creation: a writer assembles a stick figure, she puts some flesh on its bones, and then she breathes upon it tenderly, as you would upon a nest of twigs and pine needles when you're building a fire and you're down to a single match, enkindling a life destined to move into clearings far beyond its maker's ken.

Had I been still more articulate, I might have said that there's a special readerly pleasure in approaching a book as you would a box. In its self-containment lies its ferocious magic; you can see everything it holds, and yet its meagre, often hackneyed contents have a way of engineering fresh, refined, resourceful patterns.[6] And Emily might have replied that she comes to a book as to a keyhole: you observe some of the characters' movements, you hear a little of their dialogue, but then they step outside your limited purview. They have a reality that outreaches the borders of the page. (870 words)

Brad Leithauser is the editor of "The Norton Book of Ghost Stories". His new and selected poems, "The Oldest Word for Dawn", will appear next February. Read his pieces on "The Turn of the Screw" and "David Copperfield".

Words and Expressions

patch	n.	补缀,碎片	auspicious	a.	吉兆的,幸运的
impoverished	a.	贫穷的	contessa	n.	女伯爵,伯爵夫人
precipitately	ad.	猛进地	destined	a.	注定的,预定的
scribble	v.	潦草地写	febrile	a.	发烧的,热病的
besotted	a.	愚蠢的,糊涂的	credulous	a.	轻信的
creep	v.	爬,蹑手蹑脚	canny	a.	谨慎的,精明的
collude	v.	串通,勾结,共谋	swindler	n.	骗子
tryst	v.	约会,幽会	replenish	v.	补充
plunge	v.	跳进,投入	tottery	a.	蹒跚的,摇摇欲倒
perch	v.	(使)栖息,就位,位于	drone	v.	低沉地说出

straddle	v.	跨骑	articulate	v.	清晰明白地说
yearn	v.	渴望，想念	twig	n.	嫩枝，小枝
enkindle	v.	点燃，使燃烧	ken	n.	视野，知识领域，见地
ferocious	a.	凶恶的，残忍的	meagre	a.	瘦的，贫弱的
hackneyed	a.	不新奇的，陈腐的			

Proper Nouns

Daphne du Maurier　　达夫妮·杜穆里埃，英国小说家、剧作家
the New Jersey Turnpike　　新泽西收费公路
imp Conscience　　良心的小鬼

News Summary

这是美国《纽约客》——一本综合性文学期刊上的一篇文章，读起来很有文学色彩，与一般的新闻报道相比是大不相同的。作者一家在参加完一个亲戚的婚礼之后驱车回家，路程有六七个小时，于是他们便听一本名叫《我的表妹瑞琪》的有声书。随着故事情节的发展，他们也深深地被吸引了，以致对于故事的结局展开了争论。但是争论没有任何结果——每个人的看法都不一样。最后，作者说，看一本小说就像从一个钥匙孔窥看房间里的人一样：当他们的活动范围超越了你的视线时，你便看不到，也就不知道发生了什么了。

Understanding Sentences

① 叙事者的监护人——他的堂兄弟安伯鲁斯阿斯利是一名英国乡村绅士。当他在意大利过冬和养病的时候，爱上了一名贫穷的女伯爵——他的远房表妹瑞琪，并很快和她结婚。

② 叙事者，年轻的菲利普，急忙赶到意大利了解他堂兄弟的死因，虽然他十分怀疑瑞琪，但仍然疯狂地爱上了瑞琪。

③ 或者，她根本就是一名精明的女人，而且，是不是她和雷诺帝勾结起来当骗子，同时又暗地里无耻地幽会情人？

④ 问题一个接一个地出现，而答案却没有找到。还有，由于菲利普的疏忽，瑞琪从一条摇摇晃晃的桥上坠桥而死，我们车上的人没一个能说出这到底是坏消息呢，还是她罪有应得。

⑤ 我回答说，也许瑞琪实际上不像什么东西，有时候作者故意把他的人物写得模糊不清。

⑥ 在它的自我包容中藏着凶险的魔术，你能看到它容纳的一切，而它那常常是不足的、陈旧的内容具有一种产生新鲜的、经过提炼的和资源丰富的模式的方法。

Exercises

Ⅰ. **Understanding Ideas in the News**

1. What are the parallel stories in this essay?

A. Their travel and the story in *My Cousin Rachel*.

B. Driving back now and a dozen years ago.

C. Driving the car and listening to the audio book.

2. What happened to Philip after he raced off to Italy to investigate?

A. He also fell in love with Rachel.

B. He found out the truth about his cousin's death.

C. He was also murdered by Rachel.

3. What can be certain about Rachel from the story?

A. She colluded with Rainaldi to cheat.

B. She was unwise and credulous in her personal relations.

C. She was put in charge of a large fortune.

4. Why can't they decide on whether Rachel in the book is good or bad?

A. Rachel took her secrets to the grave.

B. Emily was only fifteen and sitting in the back seat.

C. The creator may want the make the ending sound unrealistic.

5. What is the process of authorial creation compared to by the writer?

A. Listening to an audio book in a car.

B. Building a fire with twigs and pine needles.

C. The god-like power.

II. Language Points

auspicious, impoverish, ferocious, destine, plunge 这些词是文章中描写瑞琪的故事时用的。

auspicious (吉兆的,幸运的) suggesting a positive and successful future e.g. *They won their first match of the season 5-1 which was an auspicious start/beginning.*

impoverished: (贫穷的) very poor e.g. *She's going out with an impoverished young actor.*

ferocious: (凶恶的,残忍的) fierce and violent e.g. *a ferocious dog*

destined: (注定的,预定的) controlled by a force which some people believe controls what happens, and which cannot be influenced by people e.g. *She is destined for an extremely successful career.*

plunge: (跳进,投入) to (cause someone or something to) move or fall suddenly and often a long way forward, down or into something e.g. *We ran down to the beach and plunged into the sea.*

III. Questions for Further Study

This is more a piece of literary writing than a news report, for it doesn't have all the characteristics of a news report. But this kind of writing is common in some more literary papers or magazines. Notice that there are two threads parallel in the writing: the one about their car drive back home, and the one about the story they are listening to.

Analyze the writing to see how the narratives are merged well, and how the writer tries to make her points by using metaphoric language.

英语报刊知识介绍

新闻漫画

漫画也是报纸的一个重要部分。漫画以政治漫画为主,通常在社论版上,与有关的评论和专栏文章放在一起。漫画可以非常深刻地表现作者的立场,讽刺政治人物的行为,而且文化内涵十分丰富。大报社一般会有好几个自己的漫画作家,他们轮流为报纸提供作品。

政治漫画一般是关于比较重大的新闻的,如美国的大选、某政治家的丑闻等。有一些关于日常生活的小漫画,也是挺有意思的。

1. A cartoon from a South African newspaper

2. A cartoon from *The New York Times*

3. Two interesting cartoon on the Internet

"On the Internet, nobody knows you're a dog."

"*Blog* is short for *bullfrog*. I hear we're very popular on the Internet now!"

Unit 17　The British Pub and Drinking Culture

The pub is one of the most important aspects of British culture. Ale, after all, existed in England long before tea. Pubs are social places where friends gather over a few pints and perhaps some food. It is said that each English village, no matter how small, has at least one pub. They are generally the centerpiece of village life, at least as much as the church is. It truly is the place to go if you really want to learn about English culture and get to know her people. There are over 60 000 pubs in the U.K. They serve, of course, a wide range of beers, wines and spirits. But food is also served. You can find everything from fish and chips to curries and lasagna. This is a relatively new development in pub history, as traditionally, they mainly served alcohol and perhaps a few bar snacks (pickled eggs, crisps, peanuts and pork cracklings). This chapter contains two reports about the pub culture in the UK, and one about the "booze" culture, too, a by-product of the pubs.

酒吧是英国文化最重要的方面之一,毕竟,啤酒早在茶之前就在英国存在了。人们在那里可以喝上几杯,或吃点东西。据说,不管村庄多小,至少都有一个酒吧。酒吧和村里的教堂一样,都是村里的中心。假如你真的想了解英国文化和英国人,那你一定要去那里。在全英国有约六万个酒吧。他们卖不同品牌的啤酒、葡萄酒和烈酒,也有食物,有炸鱼和薯条、咖喱和烤宽面条。这在酒文化里是新的,传统的英国酒吧只卖烈酒和下酒的小菜,如腌蛋、薯片、花生等。本单元收集了两篇关于英国酒吧文化的新闻,还有一篇关于"狂饮"的报道,那是酒吧的副产品。

1. A Pub Crawl through the Centuries

Old Bookbinders in Jericho

By HENRY SHUKMAN
The New York Times

April 13, 2008

DR. JOHNSON declared a tavern seat "the throne of human felicity". The Frenchman Hilaire Belloc, who spent his life in England, said: "When you have lost your inns, drown your empty selves. For you will have lost the last of England."

A good pub is a ready-made party, a home away from home, a club anyone can join. Some British pubs began as simple meeting places, some as coaching inns — hostelries where stagecoaches stopped for the night for fodder, bed and stable. ① Generally these were larger, and had a secondary pub at the back for ostlers, farriers and other riffraff.

In Oxford, which has some pubs — like the Bear, on Blue Boar Lane, and the Mitre, on the High Street — that date back to the 1200's, many of the names echo the Middle Ages. The White Hart (a stag, Richard II's heraldic emblem), the Kings Arms (named for James I, during whose reign neighboring Wadham College was founded), the Bear, the Wheatsheaf: all are names that call up a past of knights, farms and forests.

A pub is a great leveler — not a workingman's club, but an everyman's club. The best are filled not only with the scent of yeast and hops, but also with banter and wit. ② Back in 1954, when the Rose & Crown on North Parade Avenue in Oxford was threatened with closure (inadequate toilet facilities), the defense that won the day called it a "home of cultured, witty and flippant conversation". Whether it's how to warm plates swiftly or use the hyphen correctly, there's no talk like pub talk. Some, like the Rose & Crown, are a kind of family. Its landlord, Andrew Hall, knows exactly how much to know of his regulars' business. But every well-behaved person who is neither a dog nor a politician is welcome too.

The Rose & Crown is an ideal pub. Half a mile north of the city center, it's only 140 years old, but the three small, wood-paneled rooms and the affable, eloquent host make it a home away from home. It also keeps the best pint of Old Hooky in town. Brewed about 20 miles away at Hook Norton, said to be the country's last "steam brewery" (i.e., very old-fashioned), it's a legend in the annals of real ale, a vessel of hazel clarity, redolent of harvest stubble lit by an evening sun, of woods drenched in rain, of dewy meadows at dawn, of cattle in dells, of Thomas Hardy and sandy-gray churches nestled in the nook of sheep-studded hills. ③ If this isn't the drinkable essence of England, nothing is.

Some say the pub is in crisis. A few years ago, *The Guardian* reported that for the first time since the Norman Conquest fewer than half the villages of England have a pub. Chains of horrendous corporate-owned "vertical drinking establishments" — giant Identikit bars — threaten the real pubs, and the real pubs are mostly owned by equally horrendous "pubcos", companies invented to dodge laws against brewing monopolies. ④ Yet somehow real ale, championed by Camra (the Campaign for Real Ale), and real pubs do survive.

A chap at the back bar of the Kings Arms, with long hair, sports jacket (slight rip in shoulder seam) and a pint of Waggle Dance at his elbow, is holding forth about Bulgaria — "I've always loved the country," he drawls — then about Falstaff. Some say the death of Falstaff in Shakespeare's "Henry V" symbolizes the death of merry old England. In come the Protestants, out go the bibulous friars, jolly yeomen and Mother Mary. After that, only in the public house did the Middle Ages continue to find shelter.⑤

The Kings Arms is a linchpin of Oxford life. Situated at a junction in the heart of the city, it has spacious, airy front rooms, and at the rear three or four small rooms, all thick with honey-colored wood and irregular in shape. It was founded in the early 17th century when adjacent Wadham College was being built (the landlord presumably hoping for trade with the masons). It used to be host to bare-knuckle and cudgel fights, almost to the death, in its courtyard.

The Bear, tucked down Blue Boar Lane at the back of Christ Church, has only two tiny wood rooms, which date from 1242. They are covered, wall and ceiling, with picture frames containing short pieces of ties. Ties of clubs, regiments, schools — the Royal Gloucester Hussars, the Imperial Yeomanry, the Punjab Frontier Force, Lloyd's of London Croquet Club — telling of an older, more powerful, more sedate England. Croquet, beer, cricket, empire and P G. Wodehouse: a snip off your tie, and you'll get a free pint.

The small Eagle and Child on the broad boulevard of St. Giles' was for decades distinguished mostly by the coziness of its nooks, and by the fact that — like its counterpart across the road, the Lamb & Flag, where Graham Greene liked to drink — it has long been owned by St. John's, a college of spectacular wealth. But in the last few years, since the "Lord of the Rings" movies, it has become a celebrity among pubs. It was here that the Inklings (Tolkien, C. S. Lewis and others) would meet of a Tuesday to drink, talk and smoke. (879 words)

Words and Expressions

tavern	n.	酒馆,客栈	stagecoach	n.	公共马车
felicity	n.	幸福,幸运	stag	n.	牡鹿
hostelry	n.	旅馆	fodder	n.	饲料,草料
ostler	n.	(旅馆的)马夫	farrier	n.	蹄铁匠,马医
stable	n.	马厩	hop	n.	蛇麻草
banter	n.	玩笑,妙语	riffraff	n.	[贬]乌合之众
flippant	a.	能说会道的	affable	a.	和蔼可亲的
redolent	a.	芬芳的	stubble	n.	断株,茬

nook	n.	隐蔽处
horrendous	a.	可怕的
drawl	v.	懒洋洋地说
friar	n.	男修道士
linchpin	n.	关键
cudgel	v.	用棍棒打
croquet	n.	槌球戏
heraldic	a.	纹章学的,纹章的
hazel	a.	淡褐色的
sheep-studded	a.	布满(羊群)的
identikit	n.	[法]拼图认人
bibulous	a.	饮酒的,嗜酒的
yeomen	n.	自耕农,仆人
bare-knuckle	a.	裸露关节的
sedate	a.	安静的,稳重的
snip	v.	剪断
emblem	n.	象征,徽章

Proper Nouns

Waggle Dance　蜜蜂跳舞(一种啤酒的牌子)
Wadham College　牛津大学瓦德汉学院
P. G. Wodehouse　伍德豪斯,英国幽默小说家
the Inklings　与牛津大学有关的一个文学社团
Tolkien　托尔金,英国作家
C. S. Lewis　刘易斯,英国作家

News Summary

这是《纽约时报》上的一篇闲情文章,文笔优雅,内容丰富。它在简单给出一个关于"酒吧"的定义之后,介绍了在英国牛津的一系列各有特点、历史悠久的酒吧。牛津的许多酒吧都有很长的历史,起源于中世纪时期,并一直保存下来。酒吧文化是英国文化的一个显著特征:那里有各种啤酒和下酒小菜,有热烈的气氛,还有无所不谈的话题,是一般英国人在空闲时间聚集和聊天的地方。接下来作者用生动的笔调介绍牛津这几间酒吧的特点和历史。

Understanding Sentences

① 有些英国的酒吧开始时只是一个简单的供人们会面的地方;有些是作为驿馆——供车马过夜停留,得到草料、睡床和马厩的旅馆。

② 最好的酒吧不仅充满了酵母和蛇麻草的气味,而且还充满了逗弄和妙语。

③ 这酒在约20英里以外的胡克诺顿酿造,据说是这里最后一家非常老式的"蒸汽酿酒厂"酿造的啤酒,它是真正啤酒历史上的传奇,一杯透明清澈的淡褐色啤酒,使人想起落日照射的收获地,泡在雨中的木材,清晨洒满露水的草地,山谷中的牛群,分布于到处是绵羊的山坡上托马斯哈代时代的、沙子般颜色的教堂。

④ 连锁公司拥有的、样子难看的"站立饮酒的地方"——那些一模一样的酒吧——威胁真正酒吧的存在,而真正的酒吧大多数由同样可怕的"酒吧公司"所拥有,它们多数是为了躲避针对酿酒垄断的法律而建立的。

⑤ 来了新教徒,走了嗜酒的方士、快乐的农夫,还有圣母玛丽亚。从那以后,只有酒吧才是中世纪继续存在的地方。

Unit 17 The British Pub and Drinking Culture

Exercises

I. Understanding Ideas in the News

1. In what way do the names of the White Hart and the Kings Arms echo the Middle Ages?
   A. They refer to objects of the Kings.
   B. They were hostelries for stagecoaches.
   C. They were located in Oxford.

2. What are the best pubs filled with?
   A. Smell of beer and witty talks.
   B. Many working men and women.
   C. Smell of flowers and noises.

3. What defense saved the Rose & Crown from closure in 1954?
   A. It was a great place for conversation.
   B. It had inadequate toilet facilities.
   C. It was a great leveler.

4. What was reported by The Guardian that threatened the real pubs?
   A. Giant Identikit bars.   B. The "pubcos".
   C. No real ale.

5. What does the collection of short ties in The Bear tell us of?
   A. An older, more powerful, more sedate England.
   B. The Norman Conquest.
   C. The history of Oxford.

II. Language Points

banter, babble, drawl, eloquent, flippant 这些是文章中谈论英国人爱在酒吧里对着一杯啤酒夸夸其谈的用词。

banter：（玩笑, 妙语）conversation which is amusing and not serious   e.g. *He considered himself a master of witty banter.*

babble：（喋喋不休）to talk or say something in a quick, confused, excited or foolish way   e.g. *The children babbled excitedly among themselves.*

drawl：（懒洋洋地说）to speak in a slow way in which the vowel sounds are lengthened and words are not separated clearly   e.g. *drawl (out) one's words*

eloquent：（雄辩的, 有口才的）giving a clear, strong message   e.g. *She made an eloquent appeal for action before it was too late.*

flippant：（能说会道的）not serious about a serious subject, in an attempt to be amusing or to appear clever   e.g. *a flippant remark/attitude*

III. Questions for Further Study

This news report appears in the "travel" section of *The New York Times*. Since it is a piece of soft news, it is more literary in nature. Read the article once again, and try to understand the different characteristics of the pubs in Oxford, and the connection between them and history.

2. Still the Moon under Water

An exploration of the national pastime

The Economist
July 30th, 2008

Every nation needs a national myth, and Britain might seem to need more than most. A modern myth has it as a country full of overworked wage-slaves. Newspapers write of a "long-hours culture", and point out that the British working week is significantly longer than the European average.

Yet walking through the afternoon streets of St James, on my way back from Friday lunch, it is hard to see much evidence of that. A legion of investment bankers and private-equity types crowd the streets, as indistinguishable from one to the next, in their open-necked shirts and luxuriantly coifed hair, as their predecessors were in their umbrellas and bowler hats.① They are the overspill from London's pubs, which have been filling up since midday. Now it seems as if half the city is outside, pint-glass in one hand and cigarette in the other, chatting up a co-worker or arguing about football. London must be the only city in the world where the journalists work harder than the bankers. Pubs are Britain's national pastime. Three-quarters of the population indulge and a third consider themselves regulars, far higher proportions than are claimed by any of the country's religions— football included.② And they are unique to the British Isles. The Germans have beer-halls, the French have cafes and most other societies have bars, but only in Britain and Ireland can you find pubs. There are procedural differences (there

Unit 17   The British Pub and Drinking Culture

is no table service at pubs, something that causes endless confusion for tourists) as well as different pastimes once you arrive (it is hard to imagine sophisticates in a Parisian bar playing darts or Scrabble). But what really sets a public house apart from its foreign counterparts is the conceit that it is not a place of business, but a part of a person's home that is open to anyone.

In 1946, George Orwell, perhaps the 20th century's best chronicler of English culture, wrote an essay describing the ideal pub, which he named the *Moon Under Water*, and the qualities that made it special.③ Many of these remain recognisable to modern readers: the architecture, he said, was uncompromisingly Victorian, infused with the "comfortable ugliness" of the 19th century. It was busy, but not noisy, with a merry atmosphere but not a drunken one. There was a fireplace for the winter and a beer garden for the summer; the barmaids were friendly and most of the clientele were regulars. Not everything would be so familiar, were Orwell to visit a pub today. There was no dinner served at the *Moon Under Water*.

Today, virtually every pub in the land advertises "traditional pub food", and an evening trip to the pub for a meal has become a classic family evening out— a "tradition" no more than a decade or two old.④ The *Moon* was unusual in that it offered draught stout; if there is a pub in Britain today that doesn't serve Guinness, I have never found it. Orwell reserved a snooty disdain for glasses without handles, preferring to drink his beer from pewter mugs. One can only imagine his reaction to the plastic cups that are becoming common in town-centre pubs now. Still, most modern pubs try to replicate Orwell's formula, knowingly or not, some more successfully than others. One example of what not to do can be found at my local, a mid-sized pub which shall remain nameless, in a nondescript part of north London. It is owned by J. D. Wetherspoon, a large firm that has built its success on following Orwell's criteria (one of its flagship pubs is even called the *Moon Under Water*, though Orwell's essay reveals that the pub it describes did not actually exist).

First impressions are good. The dark, wood-paneled walls look suitably Victorian, and there is a nice mix of tables and booths. A pair of high-backed red leather armchairs, seemingly salvaged from the Reform club from the time of Queen Victoria's Diamond Jubilee, occupy pride of place in front of the fire.⑤ The walls in one corner are covered with bookshelves, suggesting the kind of place where one can while away a few hours reading quietly. As soon as you sit down, those good impressions start to go sour. The tables are sticky with half-dried beer.

There is a wide range of beers to choose from, but often it tastes as if the pipes have not been cleaned for weeks. The food is cheap because it comes pre-made in plastic sachets and is reheated in a microwave — that is, assuming the overworked staff can remember your order. Until smoking was banned from pubs in 2007, the front half of this Wetherspoonerism stank of cigarettes while the back half was suffused with a smell from the toilets. After three disappointing trips I swore never to return, a promise that I break now only in the interests of journalistic inquiry. Sadly, the tables are as sticky as ever and, while the cigarette smoke has gone, that has only allowed the toilets' odour to pervade the entire place. (855 words)

Words and Expressions

legion	n.	众多，大批	private-equity	n.	股票
indistinguishable	a.	不能辨别的	luxuriantly	ad.	繁茂地，丰富地
coif	v.	整理或梳理头发	indulge	v.	纵容
bowler hat		圆顶硬礼帽	predecessor	n.	前辈，前任
procedural	a.	程序上的	overspill	n.	溢出的东西
conceit	n.	奇想	dart	n.	飞镖
chronicler	n.	年代记编（记录）者	infuse	v.	泡，沏
clientele	n.	诉讼委托人，客户	draught stout		生啤酒，烈性啤酒
snooty	a.	傲慢的，自大的	disdain	n.	蔑视，鄙弃
pewter mug		白蜡杯	replicate	v.	复制
uncompromisingly	ad.	坚决地，不妥协地	salvage	v.	抢救，打捞
sticky	a.	黏的，黏性的	sachet	n.	小袋
nondescript	a.	难以区别，无特征的	stink	v.	发出臭味
suffuse	v.	充满	pervade	v.	遍及

Proper Nouns

Scrabble　一种英文单词拼写游戏
Guinness　健力士（爱尔兰的一种啤酒公司，其黑啤出名）
Wetherspoon　英国一家酒吧连锁集团

News Summary

这篇文章是一名英国记者写的关于英国酒吧文化的报道。文章一开始就说人们以为英国人都是拼命干活的，但记者发现，每到星期五，中午一过酒吧就坐满了人。接着作者指出酒吧是英国人主要的消遣去处，英国人把酒吧当作他们家里可以向任何人开放的地方。然后作者谈到20世纪作家乔治·奥威尔所描述的理想中酒吧的样子，以后很多英国酒吧都试图按照他所说的样子来装修酒吧。最后作者描写了他家乡一间蓄意模仿奥威尔描述的酒吧，但是并不成功。

Understanding Sentences

① 一群投资银行职员和私人证券商坐满了街边摆着的桌椅，他们衬衫的领扣都松开着，头发梳得整齐，看起来一模一样，犹如他们那戴着清一色的圆顶硬礼帽和拿着雨伞的前辈一样。

② 人口的四分之三沉溺于饮酒，三分之一的人说他们是酒吧的常客，比这个国家包括

Unit 17 The British Pub and Drinking Culture

足球在内的任何宗教的信徒占人口的比例都高出很多。

③ 1946 年,也许是二十世纪英国文化最好的编年史家——乔治·奥威尔写了一篇文章描述了他心目中一间名叫"水下月亮"的酒吧,以及使它变得那么特别的地方。

④ 今天,几乎全国每一家酒吧都打广告宣传他们的"传统酒吧食物",同时晚上去酒吧吃一顿饭已经成为经典的"家人傍晚外出项目"——所谓"经典"也就是不到十年二十年的事情。

⑤ 一对高靠背的红皮扶手椅,似乎是从维多利亚女皇钻石婚大庆时期的改革俱乐部抢救出来的,放在正对壁炉的位置。

Exercises

Ⅰ. **Understanding Ideas in the News**

1. What is the modern myth about Britain?
A. Many people are overworked wage-slaves.
B. Its streets are crowded by bankers Friday afternoon.
C. Journalists work harder than the bankers.
2. What is unique of the British pubs as against their foreign counterparts?
A. They are believed to be part of a person's home.
B. Their procedures are different from foreign ones.
C. You cannot see sophisticates playing darts or Scrabble.
3. What was the atmosphere of the British pub like as described by George Orwell?
A. Merry but not drunken.
B. Friendly but not regular.
C. Recognisable but not special.
4. What did Orwell like to drink his beer from?
A. Pewter mug.
B. Glasses without handles.
C. Plastic cups.
5. What is the writer's total impression about the pub in north London?
A. It looks good, but the quality is not good.
B. It serves a wide range of beers to be chosen from.
C. It was suffused with a smell from the toilets.

Ⅱ. **Language Points**

luxuriantly, conceit, disdain, infuse, indulge 这些词用来描写英国人对酒吧的喜爱。

luxuriantly:(繁茂地,丰富地)growing thickly, strongly and well e.g. *Tall plants grew luxuriantly along the river bank.*

conceit:(奇想)an unusual cleverly expressed but not very serious comparison, esp. in poetry e.g. *the use of conceits in Elizabethan poetry.*

disdain:(蔑视,鄙弃)used when you dislike someone or something and think that they do not deserve your interest or respect   e. g. *He regards the political process with disdain.*

infuse: (泡,沏) If you infuse a drink or it infuses, you leave substances such as tea leaves or herbs in hot water so that their flavour goes into the liquid.   e. g. *Allow the tea to infuse for five minutes.*

indulge: (纵容) to allow yourself or another person to have something enjoyable, especially more than is good for you   e. g. *The soccer fans indulged their patriotism, waving flags and singing songs.*

III. Questions for Further Study

This is also a piece of travel writing. The writer first presents a scene in the streets of London on Friday afternoon, then raises the issue of the British pub, and describes a place that is not so nice as a pub. Analyze the language of this writing to see how the writer uses words to express his ideas.

3. Booze buses and drunk tanks to tackle Britain's drinking culture

A fleet of "booze buses" staffed with paramedics could be deployed across UK towns to tackle the problem of late night drunkenness, as part of the Prime Minister's agenda to curb excessive drinking.

By Robert Winnett, Political Editor
The Daily Telegraph
10:24 a. m. GMT, 15 Feb., 2012

Next month, the Government publishes its alcohol strategy which is expected to recommend higher "minimum" prices for drink, potentially by increasing duties on many alcoholic beverages.①

The Prime Minister will today visit a hospital in the North East where he will discuss the growing problems caused by alcohol with doctors, nurses, paramedics and police

Unit 17   The British Pub and Drinking Culture

officers.

Mr. Cameron will say: "Every night, in town centres, hospitals and police stations across the country, people have to cope with the consequences of alcohol abuse. And the problem is getting worse. Over the last decade we've seen a frightening growth in the number of people — many under age — who think it's acceptable for people to get drunk in public in ways that wreck lives, spread fear and increase crime. ②

"This is one of the scandals of our society and I am determined to deal with it."

He will begin to set out the Government's thinking on how to tackle binge drinking. Mr. Cameron will say: "Whether it's the police officers in A&E that have been deployed in some hospitals, the booze buses in Soho and Norwich, or the drunk tanks used abroad, we need innovative solutions to confront the rising tide of unacceptable behaviour."

Official figures show that the cost to the NHS of treating alcohol abuse is about £ 2.7 billion a year — equivalent to £ 90 for every taxpayer—including £ 1 billion on A&E services. A recent Government report estimated that the total cost of alcohol to society, including crime and lost work, was between £ 17 billion and £ 22 billion annually. ③

Last year, there were 200,000 hospital admissions caused primarily by alcohol, a 40 per cent rise in the past decade. The number of patients admitted with acute intoxication has more than doubled to 18,500 since 2002-03.

Medical professionals are virtually united in calling for a minimum price per unit of alcohol in England.

A study found that a minimum price of 30p per unit would prevent 300 deaths a year, 40p about 1,000 deaths, and 50p more than 2,000 premature deaths. ④ Scotland is proposing a minimum price of about 45p a unit and several councils in England, including Greater Manchester and Merseyside, are considering bylaws to set minimum prices.

Scottish estimates suggest that a minimum price per unit of 45p would result in the steepest price increases for cider, gin and vodka. A bottle of own-brand gin with around 37.5 per cent alcohol content would go up from £ 6.95 to £ 11.85. ⑤ A two-litre bottle of own-brand cider would more than triple in price from £ 1.20 to £ 3.75.

Mr. Cameron is thought to be in favour of increasing the price of alcohol, as part of a "big bang" approach. However, Andrew Lansley, the Health Secretary, is thought to be pushing for a voluntary approach. The Lib Dems are also understood to be resistant to raising the price of cider and whisky—as their heartlands are in the South West and Scotland.

Mr. Cameron is also expected to mount a robust defence of controversial NHS reforms. Last night, more than 80,000 people had signed an official petition calling for the reforms to be abandoned. (523 words)

Words and Expressions

fleet	n.	舰队		booze	n.	酒精饮料
alcoholic	a.	含酒精的		beverage	n.	饮料
paramedic	n.	护理人员		abuse	n.	滥用
cider	n.	苹果酒		whisky	n.	威士忌酒
heartland	n.	中心地带		binge	n.	狂闹，狂欢
acute	a.	急性的		intoxication	n.	醉酒

Proper Nouns

A & E 事故和紧急部门(英国警察的一个部门)

News Summary

这是一篇关于卡梅隆政府决定提高对各种酒的税收，从而提高零售价，以遏制经常发生的酗酒行为的新闻。新闻说，政府将同时在各地布置深夜出动"醉酒巴士"，以收留那些常常在深夜狂饮以致醉而忘归的人。新闻提到了一些具体数字，说明目前英国的酒类价格还是偏低，还可以再提高一点。毕竟，酒吧文化是典型的英国文化，英国人爱喝酒也是出了名的。

Understanding Sentences

① 下个月，政府将出台它的对付饮酒的策略，其中将建议提高各种酒类的"最低价格"，很可能是通过提高对许多酒精类饮料的征税来实现。

② 过去的十年里，那些认为可以在公共场合以危害生命、制造恐慌和增加犯罪的方式饮酒的人数大增，其中许多还未到法定年龄。

③ 一份最新的政府报告估计，每年酒精对整个社会所造成的损失，包括犯罪和偷窃等，在170亿到220亿之间。

④ 一份研究发现，以30便士一单位的最低价格，每年可以防止300人死亡；如果提高到40便士则可以防止1000人死亡；而50便士则可以防止2000人死亡。

⑤ 一瓶自有品牌的、酒精含量37.5%的杜松子酒的价格将从6.95英镑提高至11.85英镑。

Exercises

Ⅰ. Understanding Ideas in the News

1. What will the government do to handle the growing problems caused by alcohol?

  A. Raise the "minimum" price for drink.

  B. Visit the hospital in the North East.

  C. Go to town centers and police stations.

2. What growth have the British people seen over the last decade?

  A. The number of people who drink irresponsibly.

B. The number of people who drink.

C. The price of alcoholic beverages.

3. What is the cost of treating alcohol abuse a year?

A. ₤2.7 billion.　　　B. ₤90.　　　C. ₤17 billion.

4. What does a study on alcoholic drinking find?

A. Higher price of drink can help reduce premature deaths.

B. The number of patients admitted with acute intoxication is high.

C. Medical professionals are virtually united.

5. What will the price of cider be if the 45p minimum price suggested by Scotland is adopted?

A. It will more than triple.

B. It will just double.

C. It will increase a little.

Ⅱ. Language Points

booze, binge, intoxication, abuse, acute 这些词是新闻在报道英国政府将对日益严重的酗酒问题采取措施时用到的。

booze：（酒精饮料）alcoholic drink

binge：（狂闹，狂欢）an occasion when an activity is done in an extreme way, especially eating, drinking or spending money　e.g. *a drinking/eating/spending binge*

intoxication：（醉酒）from intoxicated　e.g. *He used to claim that he had his best ideas after several days of intoxication* (= being drunk)

abuse：（滥用）wrong use　e.g. *Drug and alcohol abuse* (= using these substances in a bad way) *contributed to his early death.*

acute：（急性的）An acute pain or illness is one that quickly becomes very severe. e.g. *acute abdominal pains*

Ⅲ. Questions for Further Study

This news report first points out that the government is going to take action against the excessive drinking problem in the country, then shows the results of drinking in figures, and mentions the possibility of raising price of drink by the government. The structure is clear, and the words and expressions used are simple. Notice the tone of "reporting" from the angle of the reporter in the article.

英语报刊知识介绍

新媒体的兴起及对传统报刊的冲击

二十世纪后期，首先是计算机的广泛应用使英语报刊的编排技术有了突破性发展。接着，互联网的出现又使通过网络传播新闻更快更有效。各种报纸纷纷设立了自己的网站，电子报刊也逐渐流行，到今天已经有很多人改变了阅读习惯，喜欢看电子报纸。另外，高速和大容量的网络传输及多媒体技术又进一步大大改变了报纸的编排方式,如今的网络报纸上图片的容量加大,现场的声音、视频也可以嵌入报纸,更主要的是可以与读者互动,读者可以随时发表自己的评论及把自己喜欢的文章转发给亲朋好友。

近年来,网络技术在传播新闻方面又有了许多新的应用,形成了一种不可忽视的"新媒体",包括交友网站、即时通讯、音乐网站、视频网站、广播、微博、微信,等等。"新媒体"对传统报纸的冲击是很大的,不过,尽管二十多年前就有预言说印刷报纸将退出江湖,今天主要报纸每天还在印刷发行。

1. An online news site "Punch"

2. Reading news on the cell phone: intelligent cell phone further pushing applications in wireless Internet

Unit 18 Entertainment News

Entertainment is a form of activity that holds the attention and interest of an audience, or gives pleasure and delight. With the development of modern technology, means for entertainment has become more diversified. From the simple story-telling and drama, we now have radio, television, movie, and the Internet. The newspaper usually has a dedicated section for entertainment news, which carries reports on celebrities, events and performances. These sometimes may be just gossiping, but it is fun and relaxing when you are tired of reading all the serious news. This chapter includes two reports on two American actresses and one on the major awards given out at the Cannes Film Festival in 2013.

娱乐是一种吸引人们的注意力和兴趣,或使人们产生愉快和快乐的活动方式。随着现代技术的发展,娱乐的方式也变得越来越多样化,从简单的讲故事和演戏,到我们现在的电台、电视、电影以及互联网。报纸上通常也有专门报道娱乐新闻的部分,刊登有关明星、事件及演出的消息。有时候,这些消息可能就只是一些"八卦"新闻,但是,当你阅读严肃的新闻感到疲倦了的时候,看一下这些新闻,也是蛮有趣和轻松的。本章包括了两篇关于两名美国女演员的新闻和一篇关于2013年法国戛纳电影节主要获奖项目的报道。

1. Scarlett Johansson in Broadway's *Cat on a Hot Tin Roof*: What did critics think?

Scarlett Johansson during curtain call at the end of Thursday's Broadway...

By Mike Boehm
Los Angeles Times
January 18, 2013, 7:19 a.m.

Scarlett Johansson is the latest star to take a shot at *Cat on a Hot Tin Roof*, Tennessee Williams' feverish 1955 classic about a wealthy Southern family with two daughters-in-law who all but scratch each other's eyes out over who'll get the loot when Big Daddy, the dying (although he's the last to know it) paterfamilias goes to his final reward. The show has now had six lives on Broadway, including three in the past 10 years.

The incarnation that opened Thursday at the Richard Rodgers Theatre finds Johansson playing the self-nicknamed Maggie the Cat, the daughter-in-law who has the biggest hill to climb because it has become extremely dubious whether her alcoholic husband, Brick, who is Big Daddy's golden-boy favorite, will ever touch her again, alluring though she be.[①] Absent that, there'll be no offspring from their marriage — a prerequisite for Brick and Maggie to qualify for a goodly share of the massive plantation Big Daddy built from nothing.

Johansson, who won a 2010 Tony for best featured (i.e., supporting) actress in her lone previous Broadway turn, a revival of Arthur Miller's *A View From the Bridge*, joins a line of Broadway Maggies that includes, in order of appearance, Barbara Bel Geddes, Elizabeth Ashley, Kathleen Turner, Ashley Judd and Anika Noni Rose (in an all-black cast in 2008). There's also Elizabeth Taylor, who starred in the 1958 film version opposite Paul Newman's Brick and the original Broadway Big Daddy, Burl Ives.

The critics were mixed regarding Johansson, and largely unimpressed with the production, which was directed by Rob Ashford, staging his first drama on Broadway after a skein of credits there as a director and/or choreographer of musicals.[②]

Ben Brantley of *The New York Times* said Johansson made "a few miscalculations... She is perhaps too forthright to be truly feline," but concluded that "she confirms her promise as a stage actress of imposing presence and adventurous intelligence[③]... Her Maggie is, as she must be, an undeniable life force and — as far as this production... is concerned, a lifeline... the only major player... who appears to have a fully thought-through idea of the character she's portraying."

Newsday's Linda Winer was miffed about the whole thing, declaring, "What a strangely unmoored production this is." For her, that included Johansson's performance: "In her much-anticipated star turn as one of the theater's juiciest women, she works so admirably to avoid Maggie-the-Cat cliches that the actress and the character almost disappear in sensitive, levelheaded, ladylike restraint.[④]" Winer said that Benjamin Walker provided some heat as Brick, but "what's left is faceless, respectable and dull".

In the *New York Daily News*, Joe Dziemianowicz slagged the show and said that Johansson as Maggie was "a compelling idea on paper, but it doesn't deliver in reality". Subsequent descriptors of her performance include "alarmingly one-note", "overwhelmed by Williams' drama and the heavy lifting demanded", "her voice... has the musicality of a foghorn. The power of the words get lost in translation."⑤

Mark Kennedy of the Associated Press was OK with Johansson and the rest of the cast, rating her performance "a nifty turn... finding humor and barely hidden desperation in her role.... She's less overtly sexy than other actresses who have played the ironic role, making her Maggie more cerebral, angry and proud." But he faulted director Ashford for inserting too much intrusive music and too many noisy sound effects. (554 words)

Words and Expressions

feverish	a.	狂热的,兴奋的	loot	n.	掠夺物,战利品
paterfamilias	n.	家长	incarnation	n.	具体化,化身,体现
dubious	a.	可疑的,不确定的	allure	v.	吸引
prerequisite	n.	先决条件	skein	n.	(一)群,一团糟
miscalculation	n.	误算,估错	forthright	a.	直接的,直率的
feline	n.	猫科动物	miff	v.	发脾气,微怒
unmoor	v.	起锚,解缆	slag	v.	使化为熔渣
foghorn	n.	雾号(浓雾信号)	musicality	n.	音感,音乐性
nifty	a.	俏皮的,极好的	cerebral	a.	诉诸理性的
levelheaded	a.	头脑冷静的,清醒的			

Proper Nouns

Scarlett Johansson 斯嘉丽·约翰逊,美国女演员,1984年生
Broadway 百老汇(纽约一个剧场集中的地方)
Tennessee Williams 田纳西·威廉斯,美国作家
Cat on a Hot Tin Roof 《热铁皮屋顶上的猫》,也译《朱门巧妇》
Tony Award 托尼奖(美国剧场界最高荣誉)

News Summary

这篇新闻报道是《纽约时报》娱乐版上对百老汇明星斯嘉丽·约翰逊和她主演的《热铁皮屋顶上的猫》的评价。新闻先介绍了该剧演出的情况和简单的剧情,以及斯嘉丽所表演的角色在剧中的地位、她演过的类似戏剧等,然后引用了几家大媒体对她的表演的评价。

Understanding Sentences

① 星期四在理查·罗杰斯剧院的演出中,约翰逊扮演绰号叫"小猫马吉"的女主角,她是剧中的"大家长"的一个儿媳妇,在争夺遗产中面临巨大的困难,因为她越来越担心,她那

位嗜酒的丈夫布里克,"大家长"最喜爱的儿子,不会再碰她了,尽管她一直想吸引他。

② 批评家们对约翰森有不同的评价,但大部分对该剧没有兴趣。这是罗伯特·艾思福执导的第一部百老汇戏剧,此前他作为音乐剧的导演和舞蹈设计已经有了一定的名声。

③《纽约时报》的本布兰尼说,约翰逊做出了"一些错误估计……她也许过于直接,看起来不像一只猫"。但是又总结说,"她具有作为一名舞台女演员的能征服观众的气质和敢于冒险的智慧。"

④ "在她期待已久的成为剧院报酬最高的女演员的转变中,她避开了'小猫马吉'的陈词滥调,如此令人赞叹,以致演员和角色的界线在一种敏感的、头脑清醒的和淑女般的控制中几乎消失了。"

⑤ 对她的表演的其他评价还有:"惊人地单调""完全受制于威廉斯的戏剧和那些过重的提升需求""她的嗓子像雾号般沉闷。语言的力量在翻译中丢失了"。

Exercises

I. Understanding Ideas in the News

1. What is the story of *Cat on a Hot Tin Roof* about?

   A. It is about how the two daughters-in-law compete for Big Daddy's properties.

   B. It is about how Maggie the Cat and her alcoholic husband, Brick.

   C. It is about how Tennessee wrote Cat on a Hot Tin Roof.

2. What did Johansson win the 2010 Tony for?

   A. The role of Maggie the Cat in "*Cat on a Hot Tin Roof*".

   B. Best supporting actress in "*Cat on a Hot Tin Roof*".

   C. Best featured actress in "*A View From the Bridge*".

3. What did Ben Brantley of *The New York Times* say about Johansson?

   A. She didn't act the role very well, though she had talents.

   B. She was the sixth actress who played the role of Maggie.

   C. She was perhaps too forthright, but she often made mistakes.

4. What did Linda Winer of Newsday comment on Johansson's performance?

   A. There is too much of the Maggie the Cat cliches.

   B. The character of Maggie the Cat almost disappears.

   C. Her performance lacks the unique style of Maggie the Cat.

5. What did Mark Kennedy of the Associated Press think of Johansson's role of Maggie compared to other actresses?

   A. More ironic and desperate.

   B. Less overtly sexy but more thinking.

   C. Less nifty but more angry and proud.

II. Language Points

forthright, nifty, cerebral, levelheaded, unmoored 这些词用来描述约翰森在剧中的表演。

forthright: (直接的,直率的)(too) honest or direct in behaviour e. g. *His forthright manner can be mistaken for rudeness.*

nifty: (俏皮的,极好的) good, pleasing or effective e. g. *a nifty piece of work/footwork*

cerebral: (诉诸理性的) demanding careful reasoning and mental effort rather than feelings e. g. *She makes cerebral films that deal with important social issues*

levelheaded: (头脑冷静的,清醒的) calm and able to deal easily with difficult situations

unmoored: (起锚的,解缆的) from moor: to tie a boat so that it stays in the same place e. g. *We moored further up the river.*

III. Questions for Further Study

This news report is about the performance of Scarlett Johansson in the play *Cat on a Hot Tin Roof*. It first introduces her staging on Thursday, and gives a brief account of the story in the play, as well as other actresses who had acted out the same role of Maggie. Then the writer puts comments and criticism from the media together. One difficulty is to correctly understand the comments. Try explaining these in the news report to see if your understanding is correct and comprehensive.

2. Story of Young Woman's Awakening Is Top Winner

Director Abdellatif Kechiche accepts the Palme d'Or for the film *Blue Is the Warmest Colour* with actresses Lea Seydoux, left, and Adèle Exarchopoulos.

By MANOHLA DARGIS
The New York Times
May 26, 2013

CANNES, France — *Blue Is the Warmest Color* — an emotionally raw and sexually explicit contemporary French drama and critical favorite about a young woman's awakening — won the Palme d'Or on Sunday evening at the 66th Cannes Film Festival here.①

From the stage, Steven Spielberg, the head of the competition jury, announced that he and the other jurists had decided to formally recognize not only the movie's director, Abdellatif Kechiche, but also its two young actresses, Adèle Exarchopoulos and Léa Seydoux. This unusual, perhaps unprecedented step acknowledged the contributions of both women, who appear naked in several sex scenes, but it also took some auteur sheen away from Mr. Kechiche, suggesting that the jury had engaged in intense back-room negotiations.② For much of the festival the critical favorite had been *Inside Llewyn Davis*, a period story from Joel and Ethan Coen about a New York folk singer trying to make it in 1961. The Coens' film won the Grand Prix, but they were not in attendance.

Mr. Kechiche, Ms. Exarchopoulos and Ms. Seydoux took the stage together to accept their award — although only one Palme was visible — and exchanged hugs and kisses as the audience cheered and clapped for several long minutes. The pillow-lipped Ms. Exarchopoulos had been widely expected to win best actress, but that award instead went to a visibly surprised and shaking Bérénice Bejo (*The Artist*) for her role in *Le Passé*, a drama set in France from the Iranian director Asghar Farhadi. Bruce Dern won best actor for Alexander Payne's *Nebraska*, a wistful, black-and-white comedy about a fading alcoholic (Mr. Dern) and his melancholic, somewhat dyspeptic son (Will Forte) who, during an increasingly absurd and touching road trip, journey into the past.

In the only real shock of the evening, the best director award went to the Mexican filmmaker Amat Escalante for his turgid, violent shocker *Heli*, which, among other staged atrocities, features a scene of a man having his groin lighted afire.③ "I wasn't expecting this," said Mr. Escalante, a sentiment shared by some critics. The jury prize went to *Like Father, Like Son*, a lovely melodrama from the Japanese director Hirokazu Kore-eda about a family almost undone by the news that its only son was accidentally swapped at birth with another child.

The prize for Un Certain Regard, a sidebar section, went to *L'Image Manquante*, a feature from the Cambodian filmmaker Rithy Panh. The award for the Camera d'Or, for the best first feature, went to *Ilo Ilo*, from the Singaporean director Anthony Chen, who said it was the first time a movie from Singapore had won at Cannes. The Palme for the best short film was won by *Safe*, from the South Korean director Moon Byoung-gon. (492 words)

Words and Expressions

explicit	a.	清楚的,直率的	sidebar	n.	其他选项
auteur	n.	〈法〉(具有自己独特风格的)电影导演	unprecedented	a.	空前的
			sheen	n.	光辉,光彩

pillow	n.	枕头状物		wistful	a.	渴望的，惆怅的
melancholic	a.	忧郁的		dyspeptic	a.	消化不良的
turgid	a.	一本正经的，浮夸的		atrocity	n.	残暴，暴行
groin	n.	腹股沟		swap	v.	交换

Proper Nouns

    the Cannes Film Festival　戛纳电影节

    Palme d'Or　金棕榈奖

    Steven Spielberg　斯蒂芬·斯皮伯格（美国电影导演）

    Grand Prix　大满贯（指大型综合比赛）

News Summary

    这也是《纽约时报》的娱乐版上的新闻，它是关于法国戛纳电影节的颁奖仪式的。新闻主要是报道了一年一度的金棕榈奖得主——法国电影《蓝色是最暖的色》。颁奖的时候，该片的导演和两名女主角都上台领奖。新闻也介绍了其他几个主要奖项的获得者。

Understanding Sentences

    ①《蓝色是最暖的色》是一部得到好评的感情上自然和有直接性描写的当代法国戏剧，故事是关于一个年轻女人的觉醒。该片在星期六晚在这里举行的第六十六届戛纳电影节上获得金棕榈奖。

    ② 这一不平常的，也许是以前没有过的步骤，承认了这两位在片中几个性镜头中裸体出镜的女性的贡献，但也抢了导演科齐科的风头，表示评审团在幕后曾经有过激烈的讨论。

    ③ 整个晚上唯一的一个意外是，最佳导演的得主是墨西哥电影制片人阿马特埃斯科朗奇，他执导了一部臃肿的、充满暴力的恐怖片《黑利》，片中的暴力镜头包括一个男人的腹股沟被点上了火。

Exercises

Ⅰ. **Understanding Ideas in the News**

  1. Which movie had been the critical favorite for much of the festival?

  A. *Blue Is the Warmest Color.*　　　　B. *The Artist.*

  C. *Inside Llewyn Davis.*

  2. What had Ms Exarchopoulos been widely expected to win?

  A. The best actor.　　B. The best actress.　　C. The best director.

  3. What movie did the best actress winner play in to qualify her for the title?

  A. *The Artist.*　　　　B. *Nebraska.*　　　　C. *Le Passe*

  4. Why is it that the best director award is a real shock of the evening?

  A. The movie is turgid and violent.

  B. There are other scenes than atrocities.

C. Some critics didn't agree with it.

5. From which country did a movie win an award at Cannes?

A. Singapore.　　　　B. Japan.　　　　C. Cambodia.

II. Language Points

explicit, sheen, wistful, melancholic, turgid　这些词用来描写获奖的一些电影。

explicit：（清楚的，直率的）showing or talking about sex or violence in a very detailed way　e.g. *a sexually explicit film*

sheen：（光辉,光彩）a bright, smooth surface　e.g. *The conditioner gives the hair a beautiful soft sheen.*

wistful：（渴望的，惆怅的）sad and thinking about something that is impossible or in the past　e.g. *a wistful smile*

melancholic：（忧郁的）(from melancholy) sad　e.g. *melancholy autumn days*

turgid：（一本正经的，浮夸的）(of speech, writing, style, etc.) too serious about its subject matter; boring　e.g. *a couple of pages of turgid prose*

III. Questions for Further Study

This news report is about the Cannes Film Festival awards. It is typical of any news of this kind, and the structure is very clear, with the most important idea at the beginning, followed by less important ones. The only difficulty is recognizing the names of people and of movies. As the Internet is very popular now, Chinese students have heard about many of the names mentioned here. Find another report on the Oscars in the current year, and see how well you can understand it.

3. Jennifer Lawrence, interview: "I do worry that I'm too in your face"

After the huge success of *The Hunger Games*, Jennifer Lawrence is learning how to cope as a superstar, she tells Will Lawrence ahead of the release of her new film *Silver Linings Playbook*.

Jennifer Lawrence stars in new film *Silver Linings Playbook*, alongside Bradley

Cooper. (Photo: Moviestore / Rex Features)

By Will Lawrence
The New York Times
21 Nov., 2012

Jennifer Lawrence has a theory about celebrity relationships. The 22-year-old star of *The Hunger Games* is in a relationship with English actor Nicholas Hoult (they met on the set of the 2011 blockbuster *X-Men: First Class*), and Lawrence has remained tight-lipped on the subject—until recently at least.

"You don't want your relationship to be in the press," says the American actress, "but at the same time, and this is only a theory, the more you try and keep it secret, the more the media tries to crack it open. ①

"Maybe there's less pressure if you admit you are dating. Admitting that is just an experiment. I'm going to see how it goes."

The relationship itself is going well, although Lawrence concedes that the phenomenal success of last March's *The Hunger Games* has made the couple's time in Los Angeles intolerable.

"My life in LA has changed a lot," she says. "I had to move out of my condo, which is infested with paparazzi, and I am still paying off my Volkswagen, which they know about and follow."

Hence she and Hoult (*About A Boy*, *A Single Man*) prefer spending time on the East Coast, or in the UK.

"In New York it's not too bad and in London it's not terrible. London's my favourite place to be. In fact," she laughs, "over here I'm like, 'What do I have to do to get papped?'"

Media interest had been simmering since 2008's *The Burning Plain*, which earned Lawrence a newcomer's award at the Venice Film Festival, and it really heated up when she scooped an Oscar nomination for the 2010 drama *Winter's Bone*. In the following year she appeared in the Sundance Film Festival favourite *Like Crazy*, as well as *The Beaver* alongside Jodie Foster.

It was with her starring role as Katniss in the adaptation of the first book in Suzanne Collins's bestselling trilogy *The Hunger Games* that interest in Lawrence really reached boiling point. ②

The film, which is set in a post-apocalyptic world where children battle to the death in a gladiatorial contest, gobbled up almost \$700 million at the international box office, the largest-ever return for a female-led action movie. ③

"You can prepare for it in certain ways," she says of her sudden rise to superstardom. "I know if I don't want to get followed I have to take a different car and

I've learnt not to leave pictures on the Internet.

"But I do worry that I'm too in your face because of the movie. There are posters of me everywhere and when I see posters of other people everywhere I think they're annoying, no matter what they're like personally or professionally. So I worry that I might start put people off."

Lawrence is locked into the franchise and must take that chance. She is currently midway through filming the second instalment, *Catching Fire*, with the new director Francis Lawrence.

"It's great to return," she beams. "It feels like being a sophomore in high school because normally the first day at work is like the first day at school and you don't know if you are going to make friends. On this movie I know that I adore everyone."

What does worry her, though, even more than her own ubiquity is Katniss's popularity. "My biggest concern in taking on this franchise was that people wouldn't be able to lose themselves in my other films — that they would only see Katniss."

Lawrence was one of the actresses to lose out to Kristen Stewart during the casting of *Twilight*, and she has paid attention to her one-time rival's subsequent career.

"I have definitely put a lot of thought into the movies I am doing that come out around *The Hunger Games*," she says. "That's why making a great film like *Silver Linings Playbook* was so important."

Directed by The Fighter's David O Russell, *Silver Linings Playbook* casts Lawrence opposite Bradley Cooper.

"Bradley gets released from a mental institution, after he was sentenced for almost killing a man who was having an affair with his wife, and then he meets me, a recovering sex addict, and the two of us form a very explosive love story," she explains. ④ "Well, not quite a love story, but almost."

She is a devoted fan of the film's director—"I love David O Russell and saw *I Heart Huckerbees* 11 times in one week"—and was excited by the prospect of working with Robert De Niro, who plays Cooper's father. In one memorable scene, Lawrence goes toe-to-toe with the legend, unleashing a forceful monologue right in his face.

"I was obviously very aware that it was De Niro," she recalls, "but I wasn't necessarily nervous. I think he has a lot to do with that—he is a very nice, normal and warm person." (805 words)

Words and Expressions

blockbuster	n.	流行佳作；票房很高的电影	ubiquity	n.	无所不在
			crack	v.	（使）破裂
concede	v.	（勉强）承认	condo	n.	一套小公寓房
infest	v.	大批滋生	paparazzi	n.	专门追逐名人的摄影记者

simmer	v.	慢煮	scoop	v.	获得
apocalyptic	a.	启示录的，天启的	gladiatorial	a.	斗剑者的，争论的
gobble up		贪婪地吃、攫取	franchise	n.	特权

Proper Nouns

Jennifer Lawrence　珍妮花·劳伦斯，美国电影演员，生于1990年
The Hunger Game　《饥饿游戏》
the Venice Film Festival　威尼斯电影节
the Sundance Film Festival　圣丹斯电影节，每年1月18—28日在美国犹他州帕克城举行

News Summary

珍妮花·劳伦斯因主演名为《饥饿游戏》的电影而出名，所以英国媒体也采访她。由于是采访，话题比较多，但记者整理归纳后写成新闻发表，也就集中在几个方面。从标题下面的内容概要句子可以知道，新闻的内容是关于珍妮花谈如何应对成名以后给她带来的麻烦，同时介绍了她的另一部新片《银衬里的剧本》。

Understanding Sentences

① 这位美国演员说，"你不想你的各种关系被公布于众，但是，同时，这只是一种假设，你越想保守秘密，媒体就越想把它撬开。"

② 正是由于她在根据苏珊娜·柯林斯的畅销三部曲《饥饿游戏》的第一本改编的电影中扮演凯特尼斯的角色，人们对劳伦斯的兴趣达到了极点。

③ 这部电影以一个后启示时代的世界为背景，那里的儿童在古罗马决斗士般的打斗中直到死亡。电影在国际票房上获取了几乎七亿美元的收入，这对于一部以女性领衔的动作片来说，是最大的回报。

④ 她解释说，"不完全是爱情故事，但差不多。布莱利因为几乎要杀死一个跟他妻子通奸的男人而被判刑，从一所精神病院出来以后遇到了我。他是一名恢复中的性狂病人，我们两人之间爆发了爱情故事。"

Exercises

I. Understanding Ideas in the News

1. Whom did Lawrence admit dating with?
   A. Nicholas Hoult.　　B. X-men.　　C. A Single Man.
2. What have made their life in L.A. intolerable?
   A. The revelation of her dating.
   B. The phenomenal success of *The Hunger Games*.
   C. The condo where they live.
3. After that, where is the ideal place for Lawrence to live?

A. Los Angeles.　　　　B. London.　　　　C. New York.

4. According to Lawrence herself, what makes it difficult for her not to be followed by the paparazzi?

A. The posters of other people everywhere.

B. The car she has been driving.

C. The posters of her everywhere.

5. What is the reason for Lawrence to take on new roles in new movies?

A. She is worried that Kristen Stewart would get the cast in *Twilight*.

B. She would like to meet new director and make friends with people.

C. She is worried that people would only see Katniss.

Ⅱ. Language Points

concede, infest, gobble, scoop, ubiquity　这些词用于描述珍妮花谈论她的电影和男友。

concede：((勉强)承认) to admit, often unwillingly, that something is true　e.g. *The Government has conceded (that) the new tax policy has been a disaster.*

infest：(大批滋生) (of animals and insects which carry disease) to cause a problem by being present in large numbers　e.g. *The barn was infested with rats.*

gobble (up)：(贪婪地吃、攫取) to take greedily; grab　e.g. *gobbled up the few remaining tickets*

scoop：(获得) to get a large number of votes or prizes　e.g. *The socialist party is expected to scoop up the majority of the working-class vote.*

ubiquity：(无所不在) from ubiquitous：seeming to be in all places　e.g. *the ubiquity of fast-food outlets* (= the fact that they are found everywhere)

Ⅲ. Questions for Further Study

This news report is an interview with the American actress, Jennifer Lawrence, who became a star at an early age. The lead paragraph reveal that Jennifer is dating a British actor, and she has to face the paparazzi now. Then the reporter introduces her new movies, and the directors whom Jennifer likes. The main part of the news is rather loosely knitted together, so there is not a main idea or an ending to the news. Analyze how this style of news writing is appropriate to the topic for reporting.

英语报刊知识介绍

报刊网站和电子报刊的订阅和阅读

报刊网站和新闻网站是近十几年来出现的新事物,它们利用互联网技术,不仅使世界各地的读者可以在几乎同一时间看到同一消息,而且还提供了照片、声音、视频、互动等多媒体效果,比传统的平面报刊更加形象生动。

电子报纸则是印刷报纸的衍生。各种报纸基本上都开发了他们的电子报纸,这是一种以 PDF 格式出现的电子文档。读者可以在互联网上进行阅读。现在的电子报纸形式已经非常成熟,大多数是出现一个跟印刷报纸一样的版面,你只要点击相关标题就弹出该新闻的窗口。在电子报纸上还包括了声音、照片展示、视频等。随着智能型手机技术的发展,电子报纸也有手机版本。但是,订阅电子报纸要收费,不过你只要有一张信用卡,一切都可以很快完成,然后你就每天可以舒服地在家或办公室查看当天的报纸,不用等送报纸的一早来投递了。

1. The e-newspaper of *Boston Globe*

2. There are many applications for the Internet on the cell phone now.

Keys to Understanding Ideas in the News

Unit 1   Regional Focuses: Domestic Turmoil and War

1.
1. A   2. B   3. C   4. C   5. A
2.
1. B   2. A   3. C   4. B   5. A
3.
1. C   2. A   3. A   4. B   5. B

Unit 2   Conflicts in the Middle East

1.
1. A   2. C   3. C   4. A   5. B
2.
1. C   2. A   3. C   4. A   5. B
3.
1. B   2. B   3. A   4. A   5. C

Unit 3   The African Scene

1.
1. A   2. B   3. C   4. A   5. A
2.
1. C   2. C   3. A   4. B   5. C
3.
1. B   2. B   3. C   4. A   5. C

Unit 4   Violence and Terrorist Attacks in the U. S.

1.
1. A   2. C   3. B   4. A   5. C
2.
1. B   2. C   3. A   4. C   5. B
3.
1. A   2. B   3. A   4. B   5. C

Unit 5   American Election 2012

1.
1. C   2. A   3. B   4. A   5. B
2.
1. A   2. C   3. C   4. B   5. A

Keys to Understanding Ideas in the News

3.
1. B 2. A 3. CA 4. C 5. B

Unit 6 Social News — the U.S.
1.
1. B 2. A 3. B 4. C 5. C
2.
1. A 2. C 3. A 4. C 5. B
3.
1. C 2. B 3. A 4. B 5. C

Unit 7 National News—the UK
1.
1. B 2. B 3. A 4. A 5. C
2.
1. A 2. B 3. C 4. A 5. B
3.
1. B 2. B 3. C 4. A 5. C

Unit 8 Social News—South Africa
1.
1. AC 2. A 3. B 4. C 5. B
2.
1. A 2. C 3. A 4. B 5. C
3.
1. B 2. A 3. B 4. C 5. A

Unit 9 Social News—Life and Lawsuits
1.
1. A 2. C 3. A 4. B 5. C
2.
1. B 2. C 3. A 4. B 5. C
3.
1. C 2. B 3. A 4. A 5. C

Unit 10 Environmental Protection—Saving Wild Lives
1.
1. A 2. C 3. C 4. B 5. A
2.
1. C 2. A 3. B 4. A 5. C
3.
1. C 2. B 3. A 4. A 5. C

275

Unit 11 Computer Technology and the Internet

1.
1. B 2. A 3. C 4. A 5. A
2.
1. C 2. B 3. A 4. A 5. B
3.
1. B 2. C 3. B 4. A 5. C

Unit 12 Science and Technology

1.
1. A 2. C 3. B 4. A 5. C
2.
1. B 2. B 3. A 4. C 5. C
3.
1. C 2. A 3. C 4. B 5. A

Unit 13 World Economy

1.
1. C 2. B 3. A 4. B 5. C
2.
1. A 2. C 3. B 4. A 5. B
3.
1. B 2. B 3. C 4. B 5. C

Unit 14 Business News

1.
1. A 2. C 3. A 4. B 5. B
2.
1. C 2. B 3. A 4. A 5. C
3.
1. B 2. C 3. C 4. A 5. A

Unit 15 The London 2012 Olympics

1.
1. B 2. C 3. B 4. A 5. C
2.
1. A 2. C 3. A 4. B 5. B
3.
1. C 2. B 3. B 4. A 5. A

Unit 16 Culture News

1.
1. A 2. C 3. C 4. B 5. A

2.
1. C 2. A 3. B 4. A 5. C
3.
1. C 2. B 3. A 4. A 5. C

Unit 17 The British Pub and Drinking Culture
1.
1. A 2. B 3. A 4. C 5. B
2.
1. C 2. A 3. B 4. B 5. C
3.
1. A 2. C 3. C 4. B 5. A

Unit 18 Entertainment News
1.
1. A 2. C 3. A 4. C 5. B
2.
1. C 2. B 3. C 4. A 5. A
3.
1. A 2. B 3. B 4. C 5. C